CREATIVE COLOURING FOR GROWN-UPS

TATTOO DESIGNS

Michael O'Mara Books Limited

First published in Great Britain in 2014 by
Michael O'Mara Books Limited
9 Lion Yard
Tremadoc Road
London SW4 7NQ

A CIP catalogue record for this book is available from the British Library.

Papers used by Michael O'Mara Books Limited are natural, recyclable products made from wood grown in sustainable forests. The manufacturing processes conform to the environmental regulations of the country of origin.

ISBN: 978-1-78243-249-4

1 2 3 4 5 6 7 8 9 10

www.mombooks.com

Designed by Billy Waqar
Cover by Claire Cater

Illustrations by Iván Cruz, Matteo Buscicchio, Erik Batista, Ezster David, Maz SpiralOut Art, Ale Abuelita, Greg Stevenson, Pachu Garcia and Shutterstock.com

Printed and bound in China

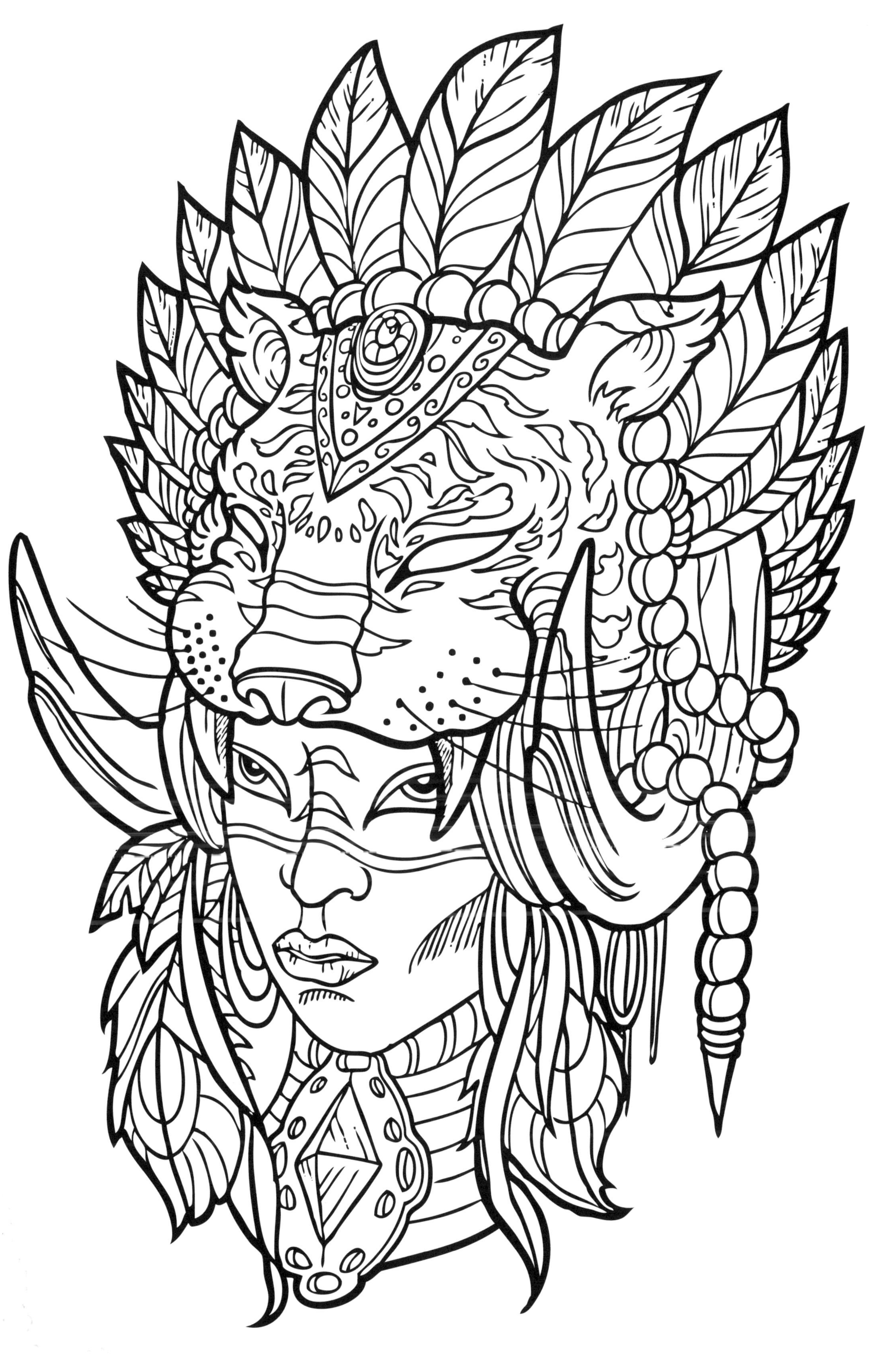

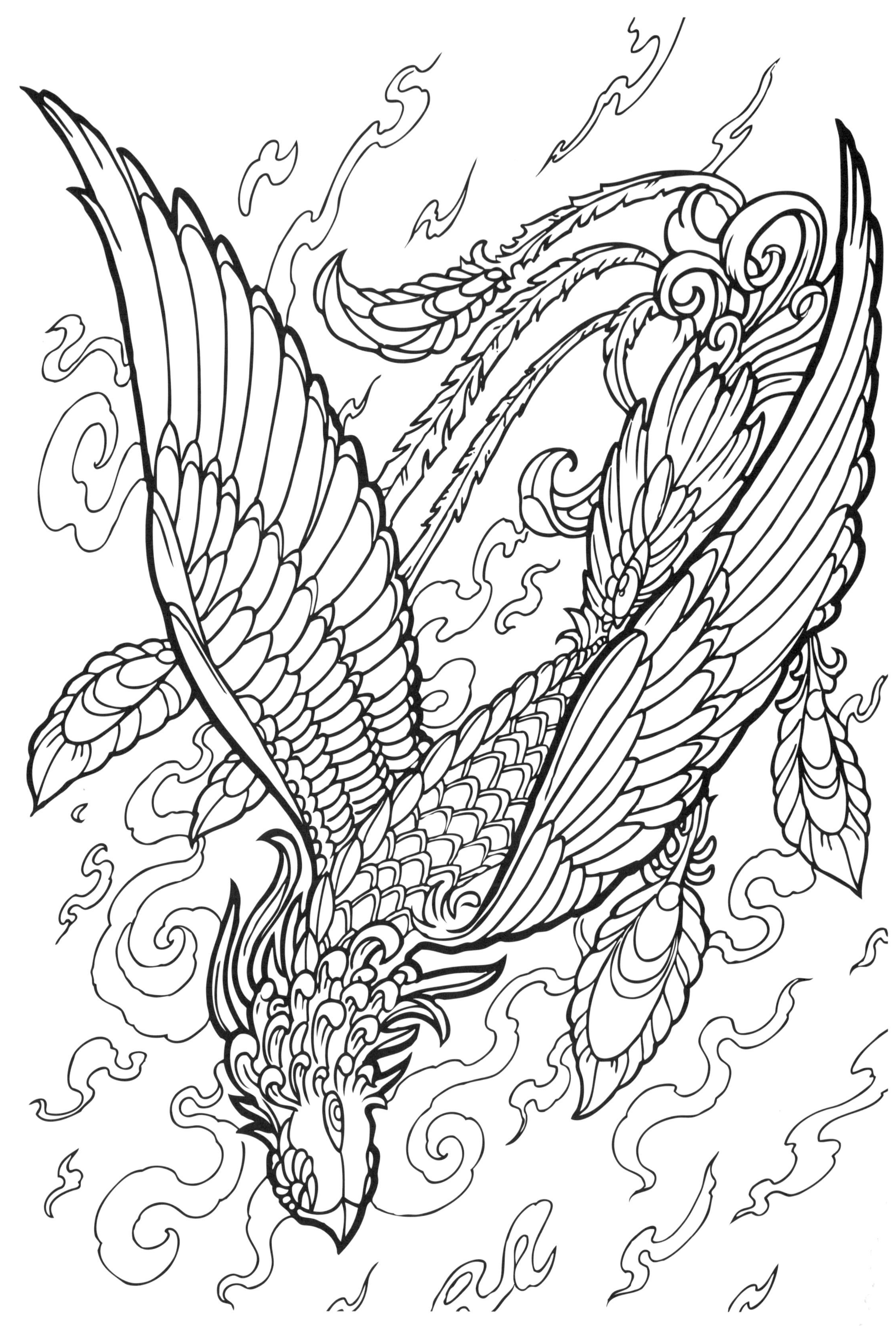

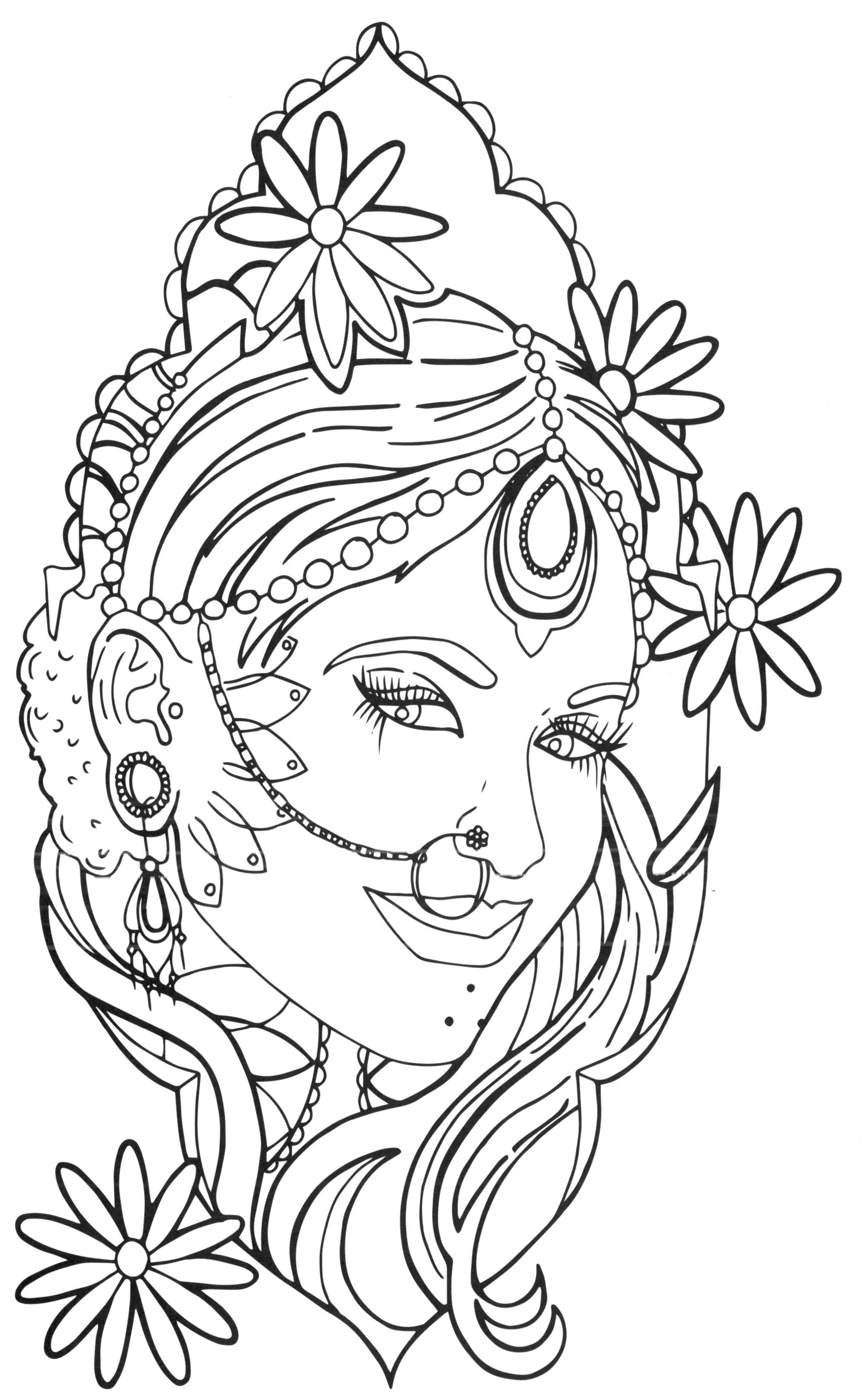

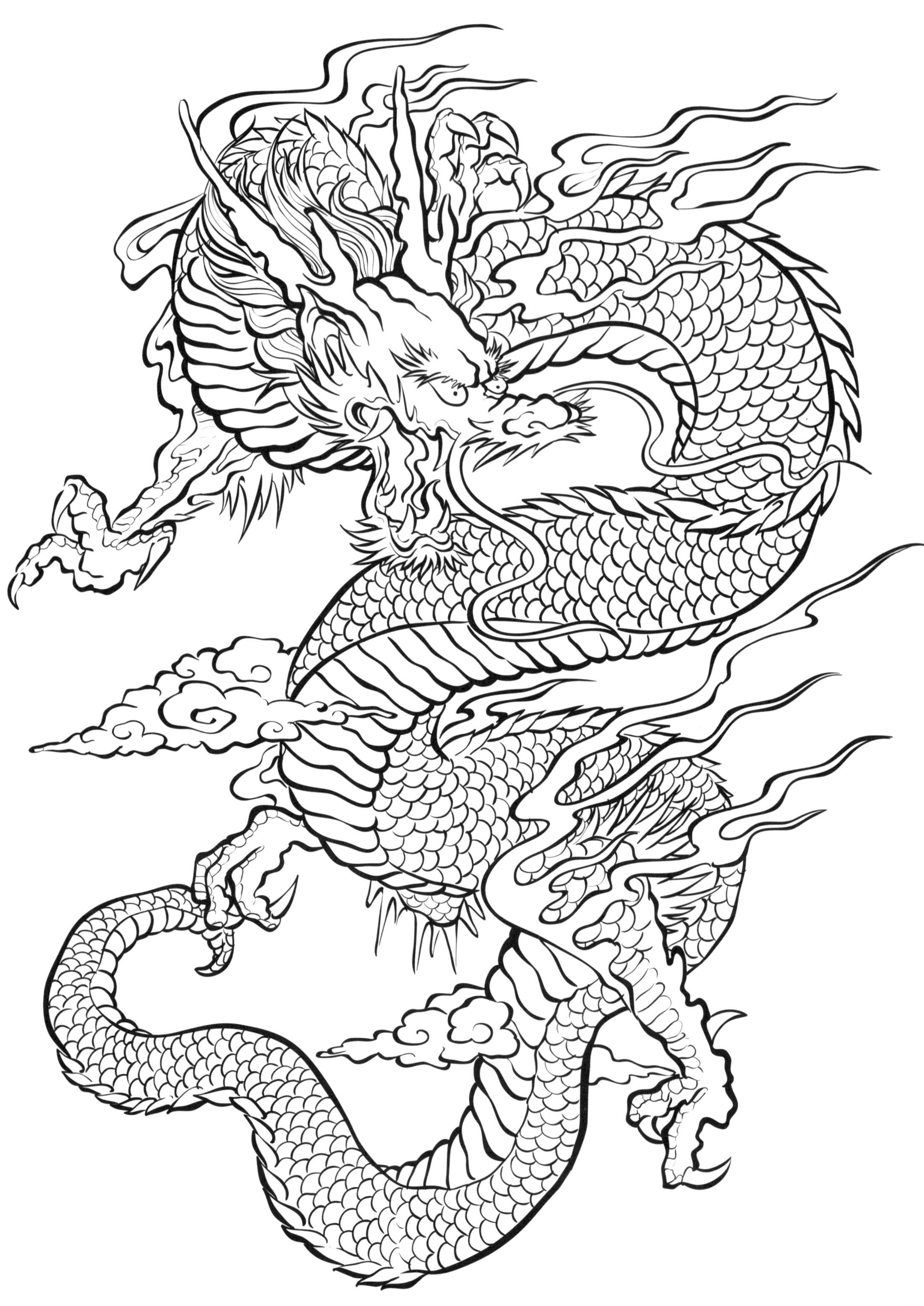

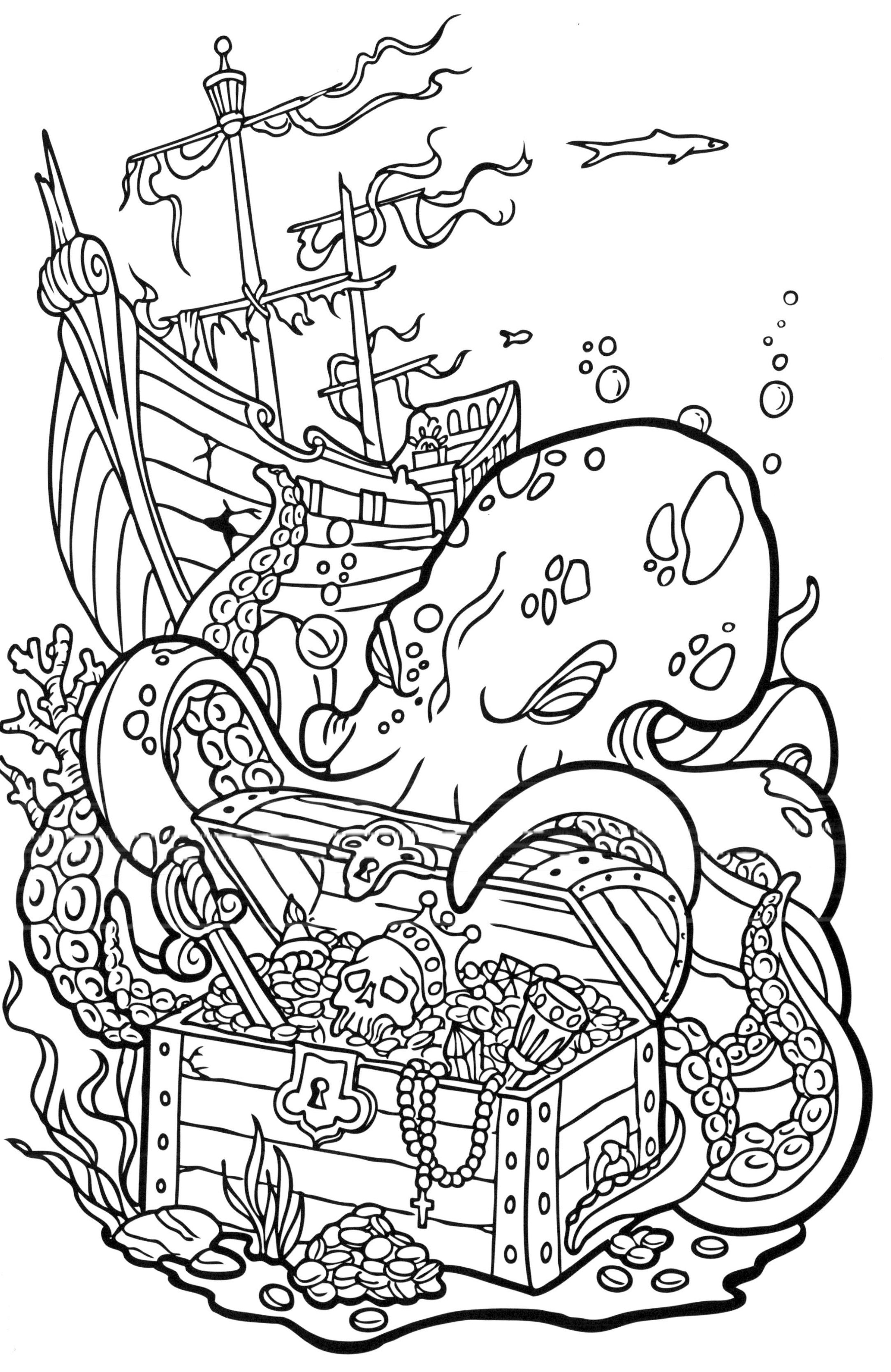

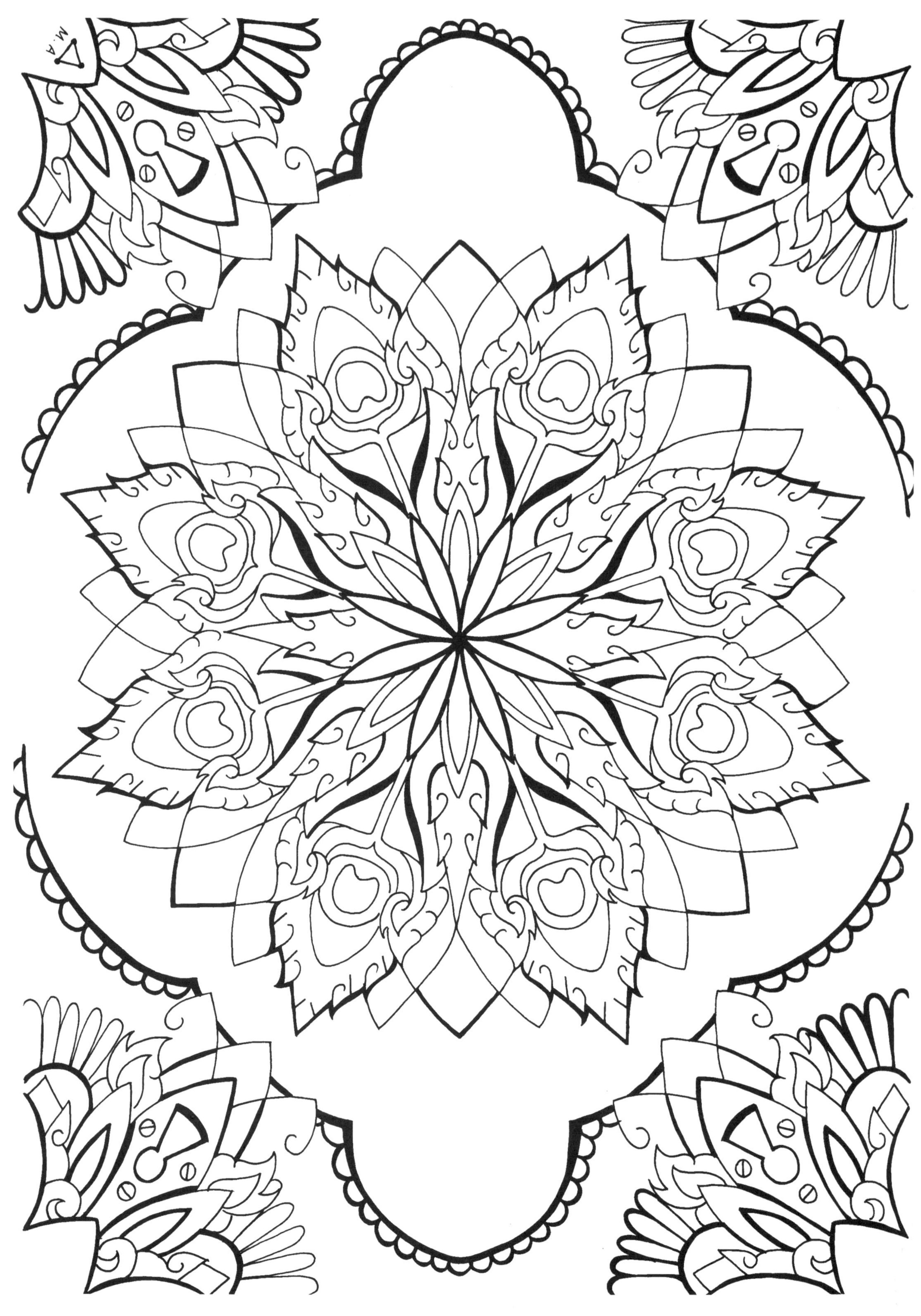
M.A

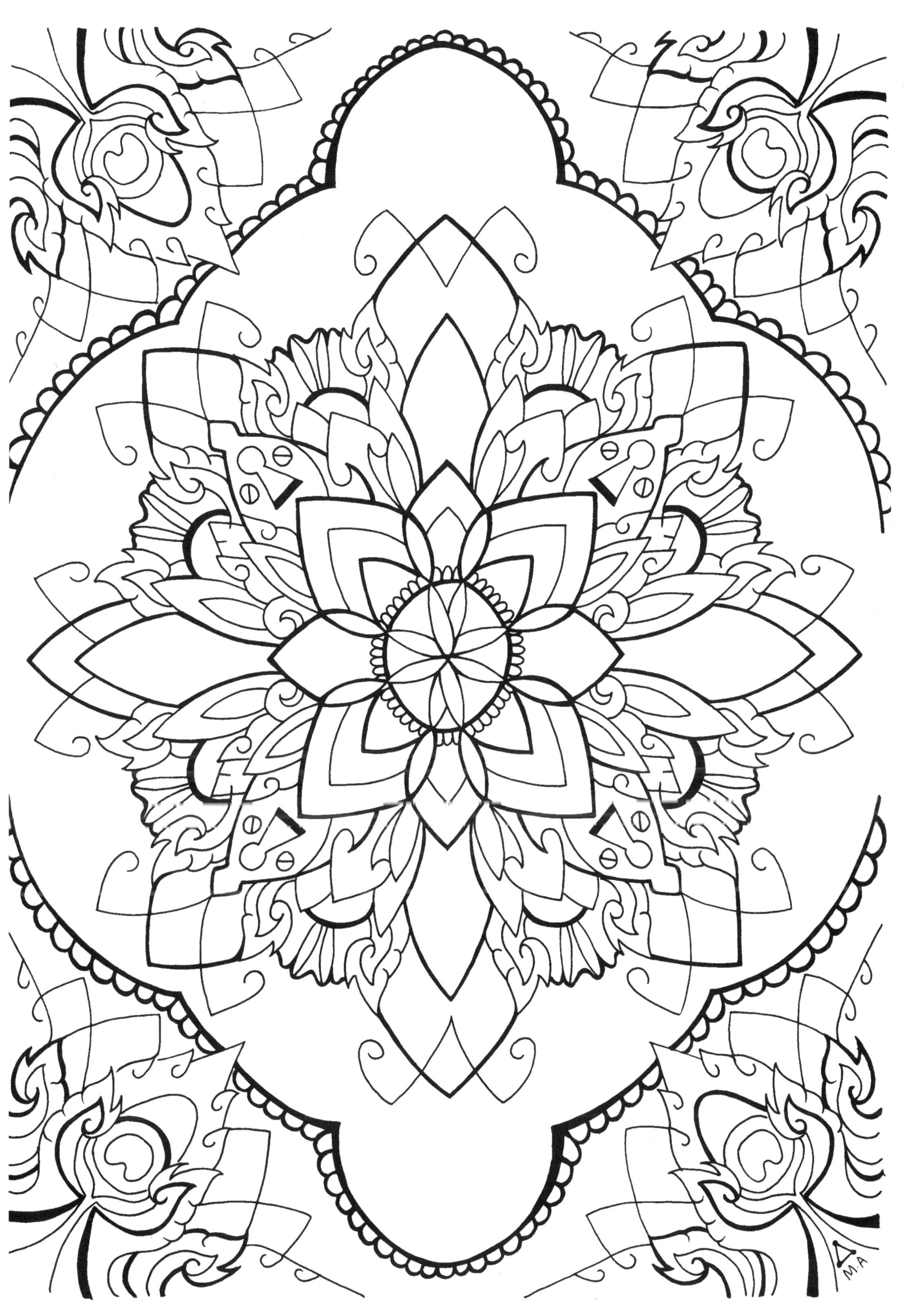
M.A

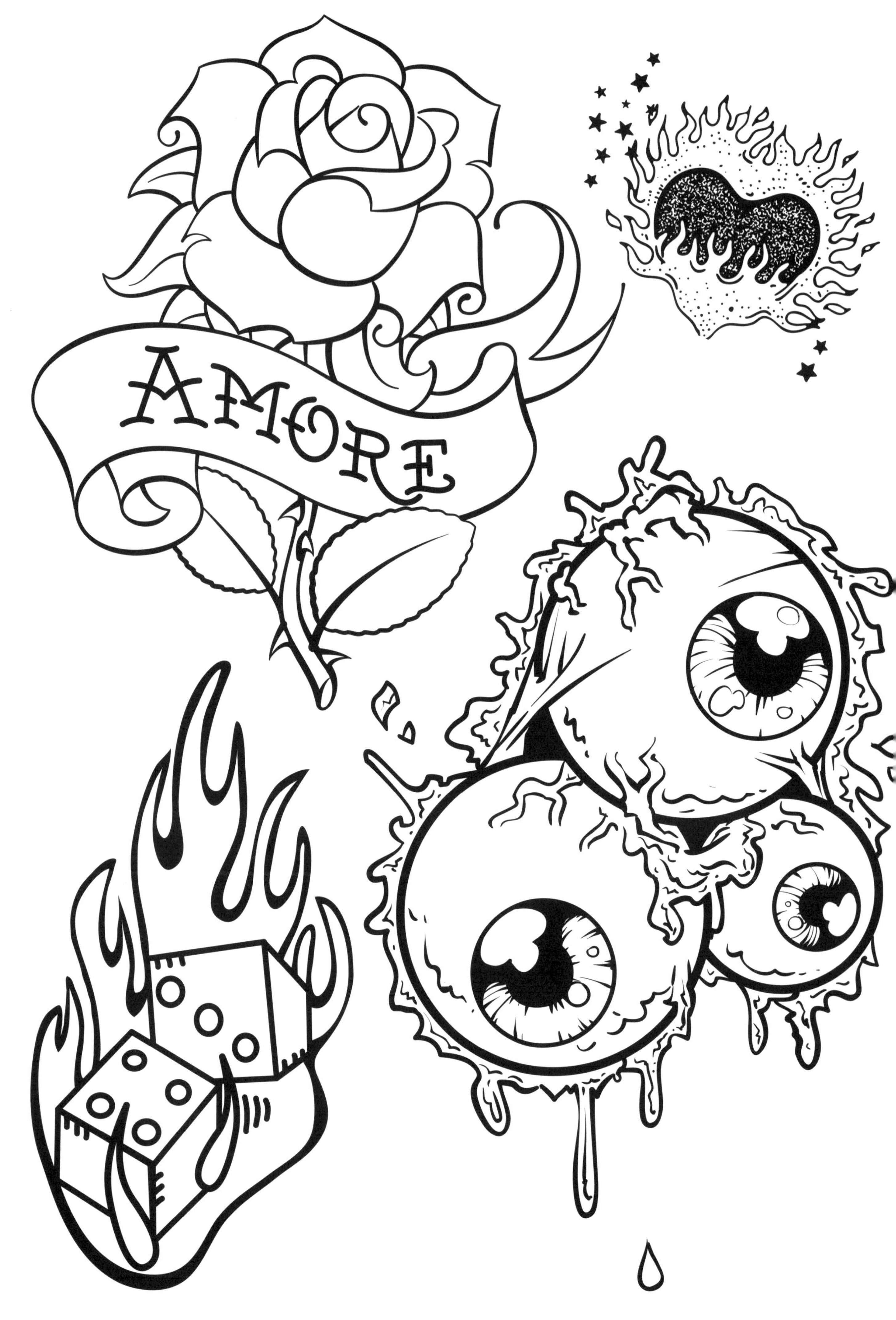
AMORE

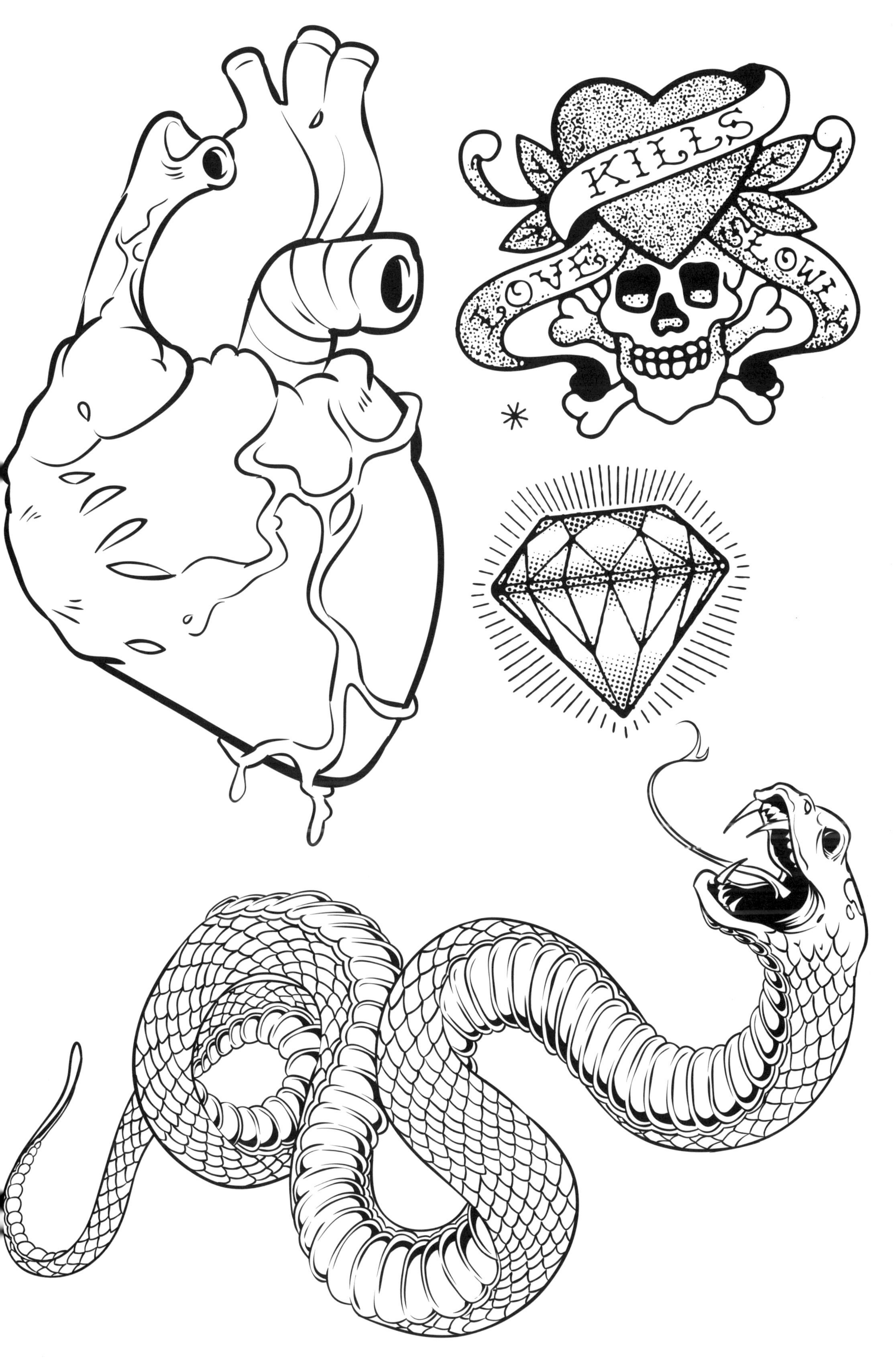
KILLS
LOVE
SLOWLY

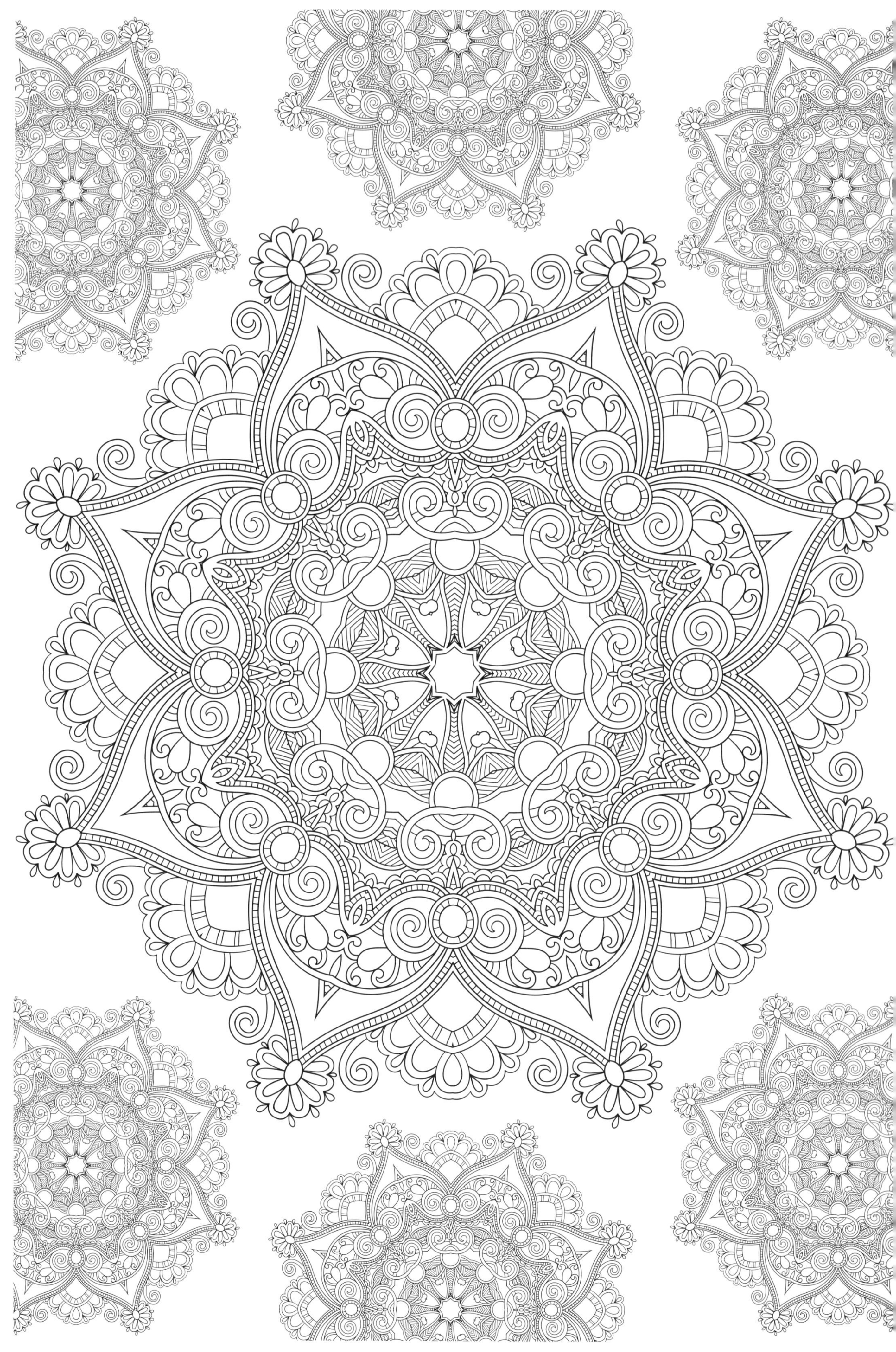

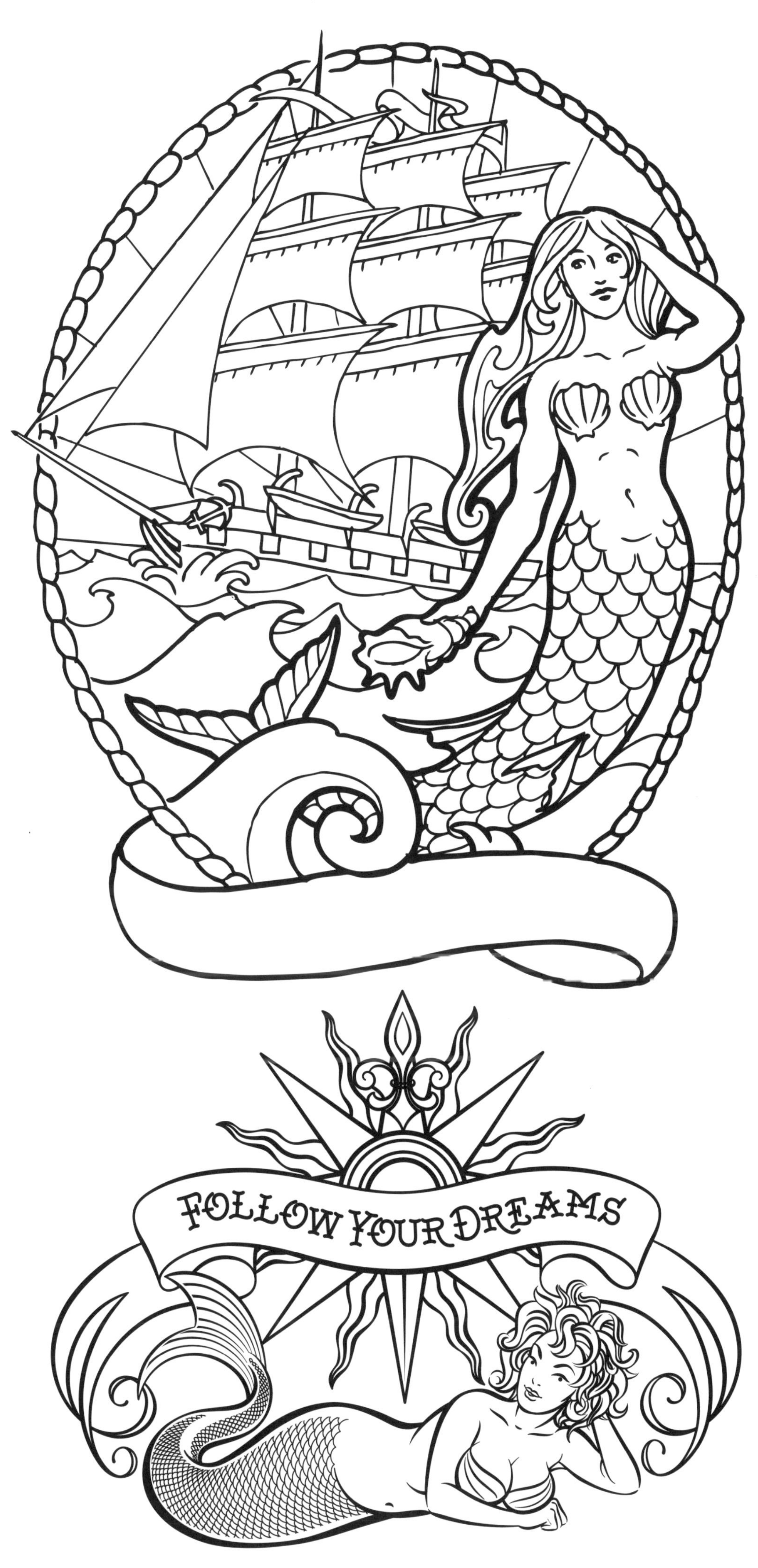
FOLLOW YOUR DREAMS

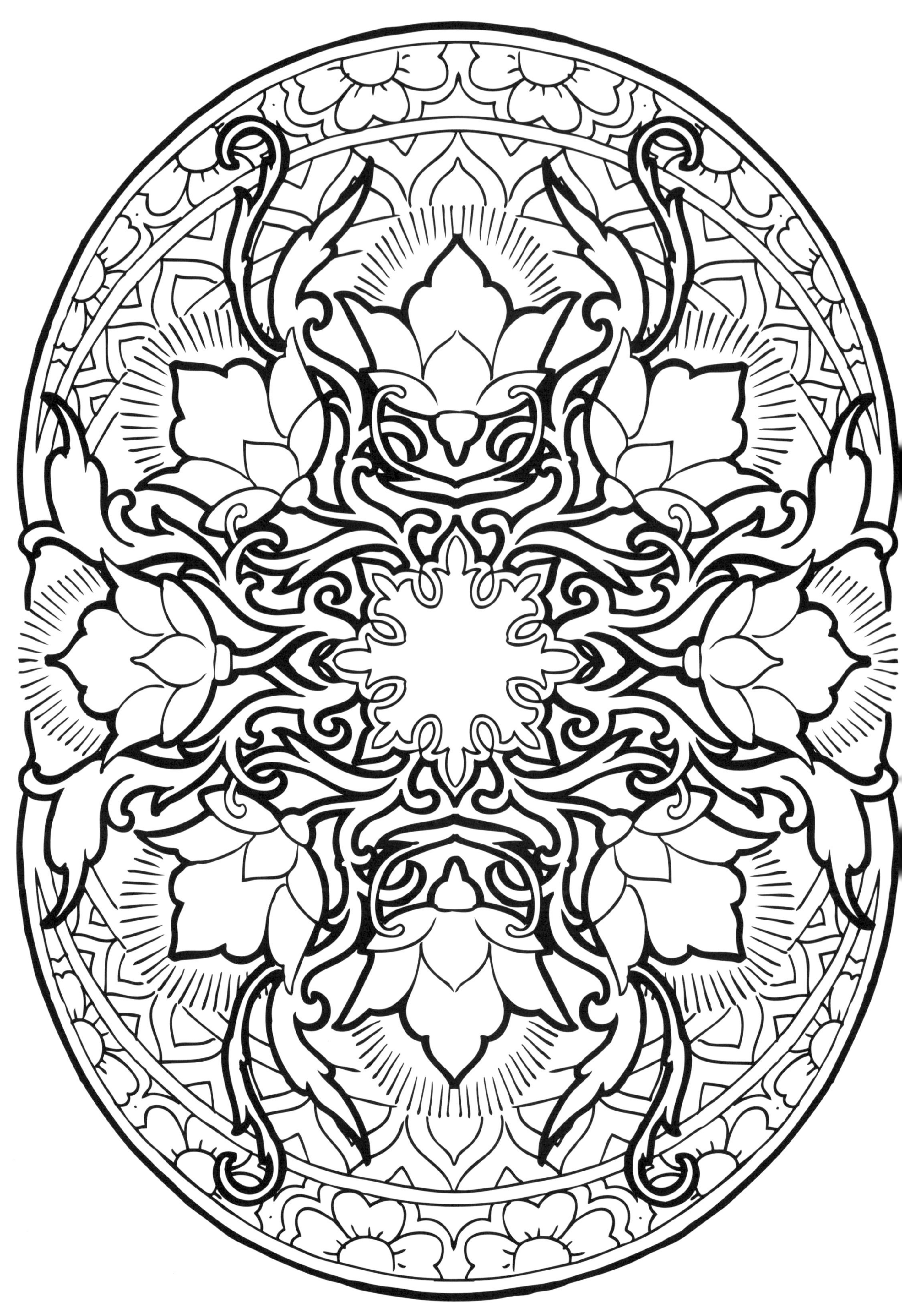

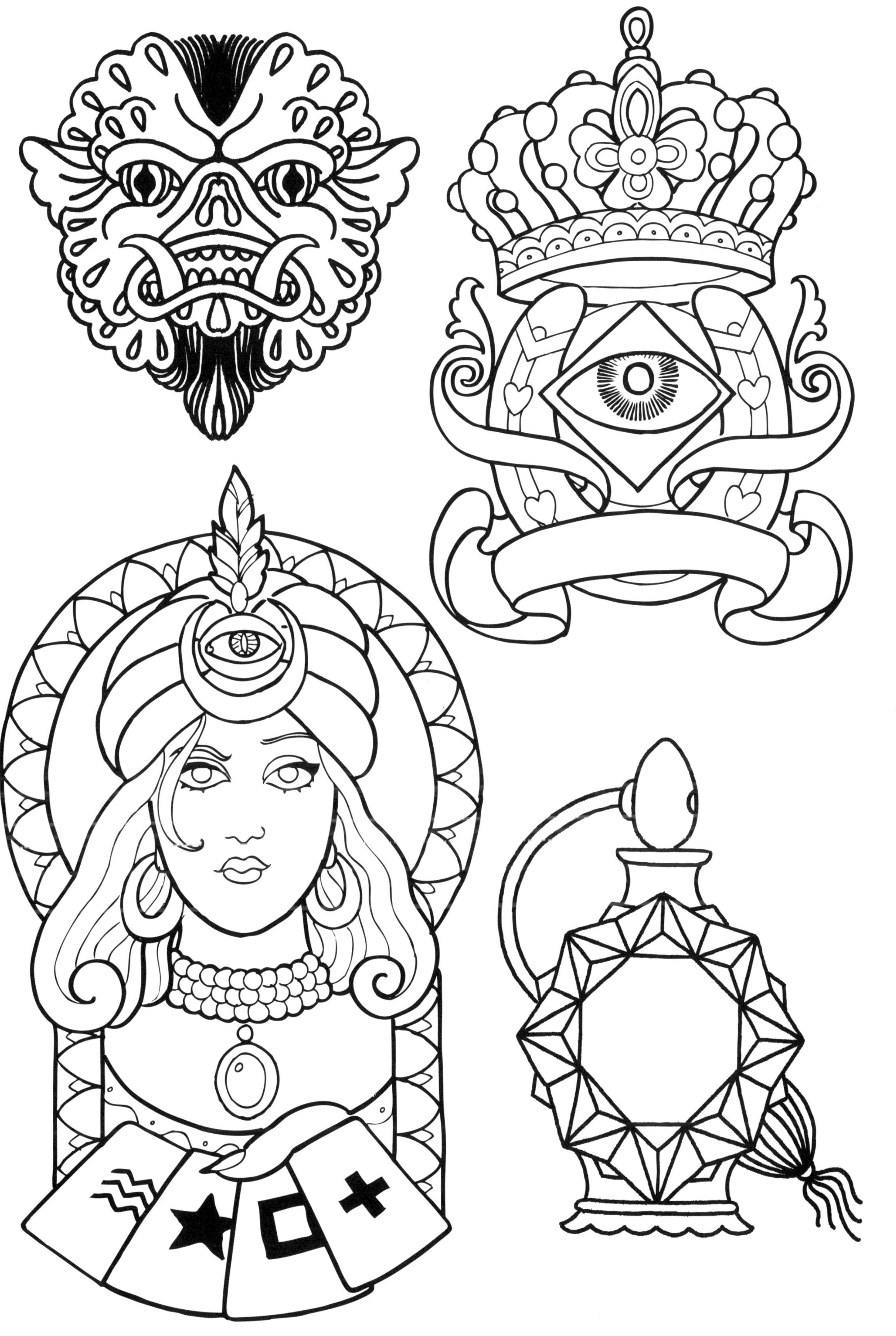

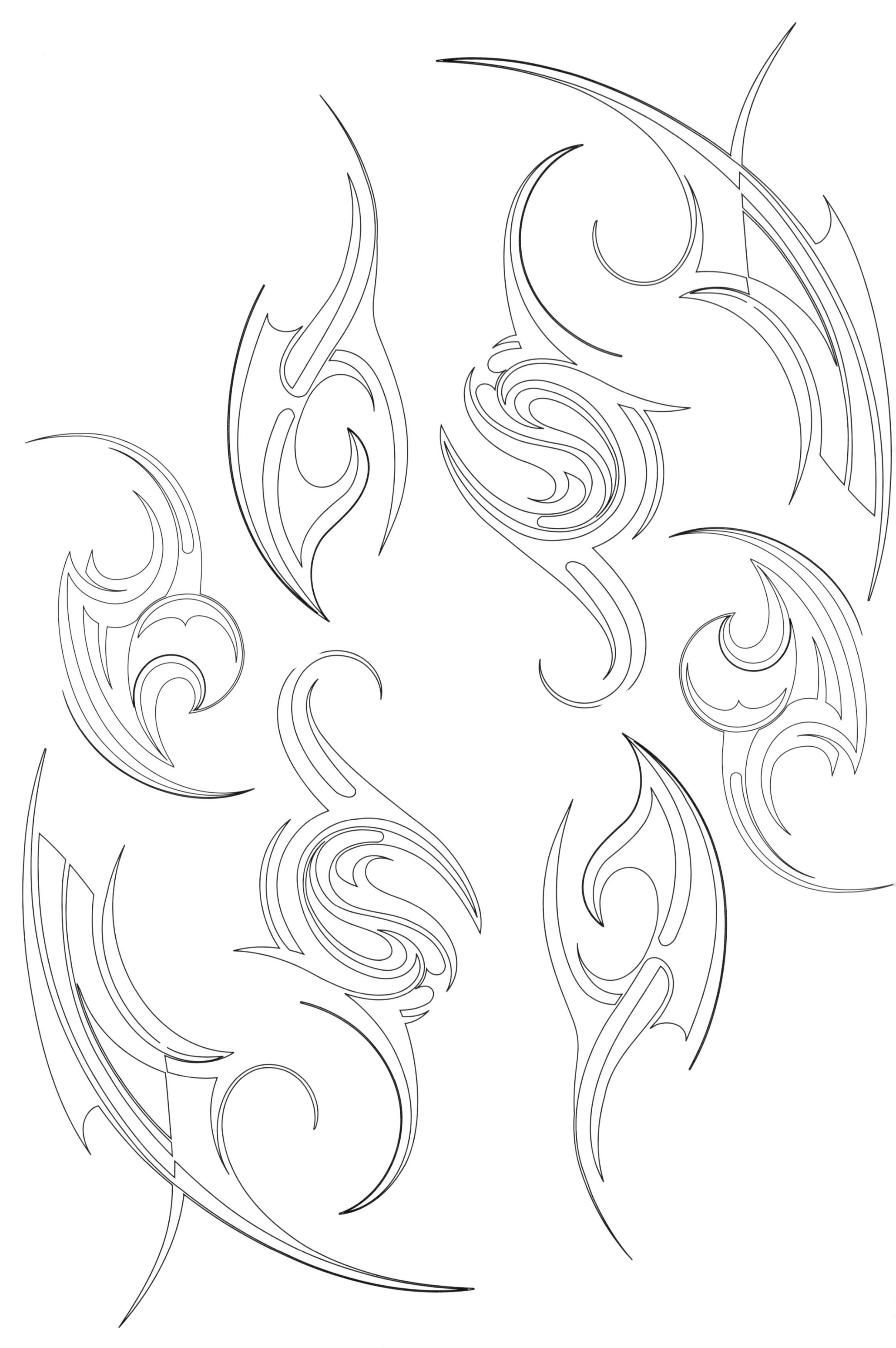

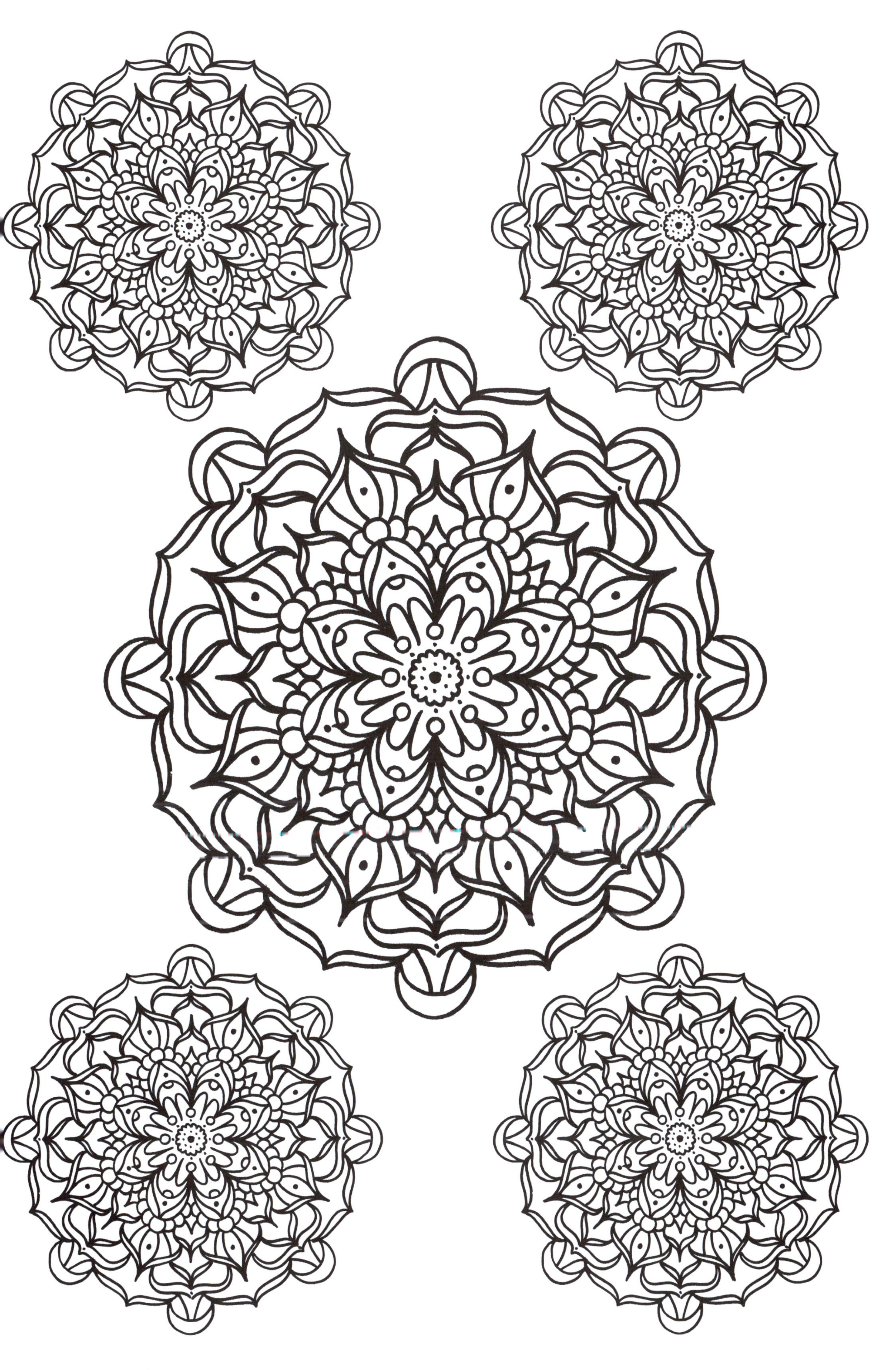

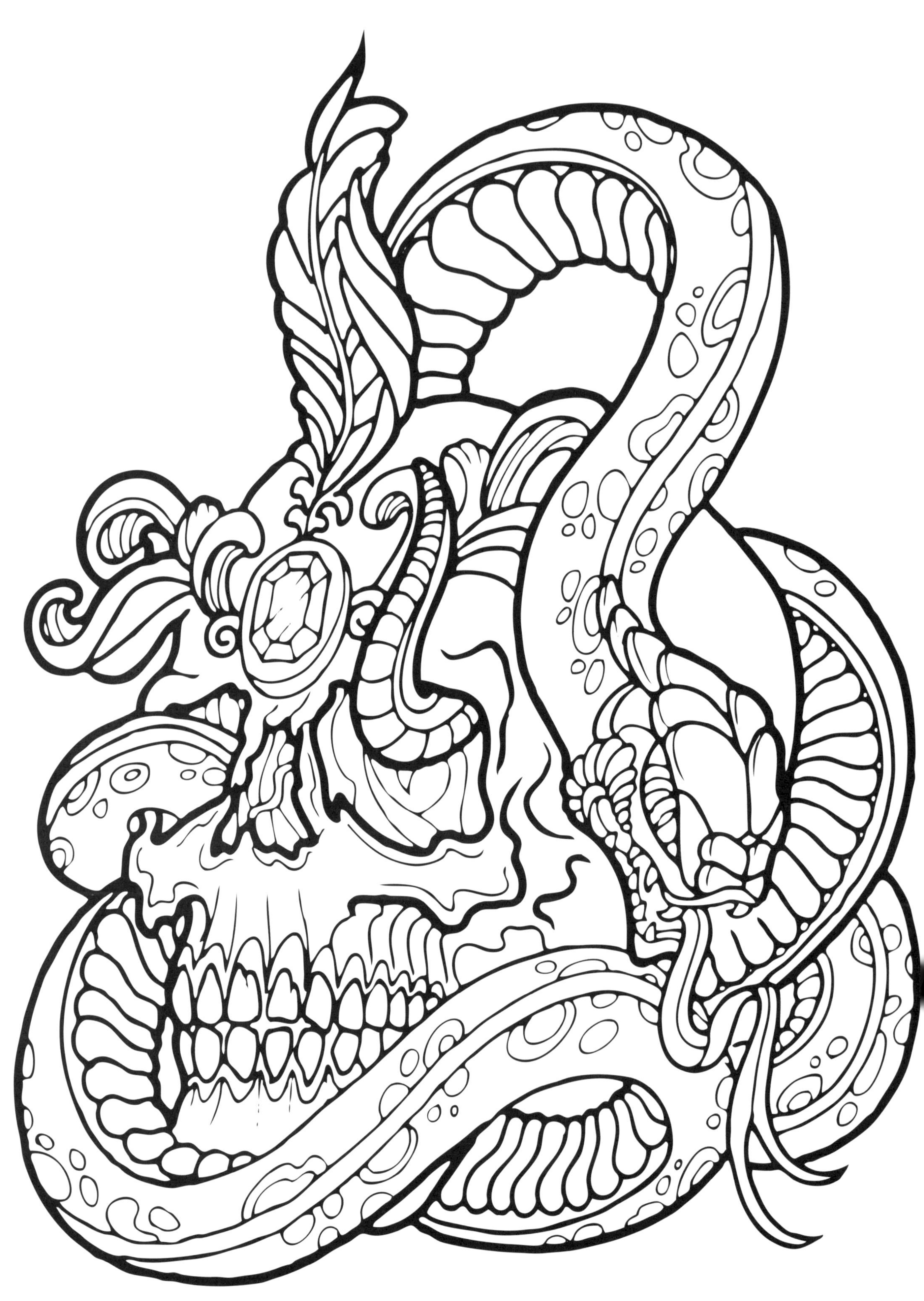

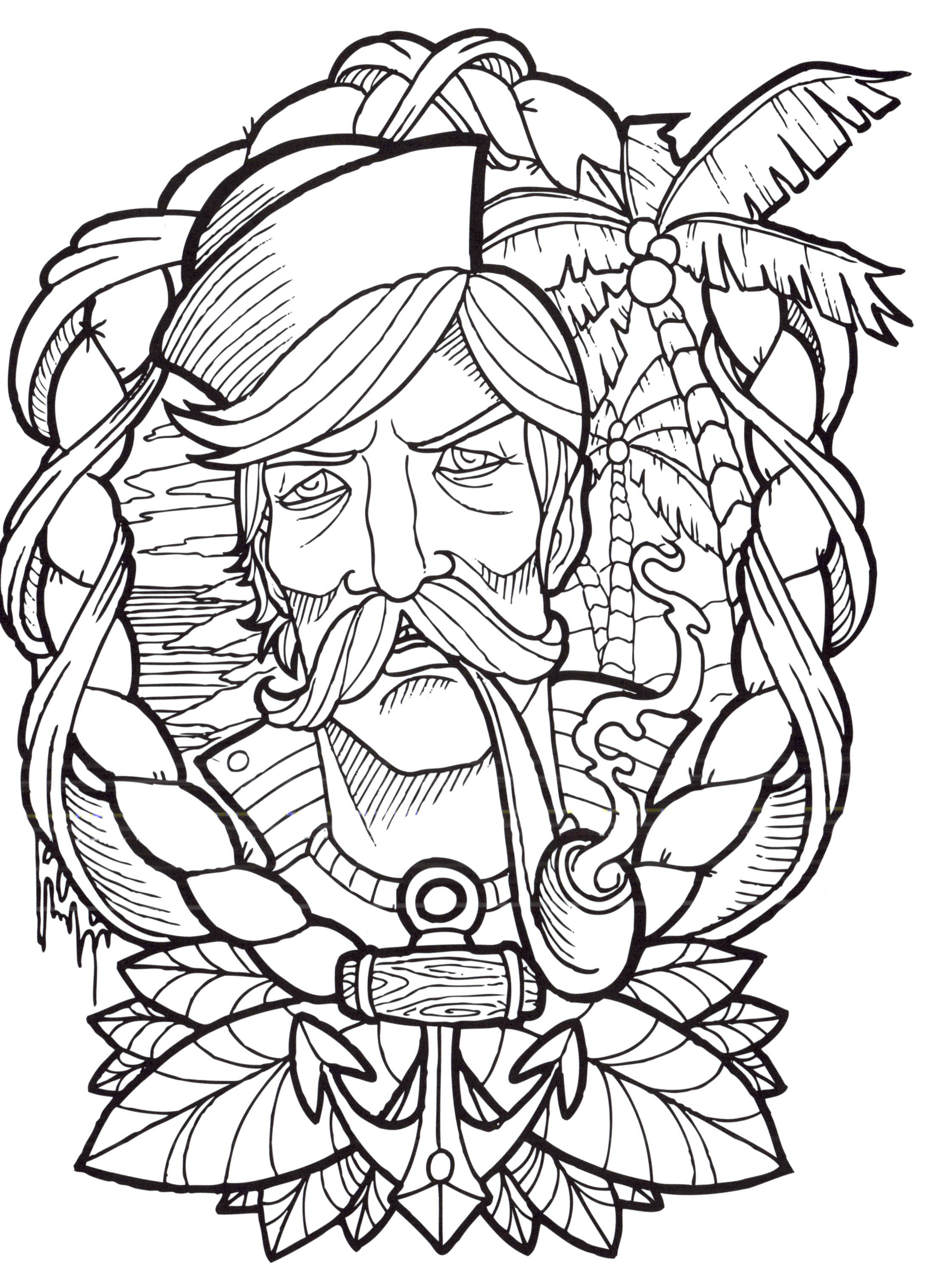

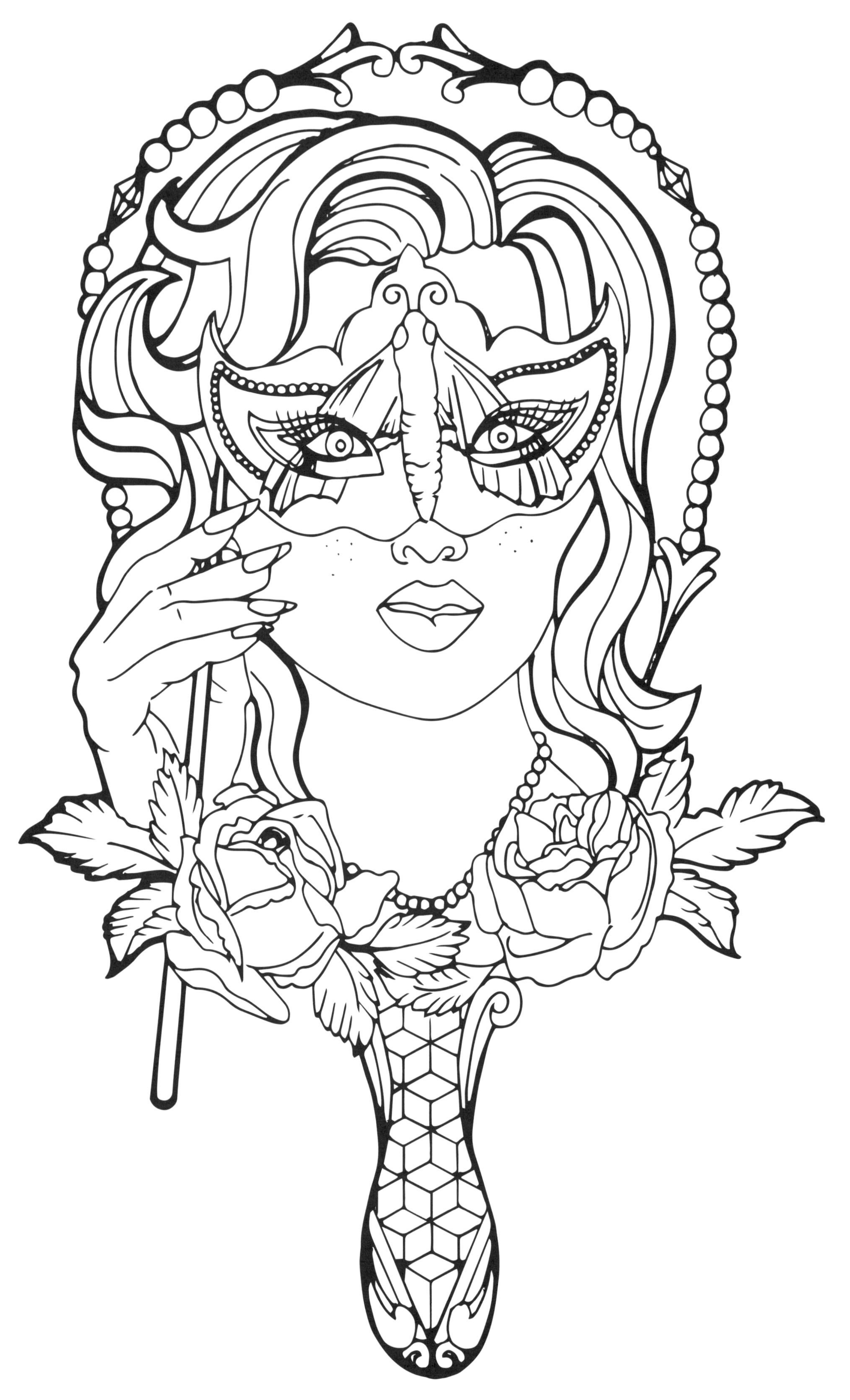

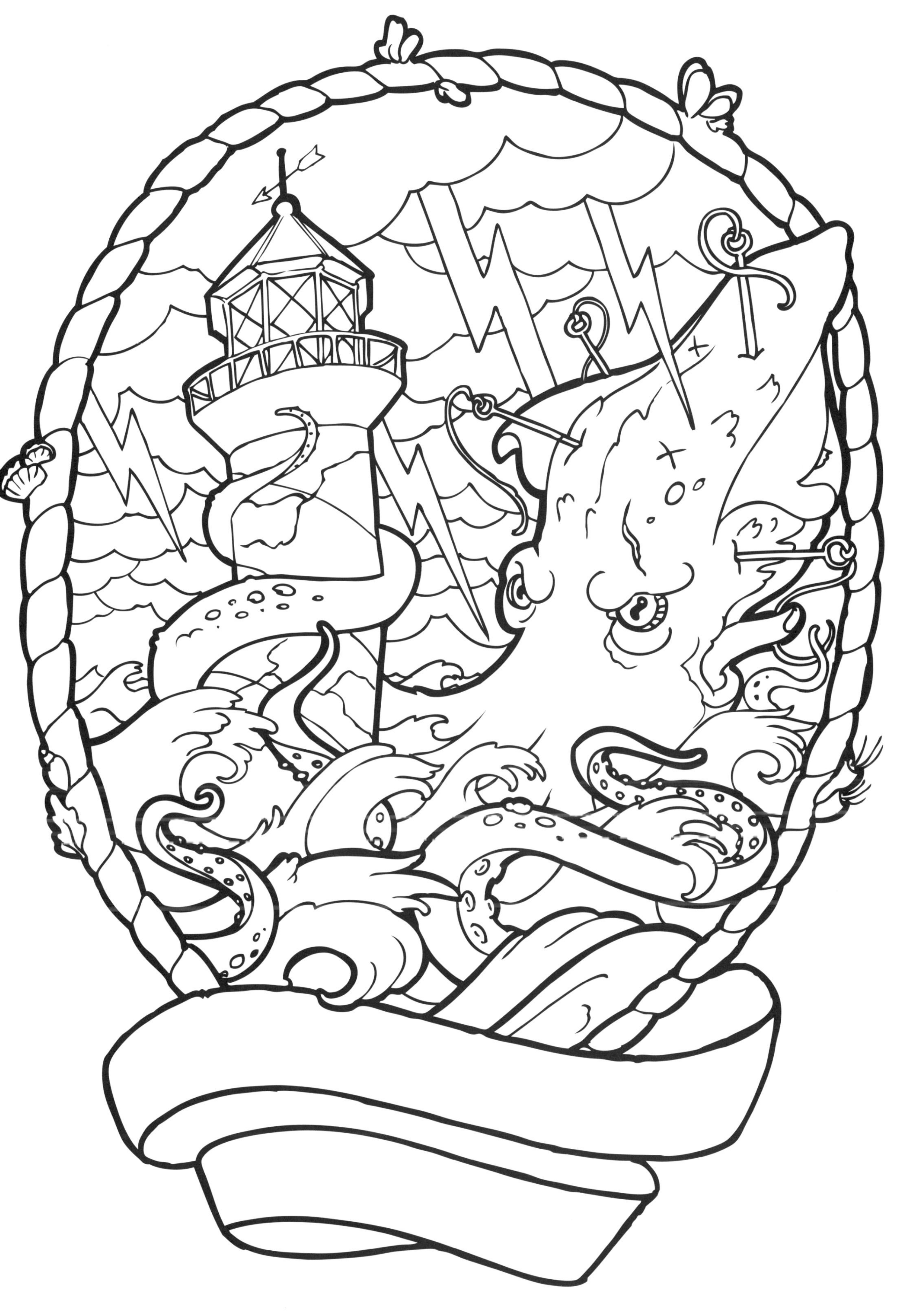

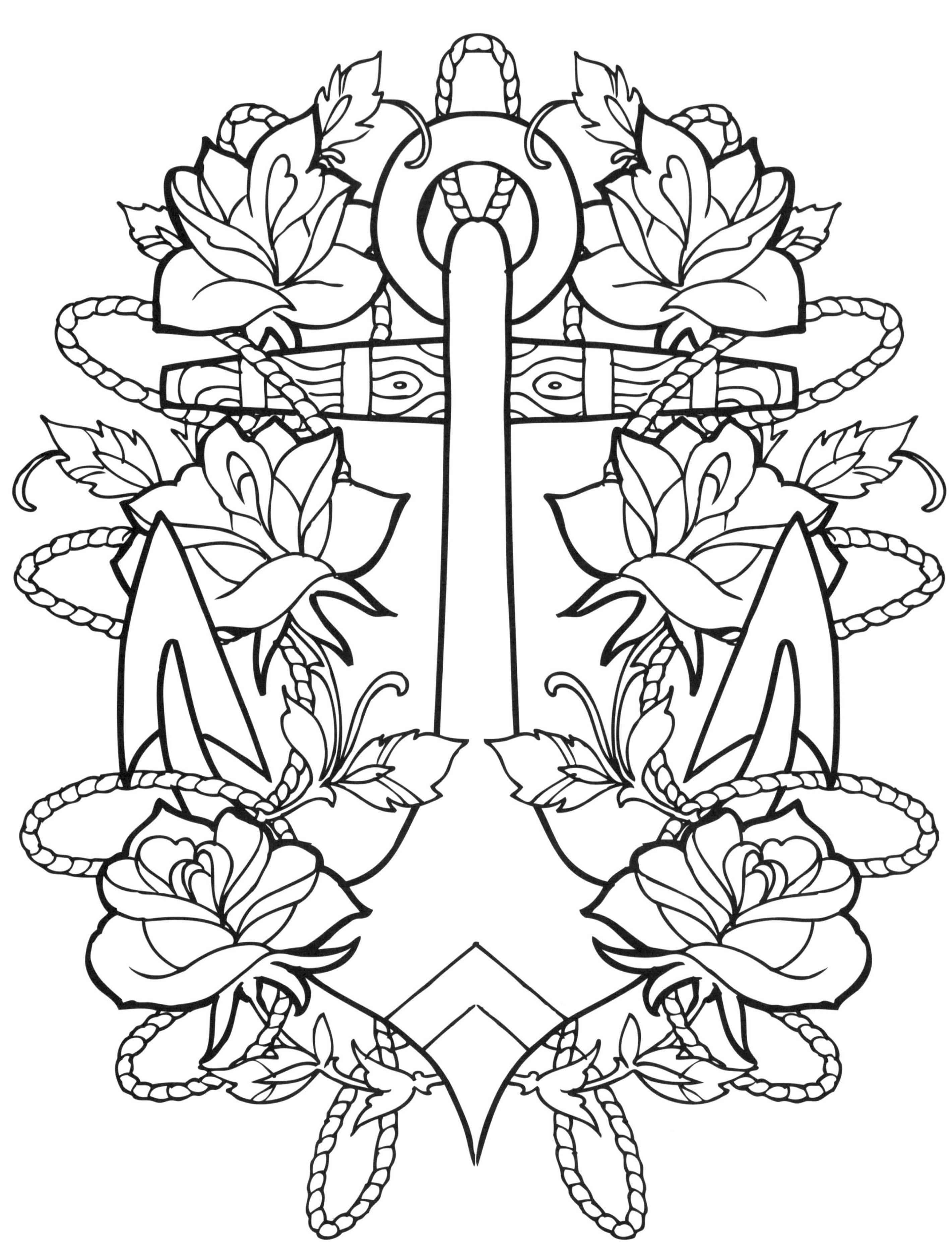

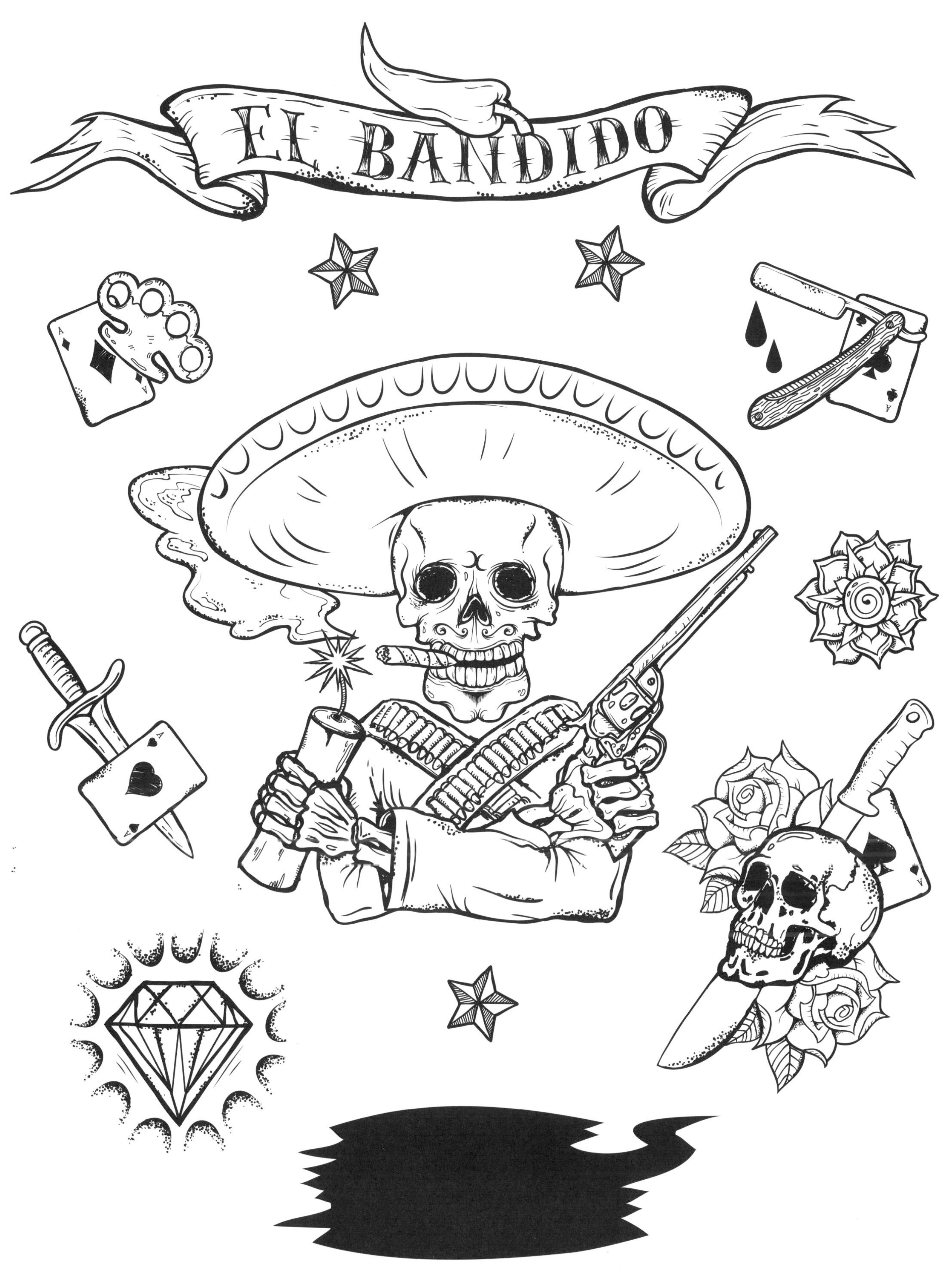
EL BANDIDO

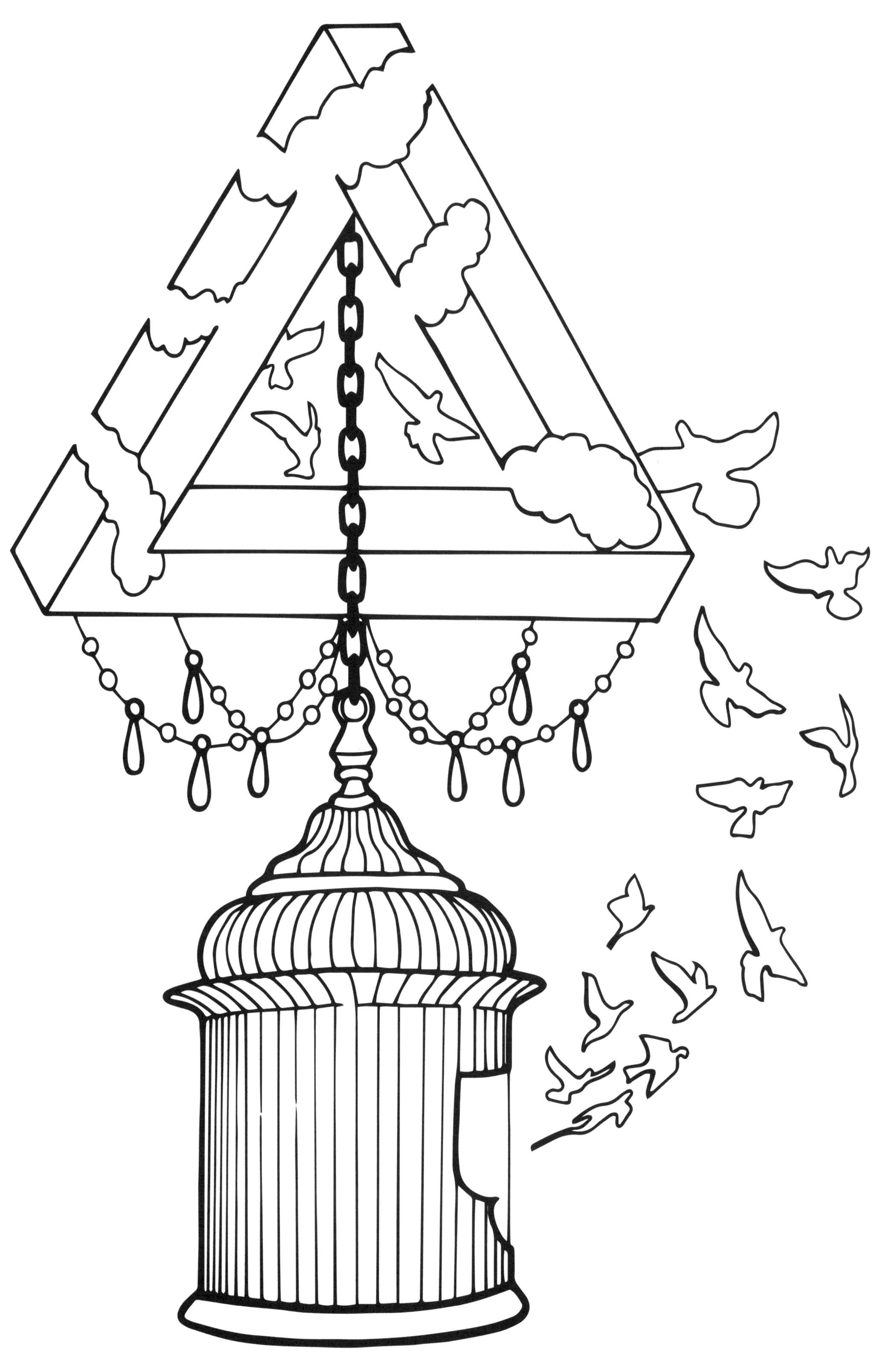

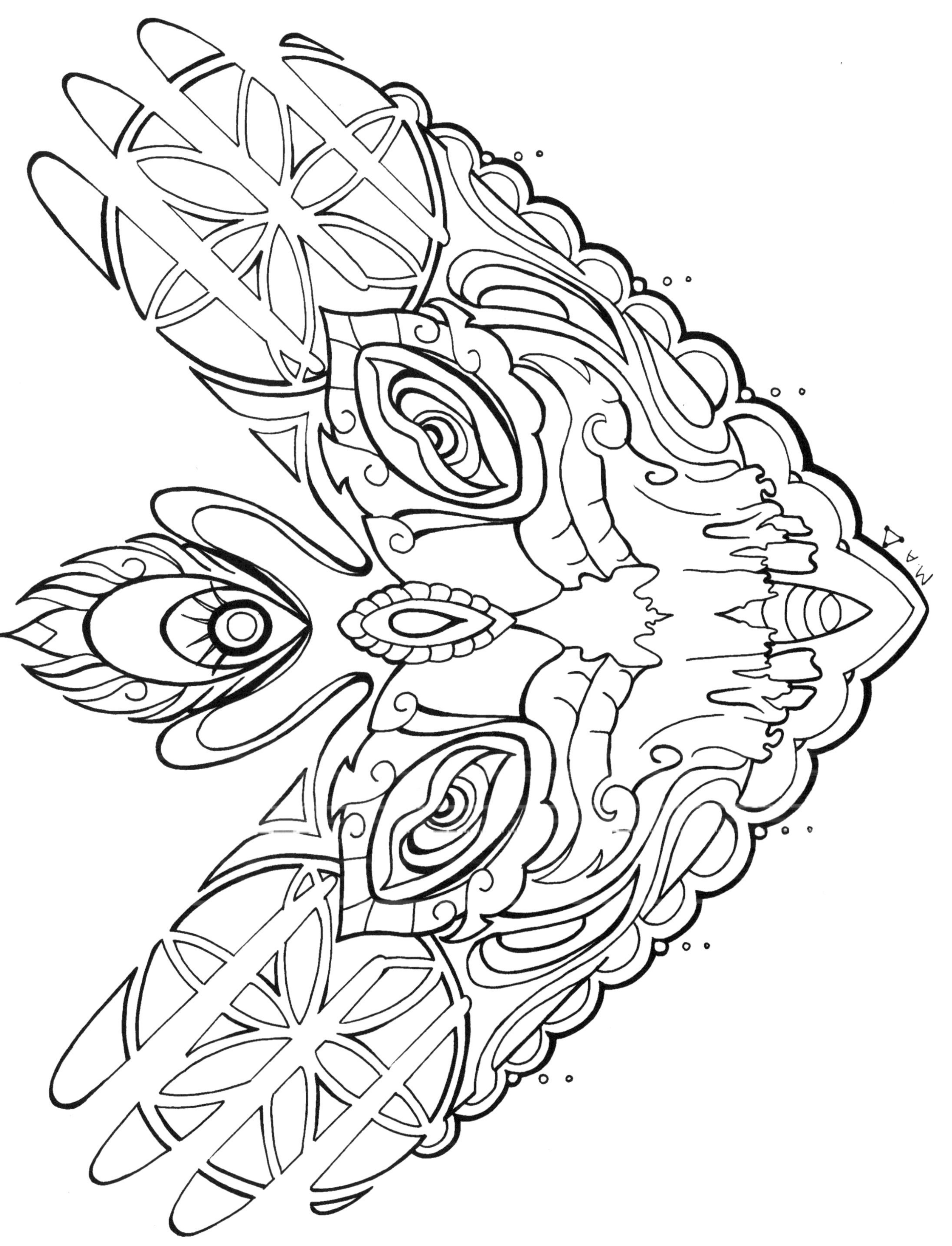

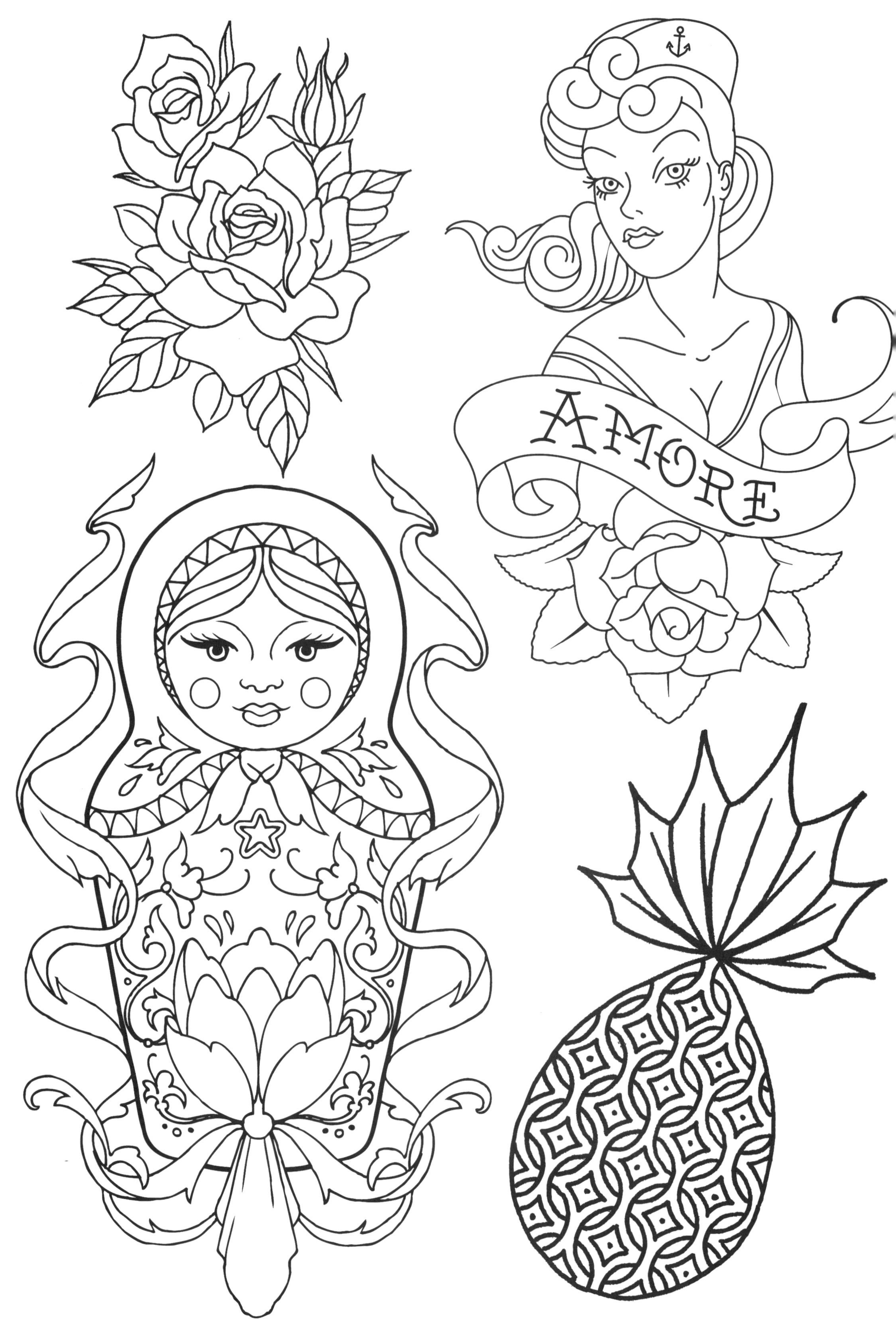
AMORE

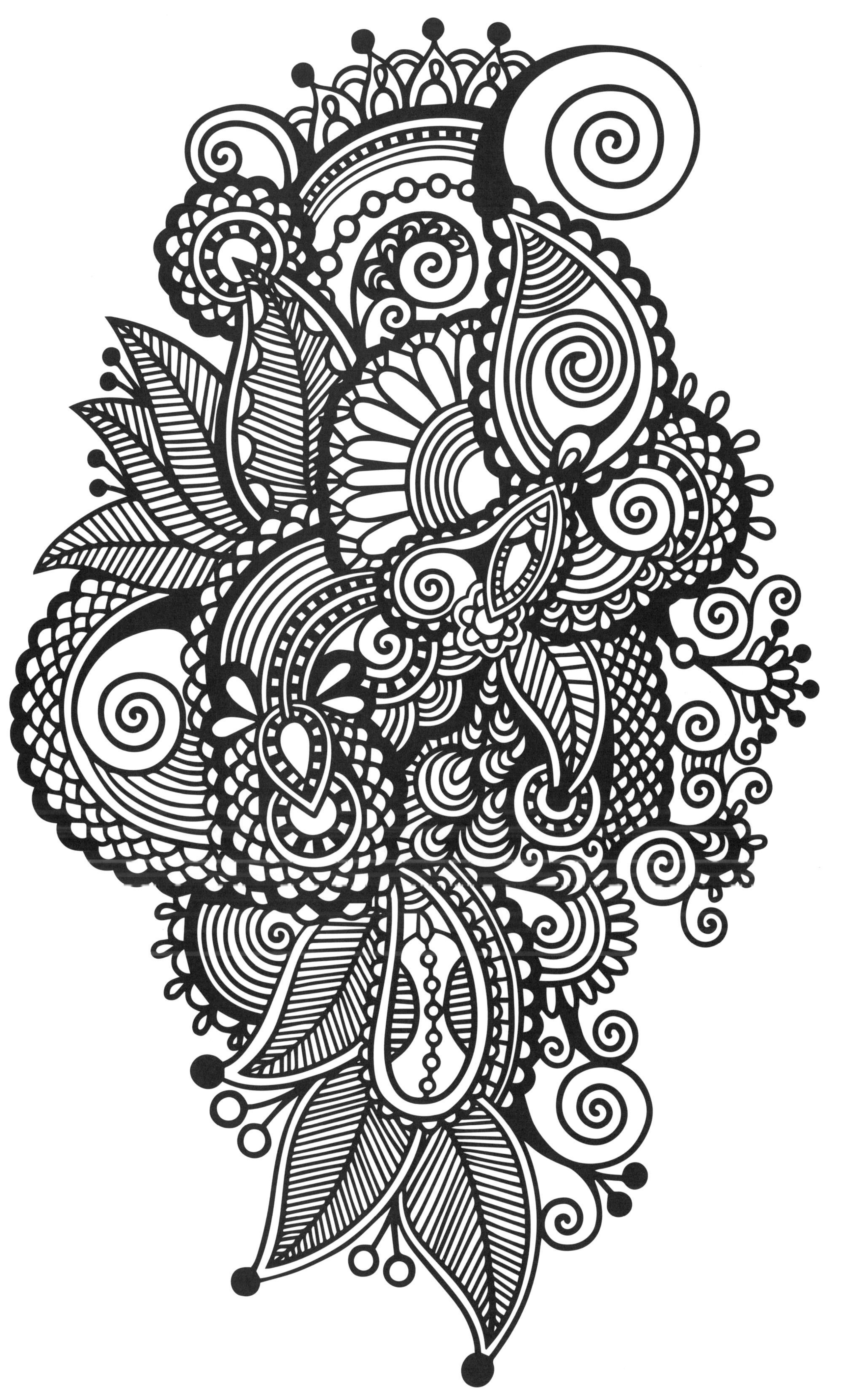

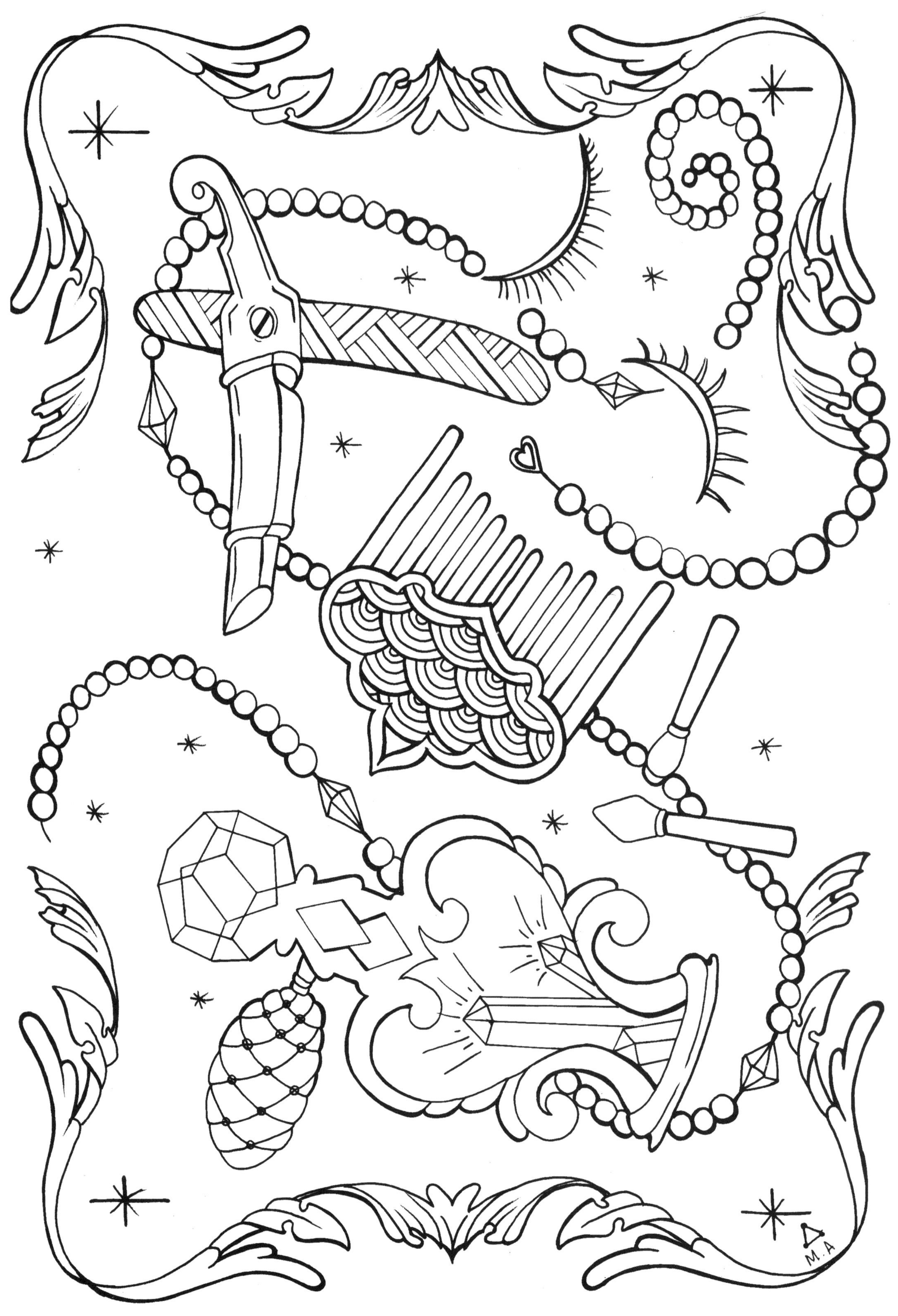
M.A

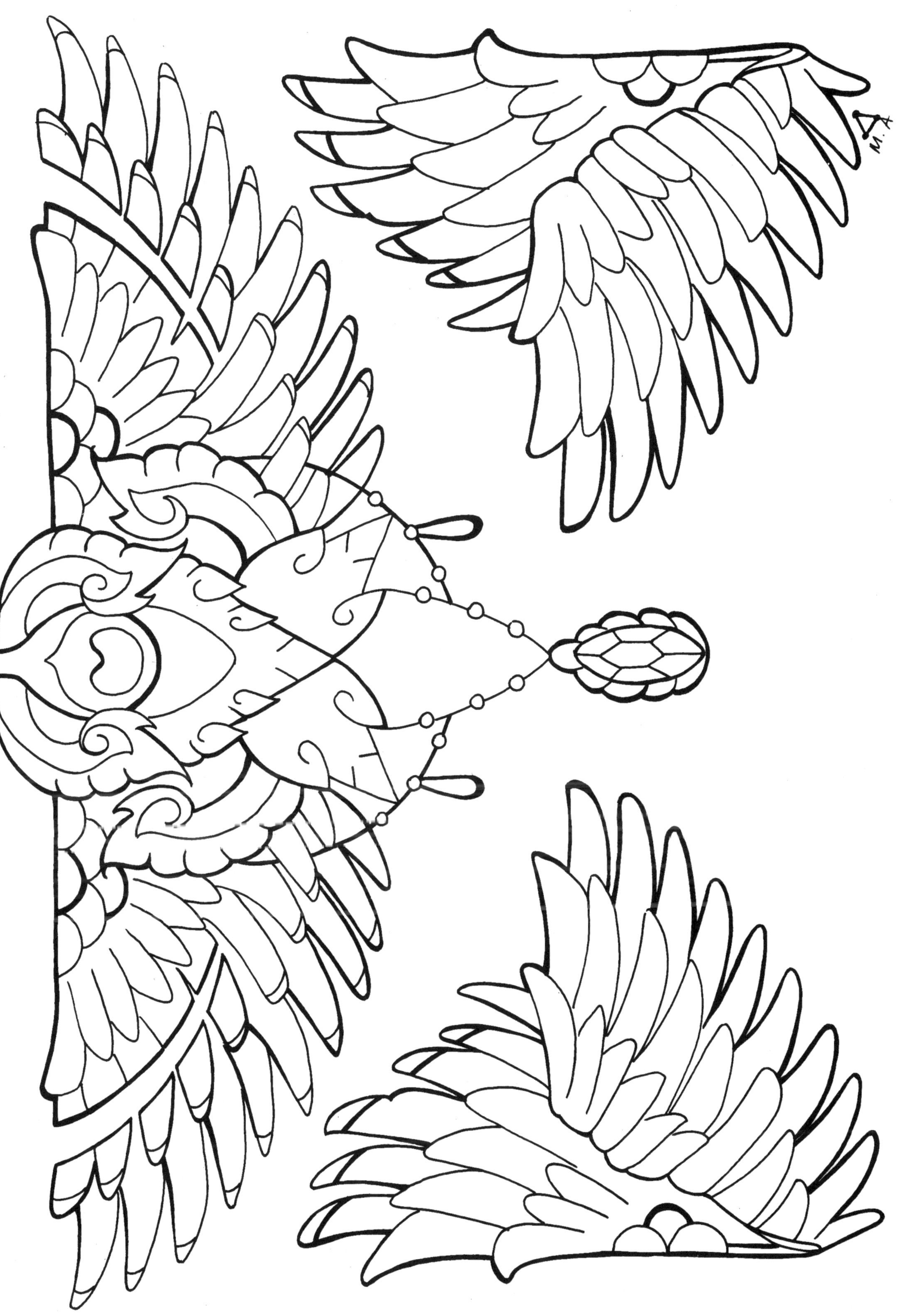

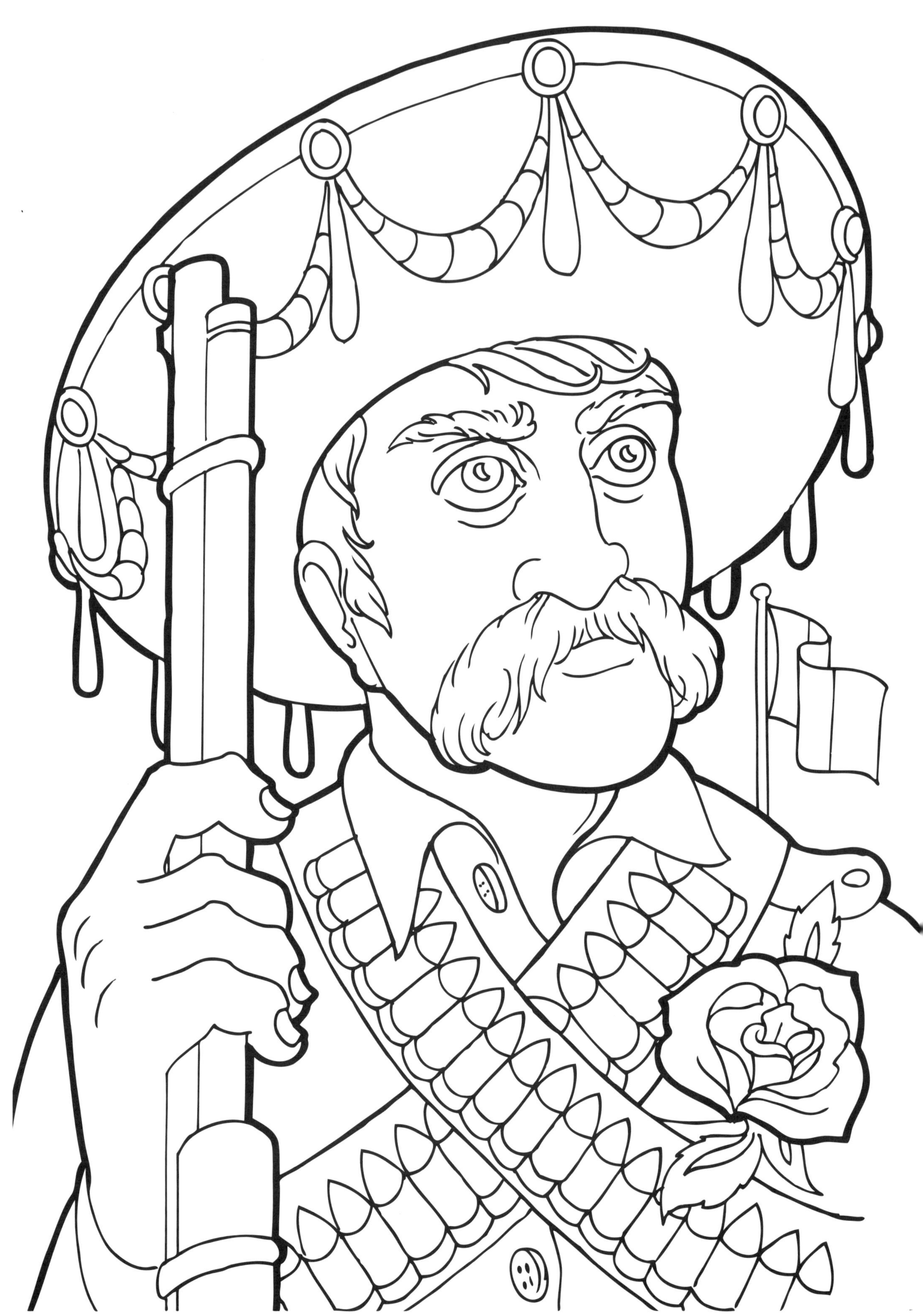

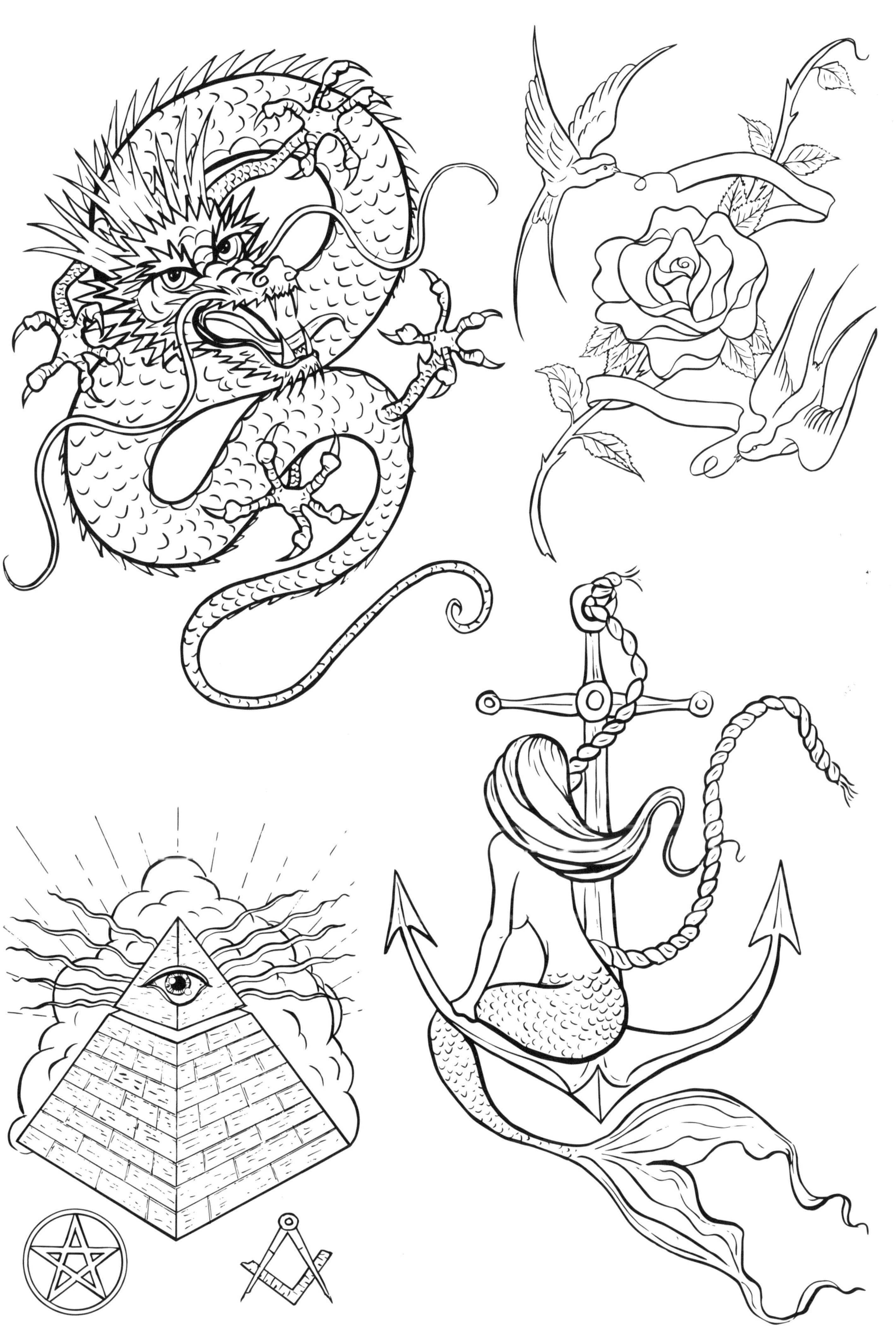

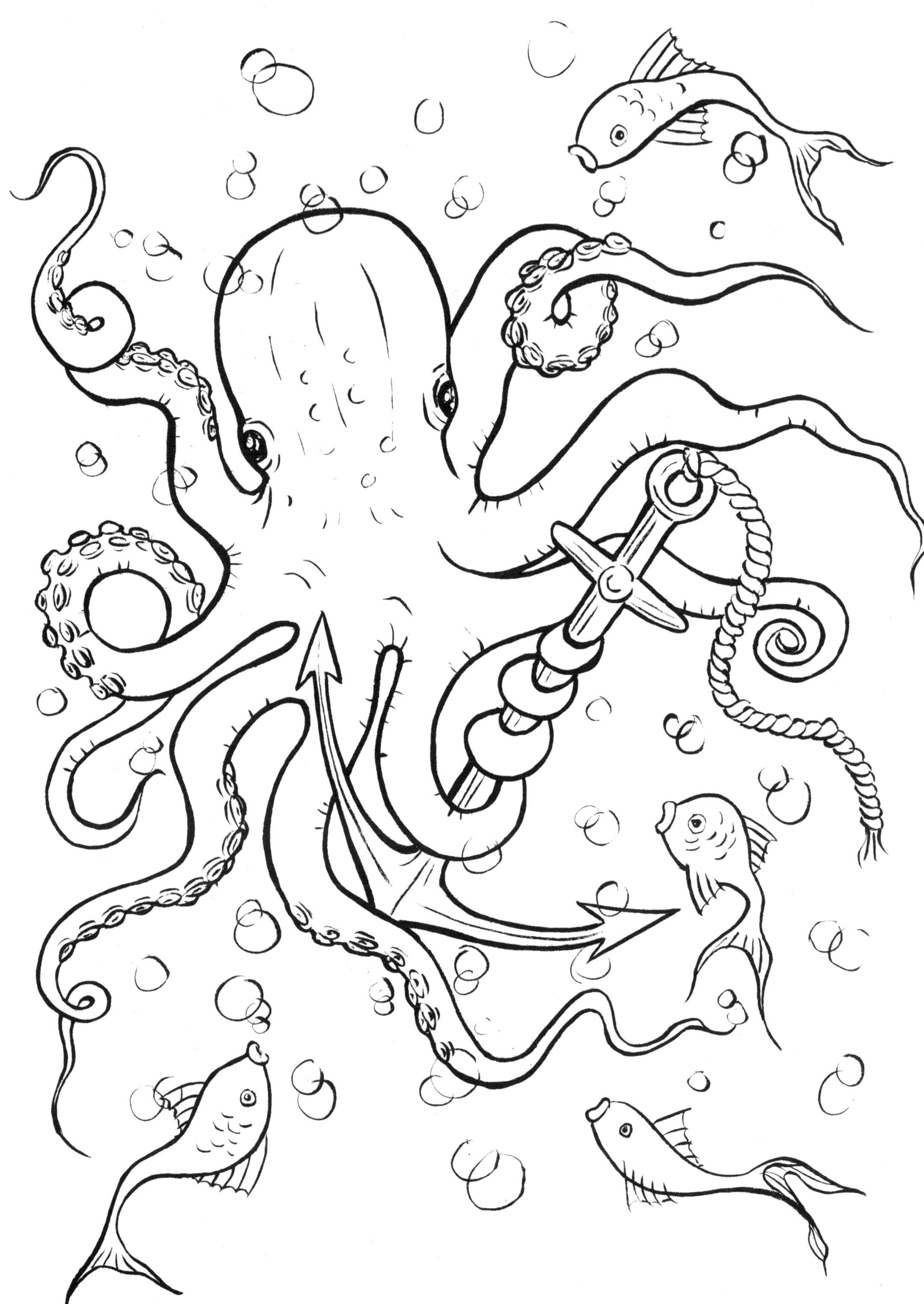

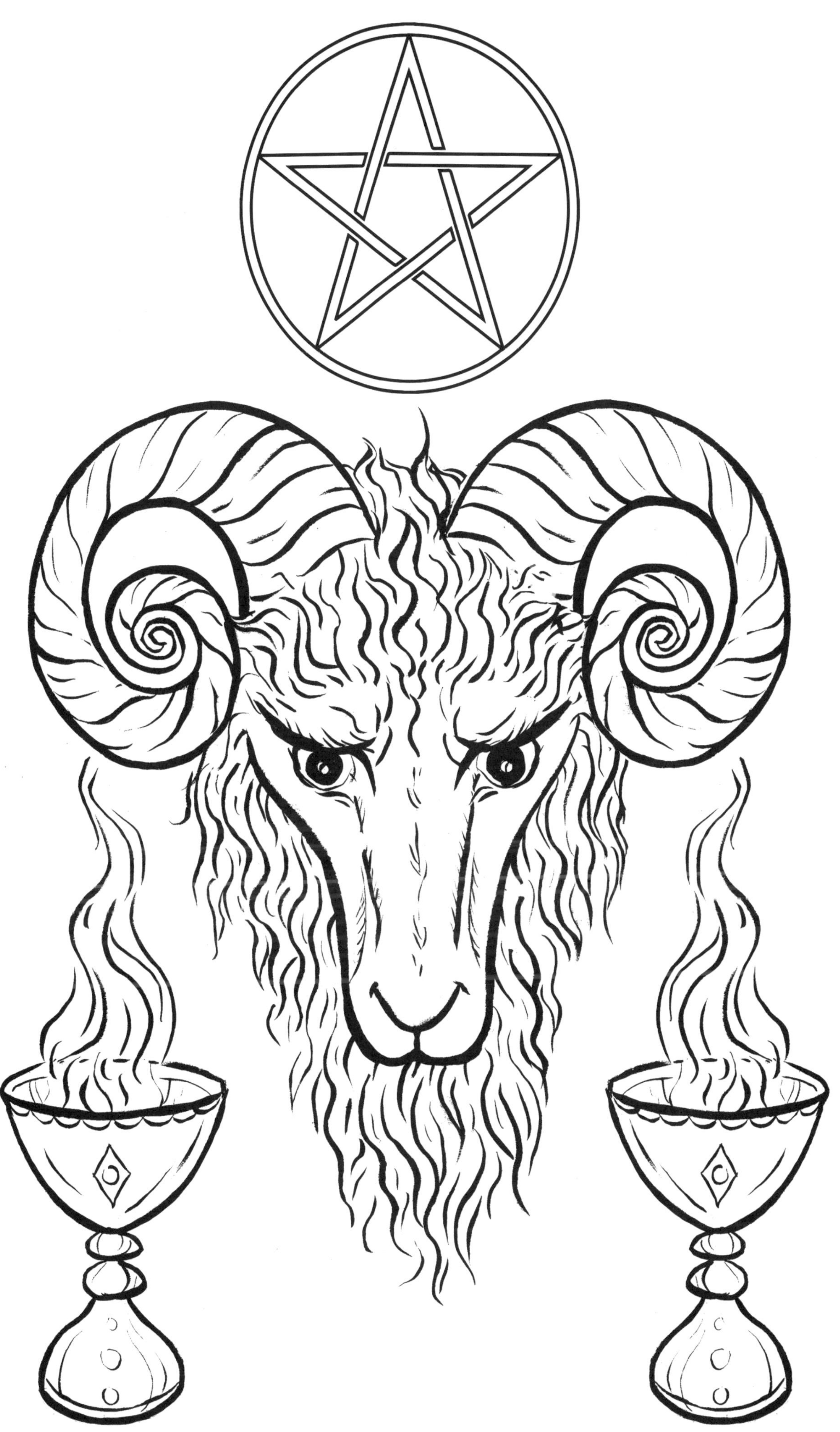

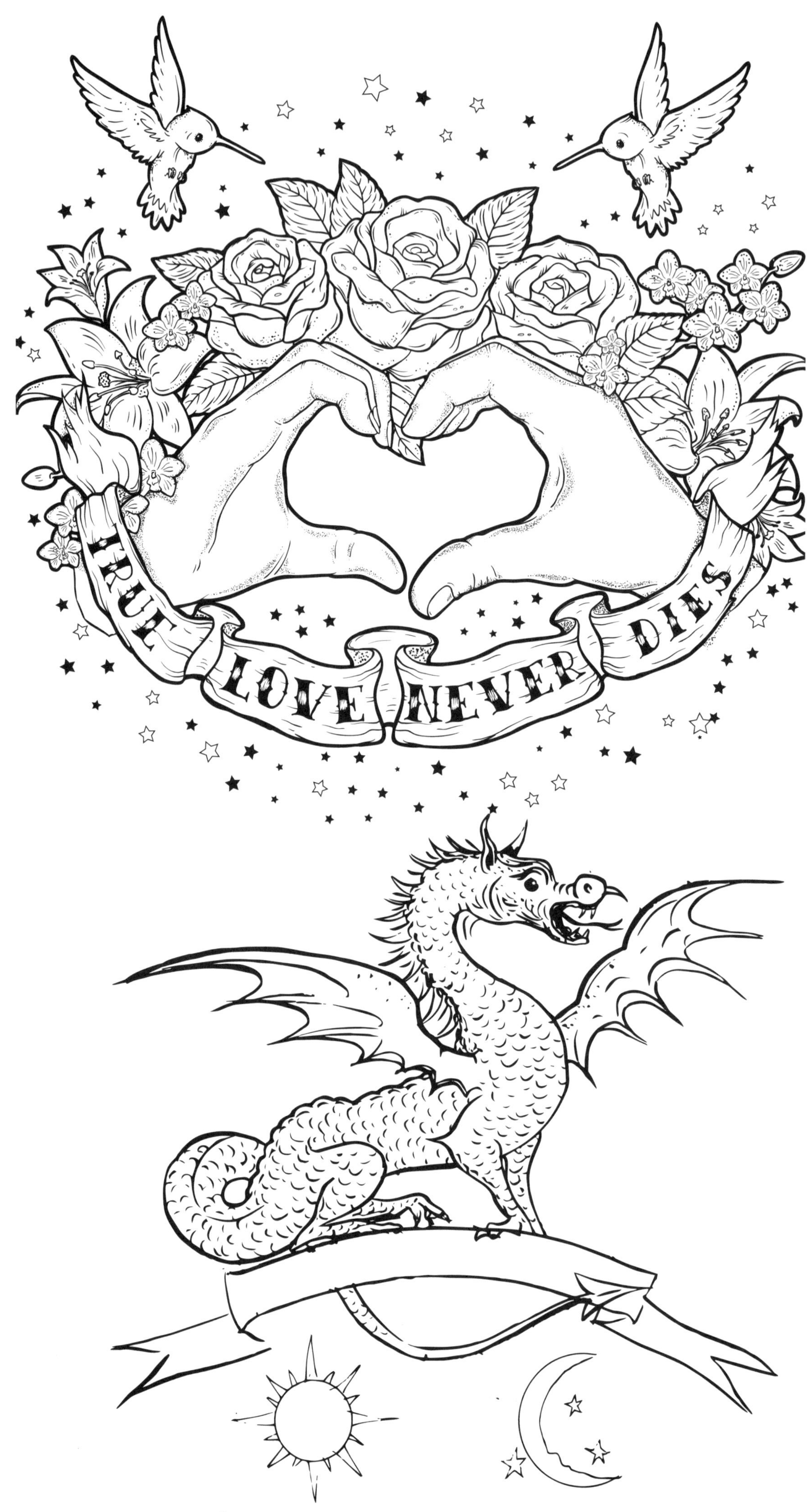
TRUE LOVE NEVER DIES

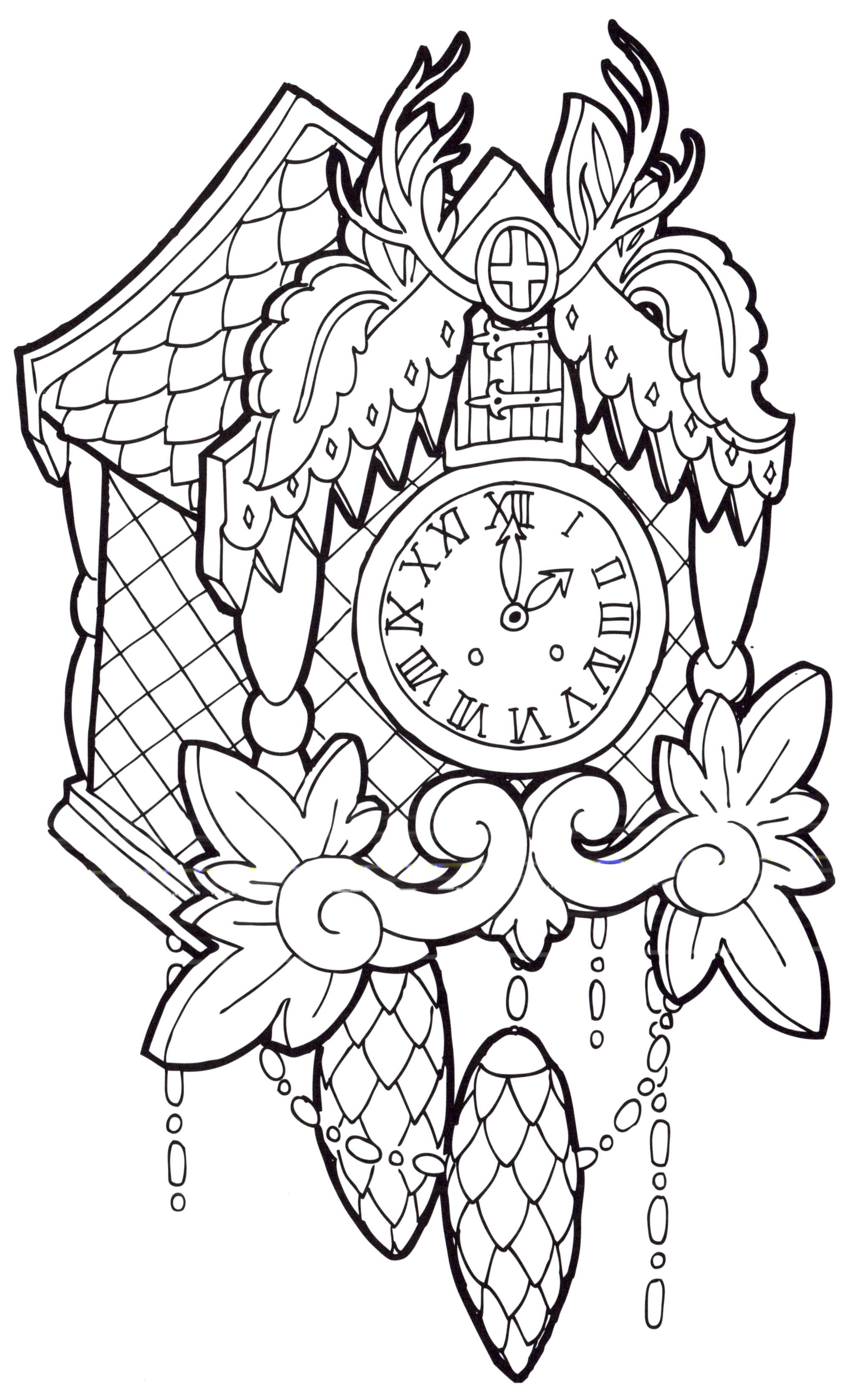

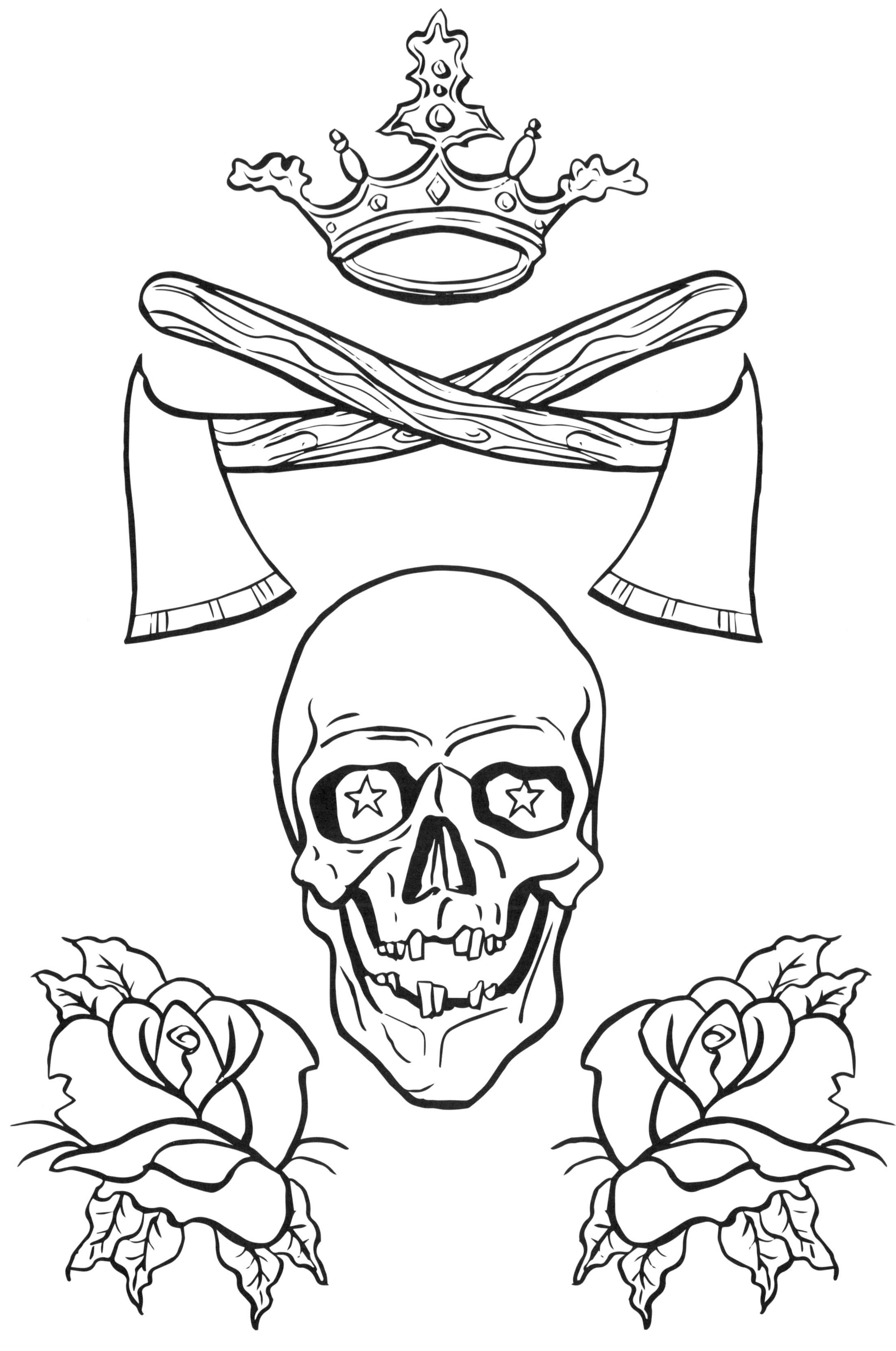

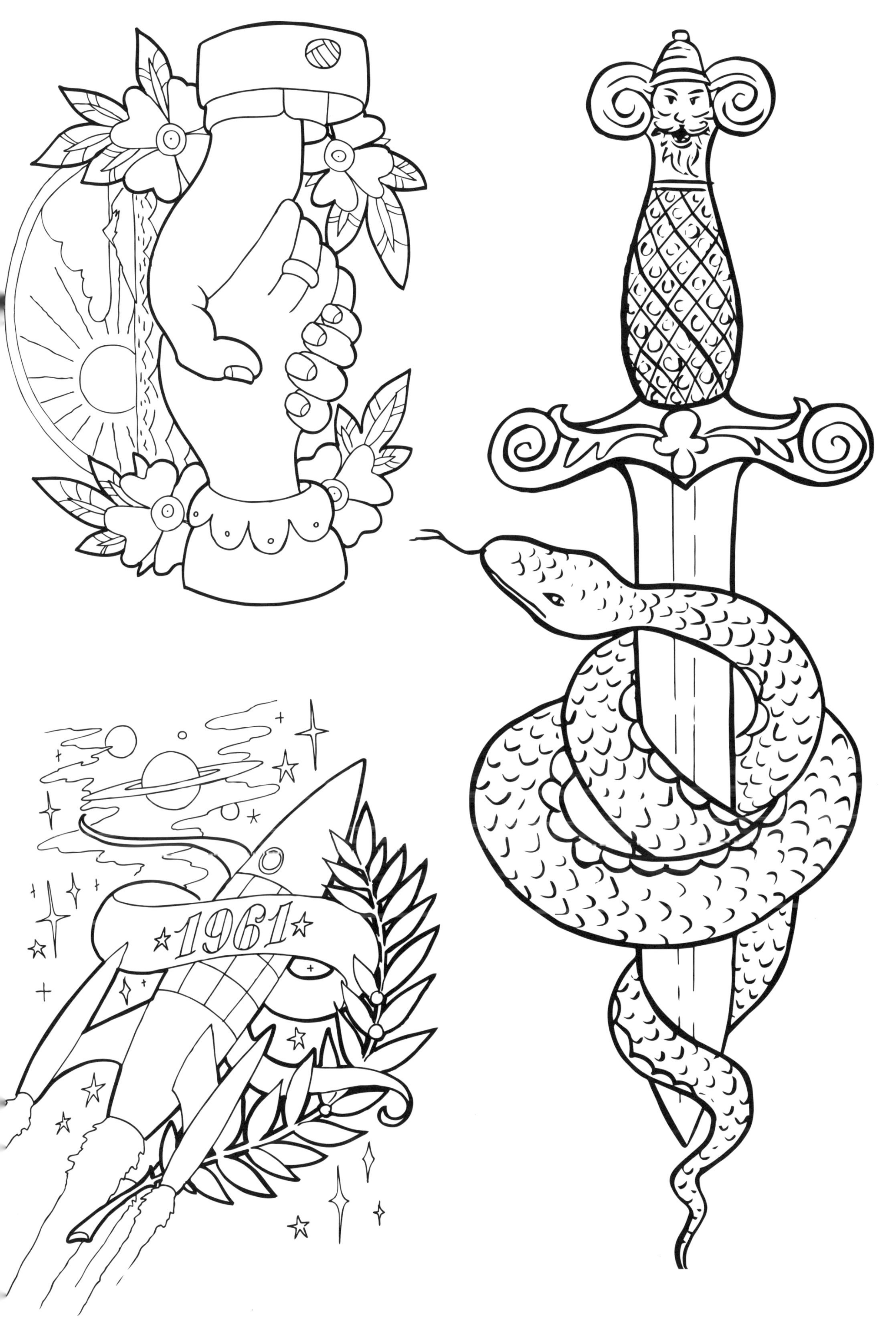
1961

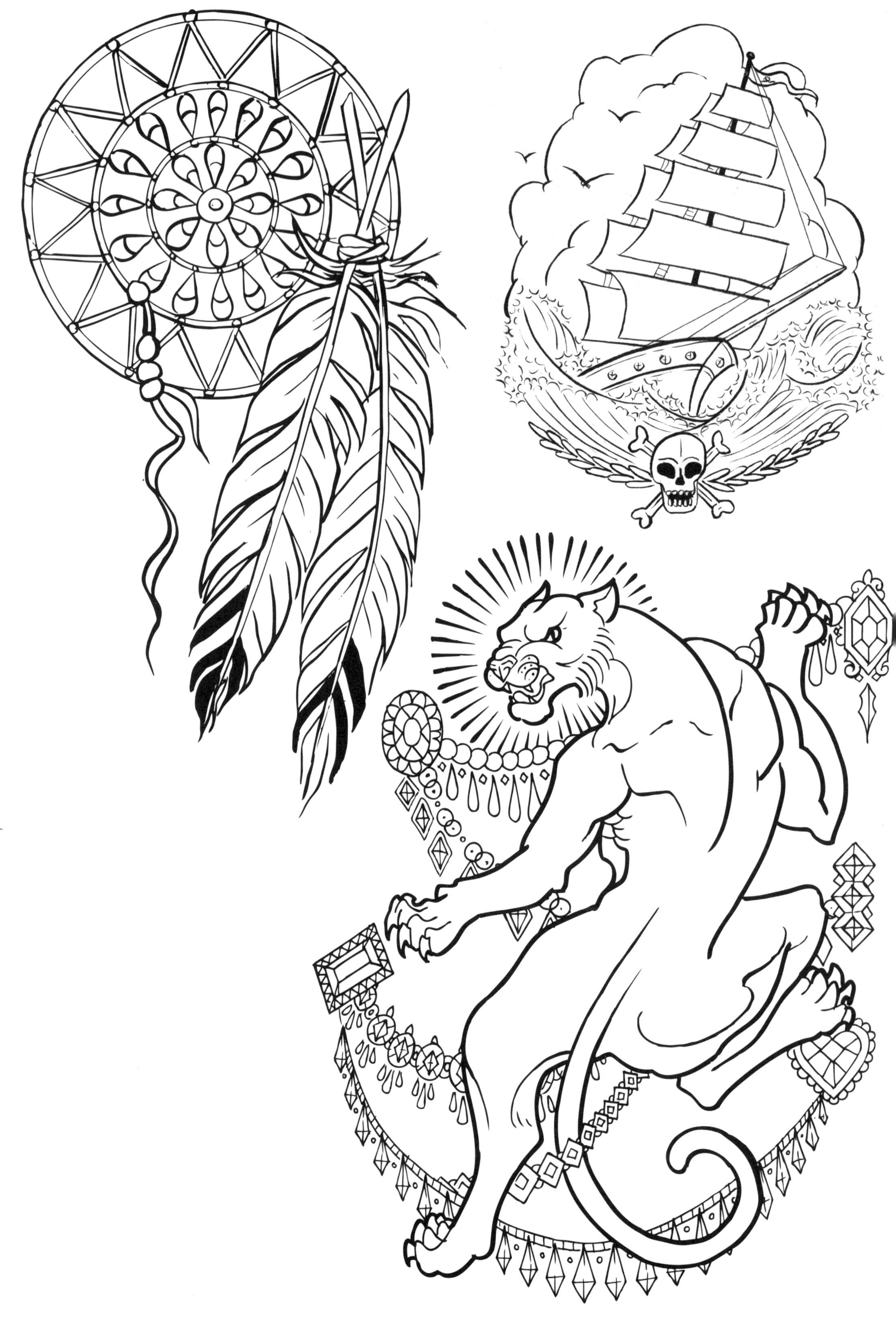

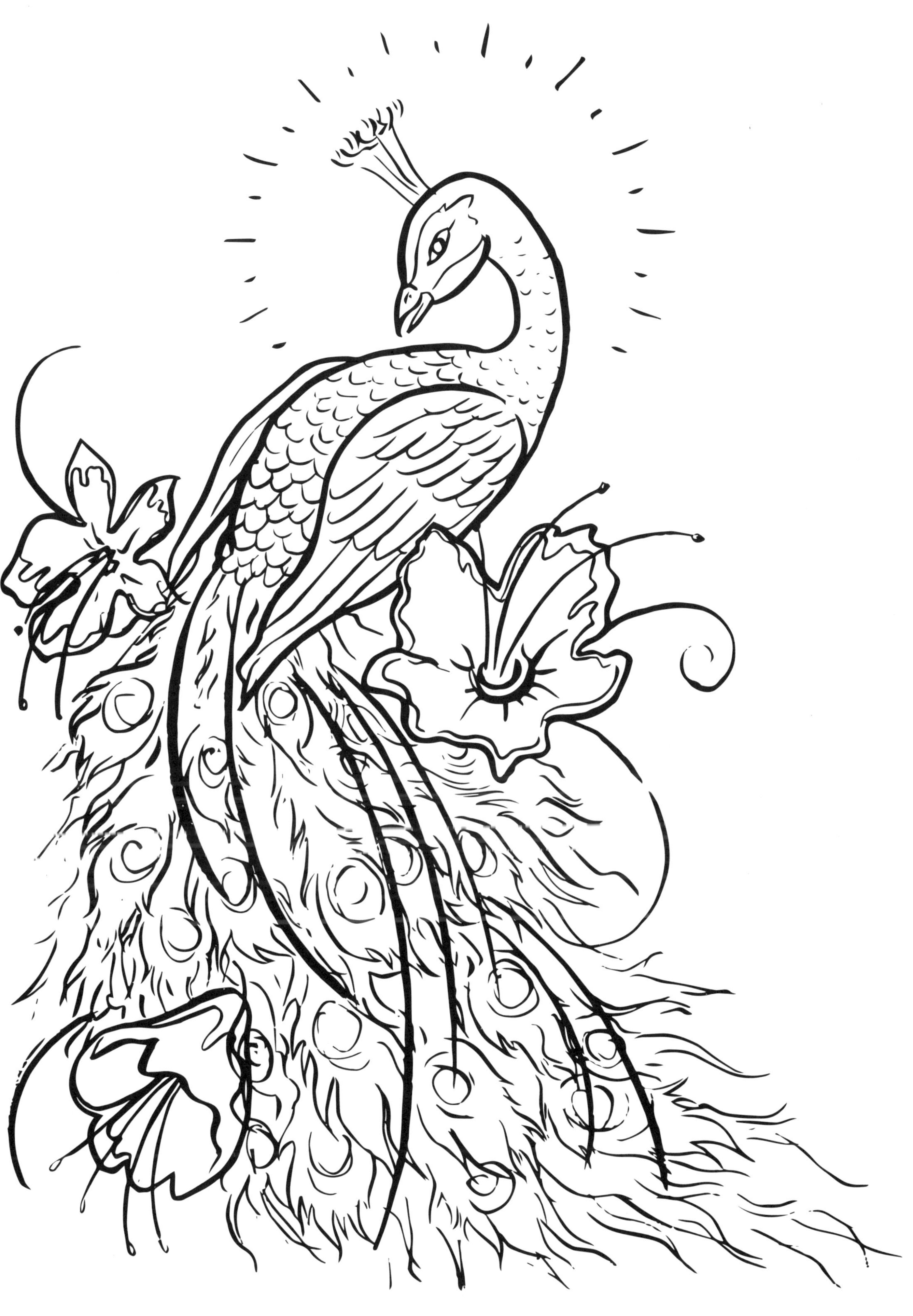

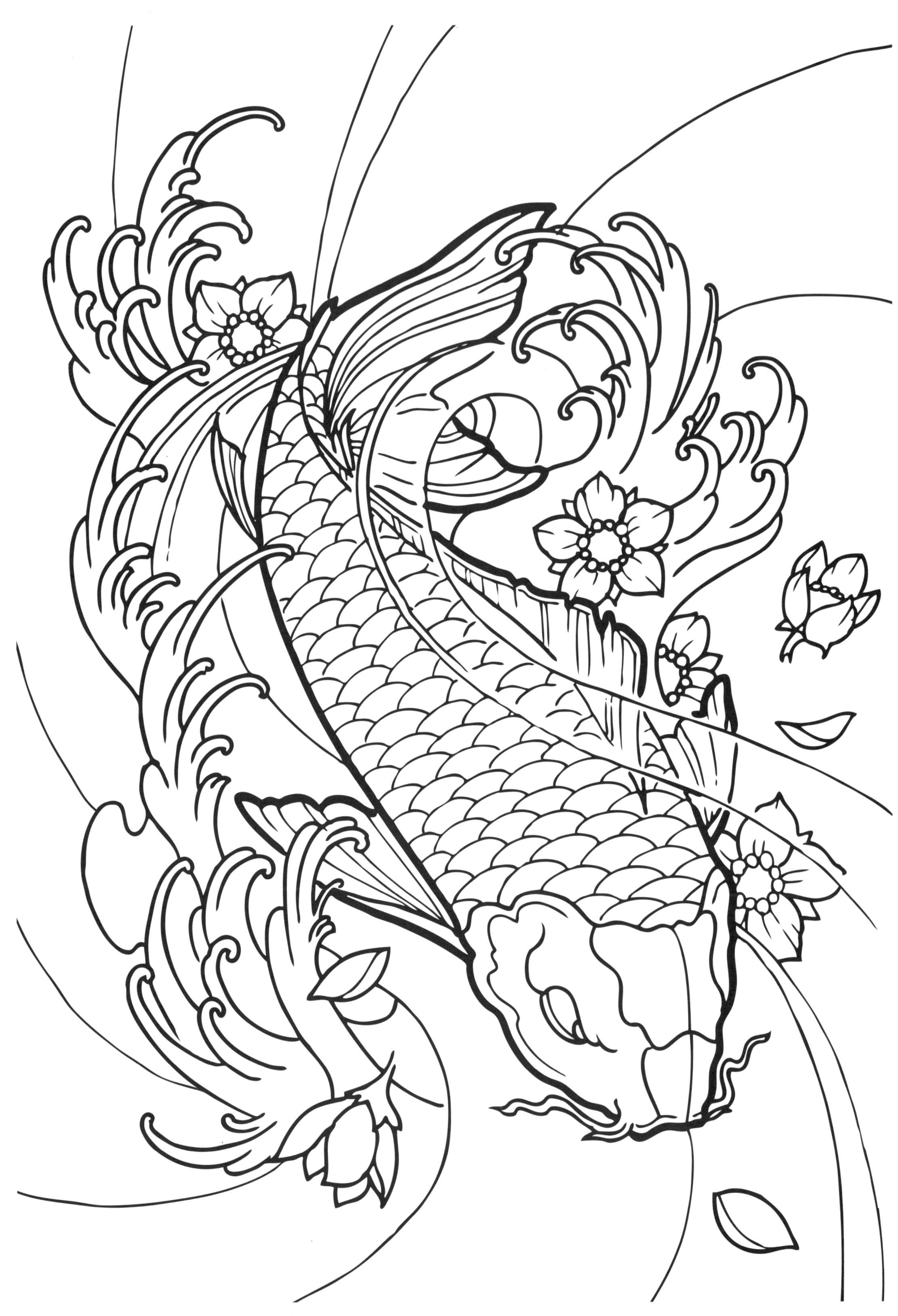

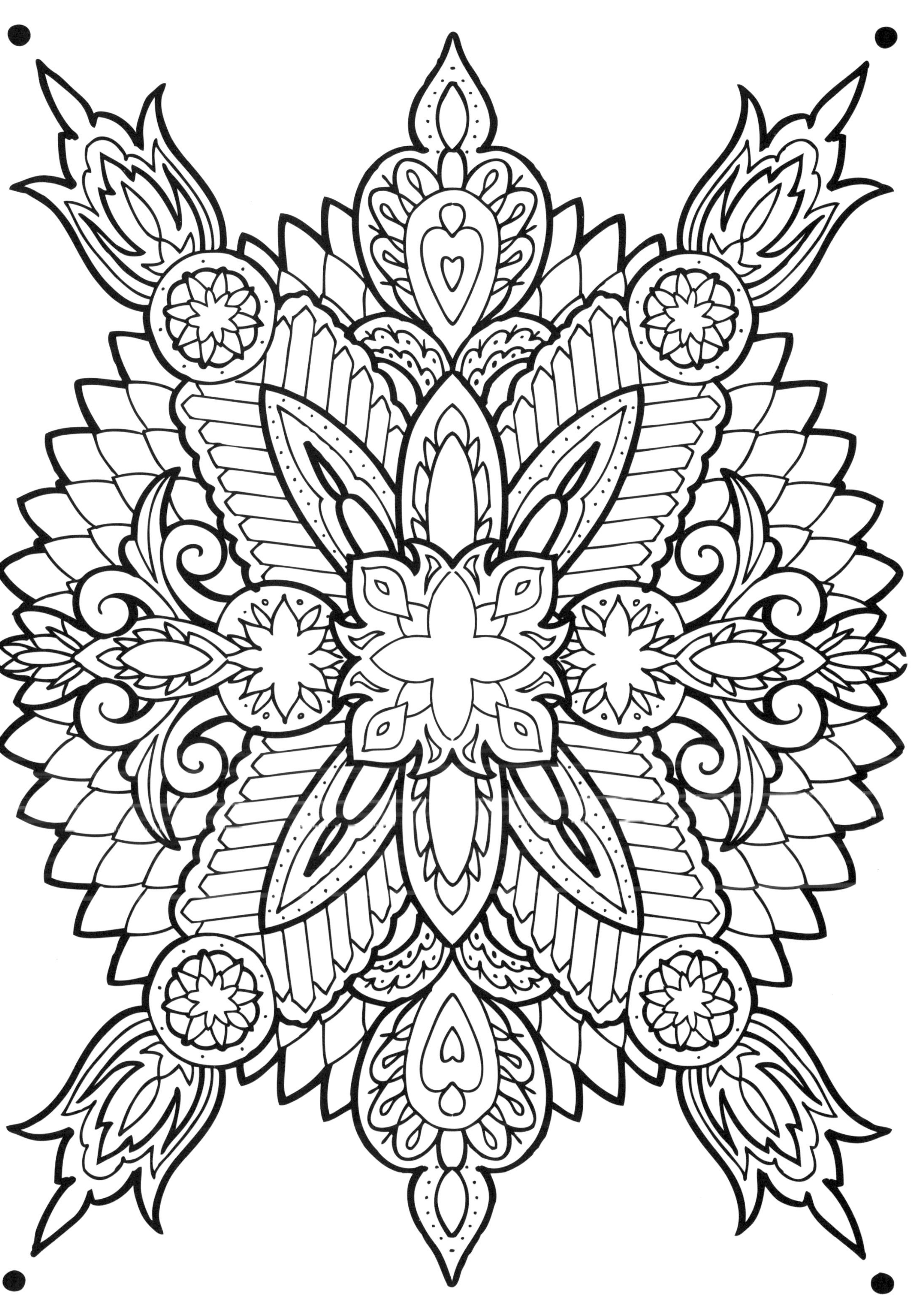

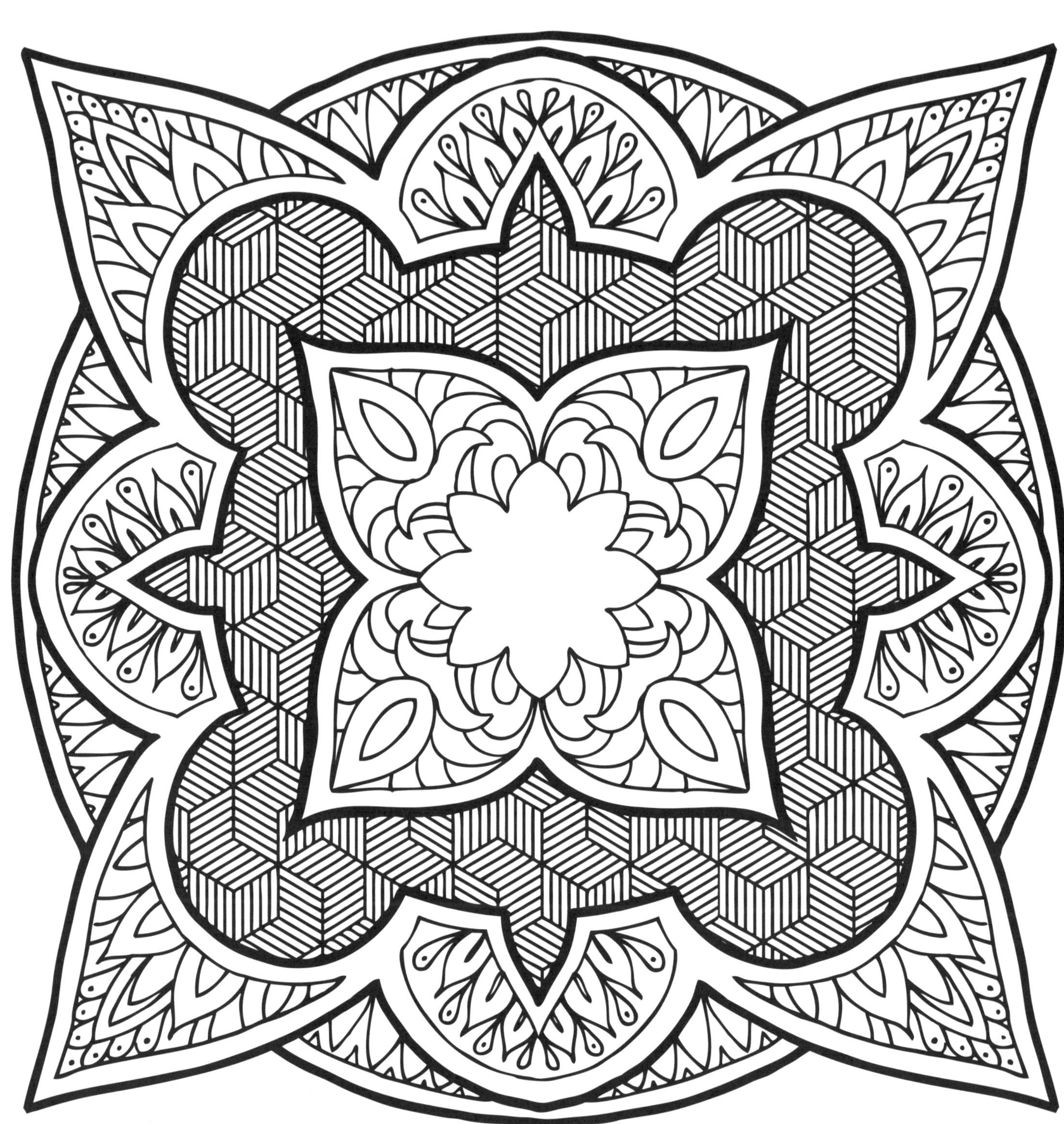

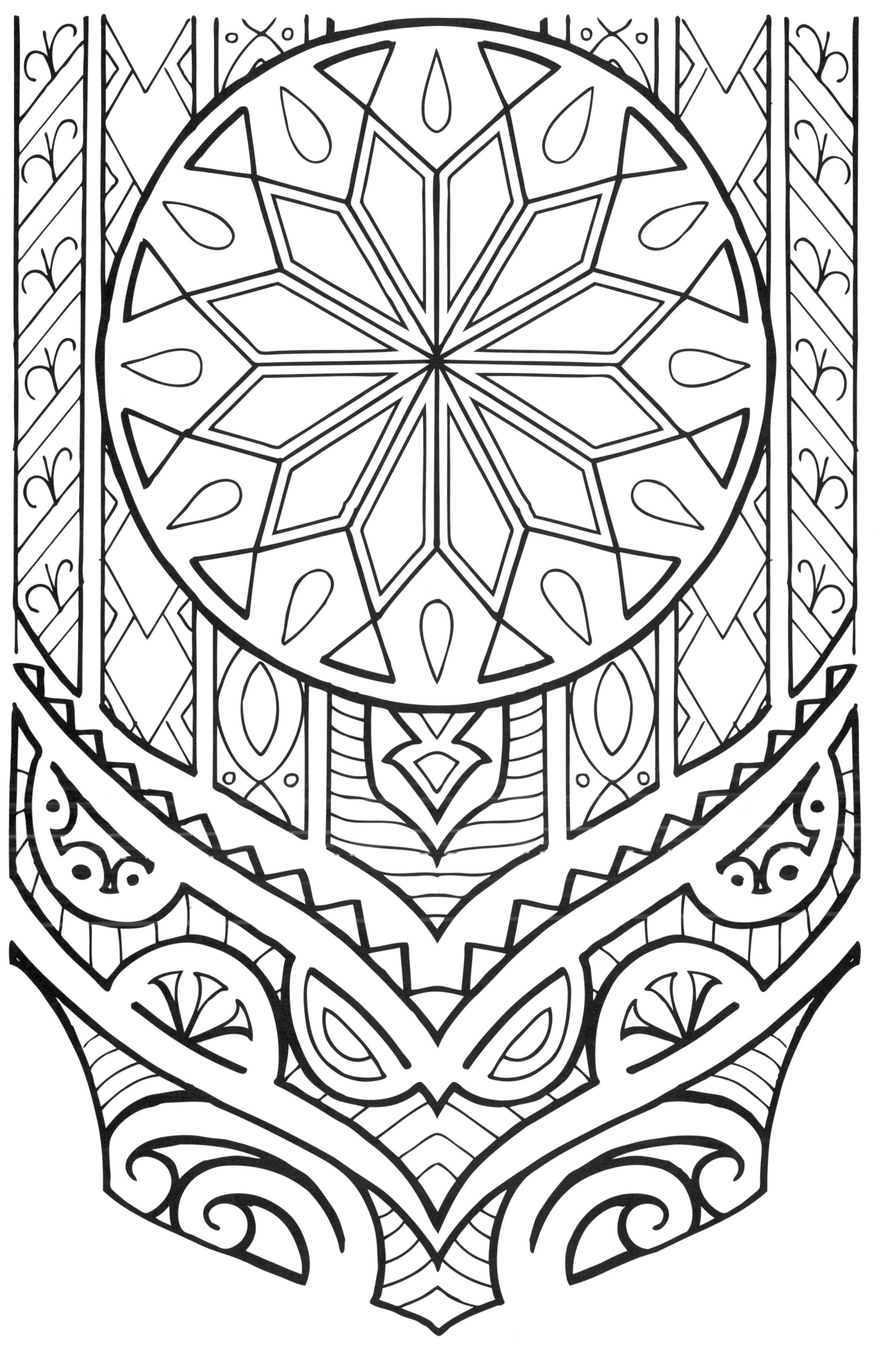

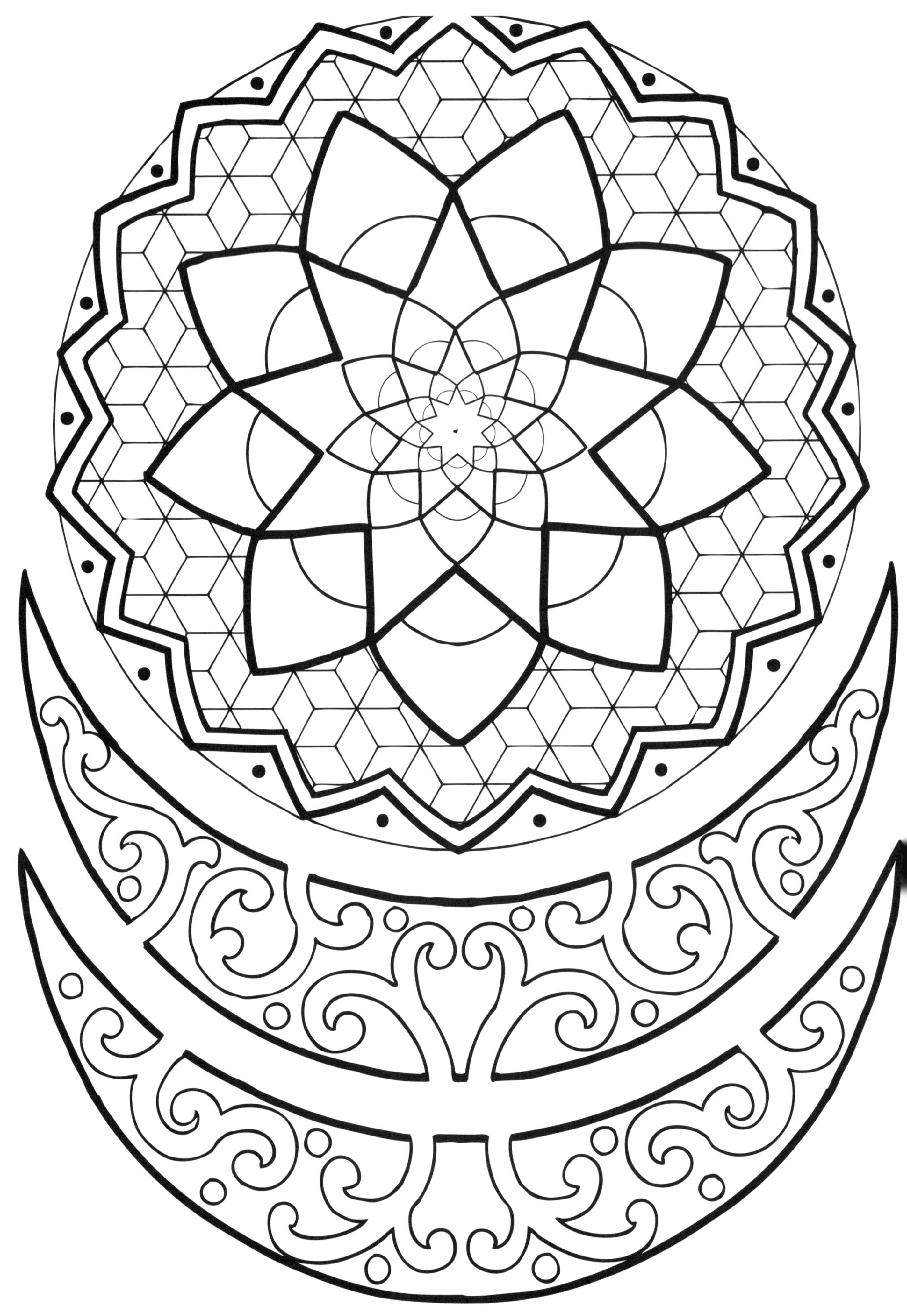

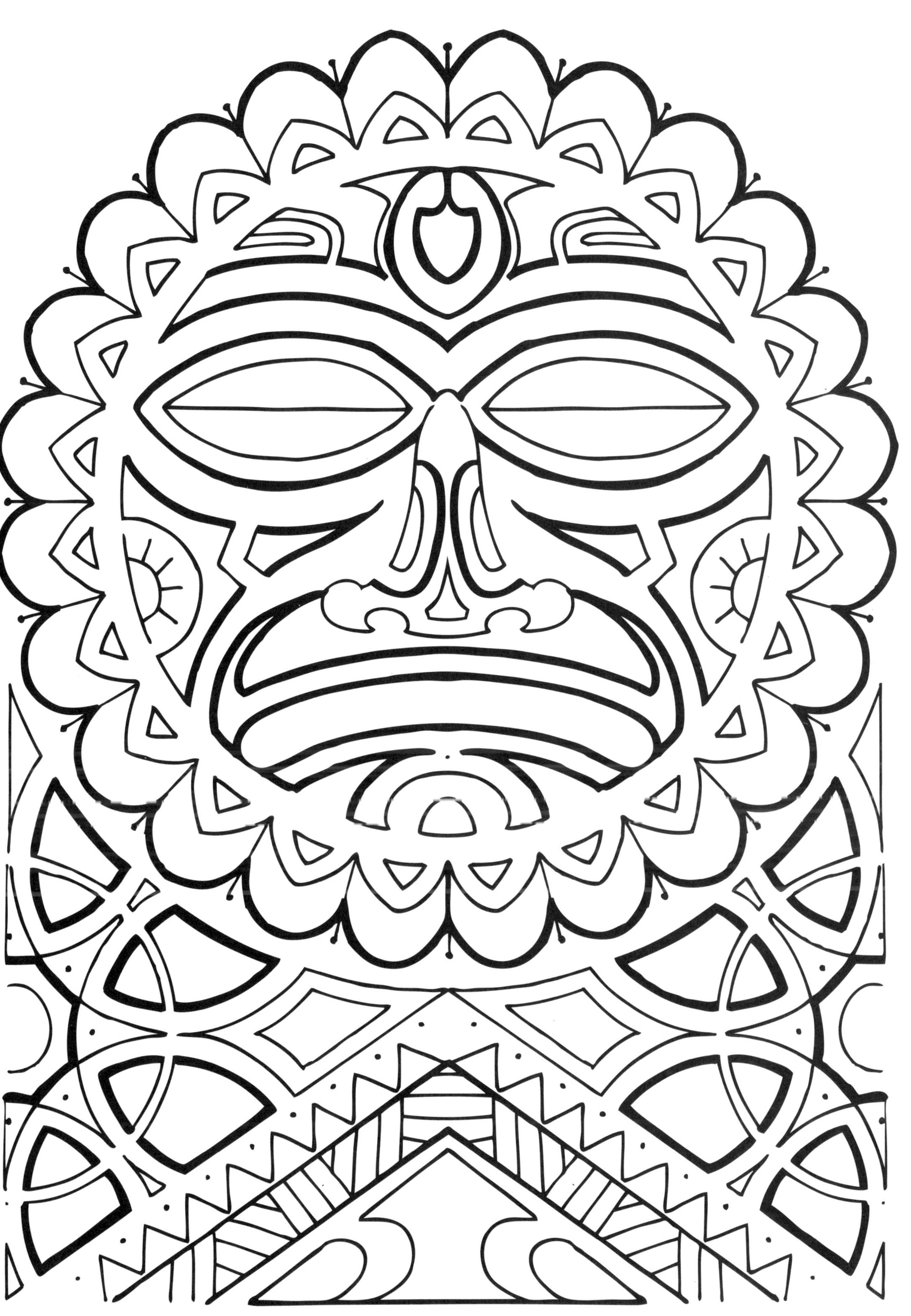

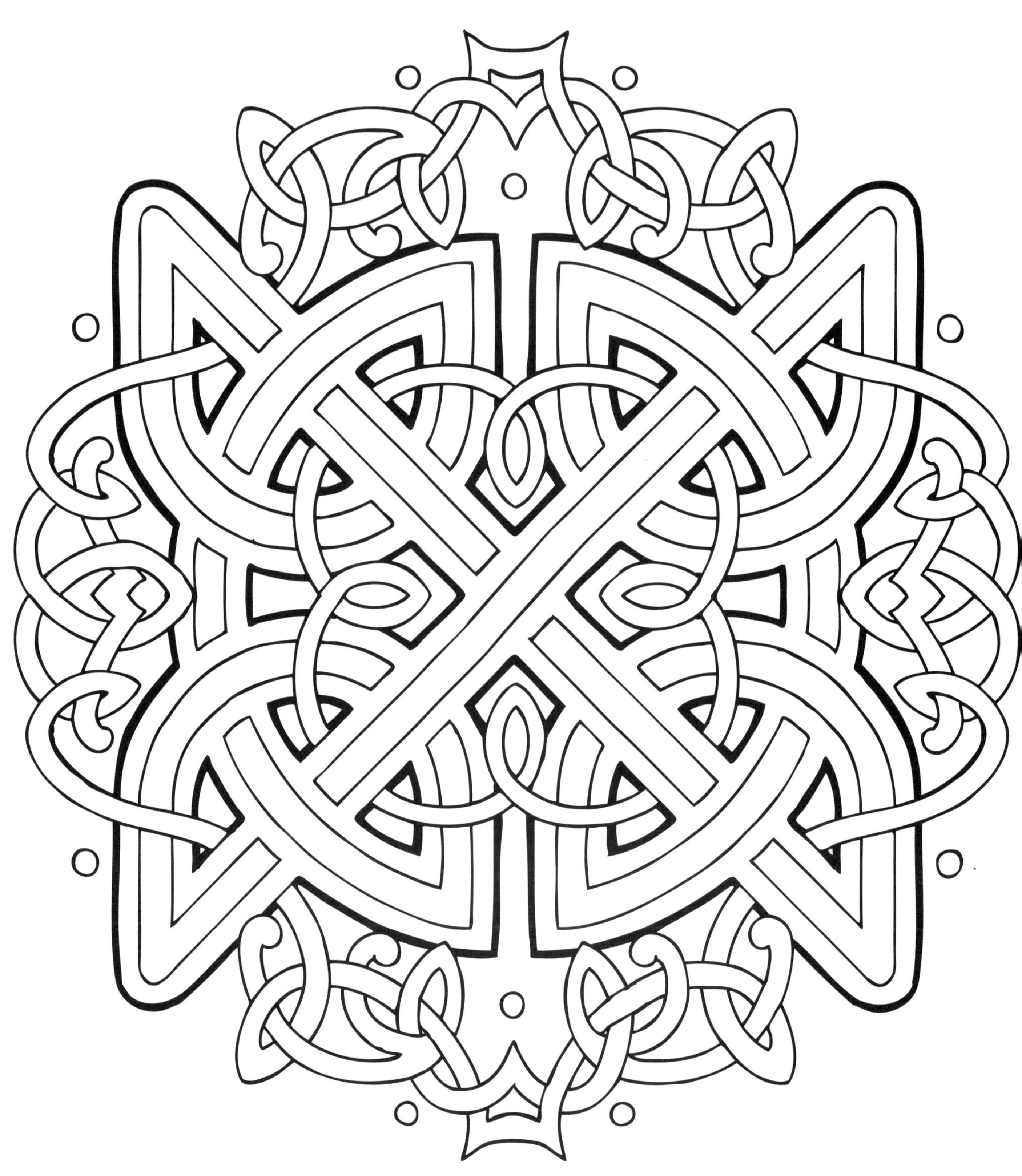

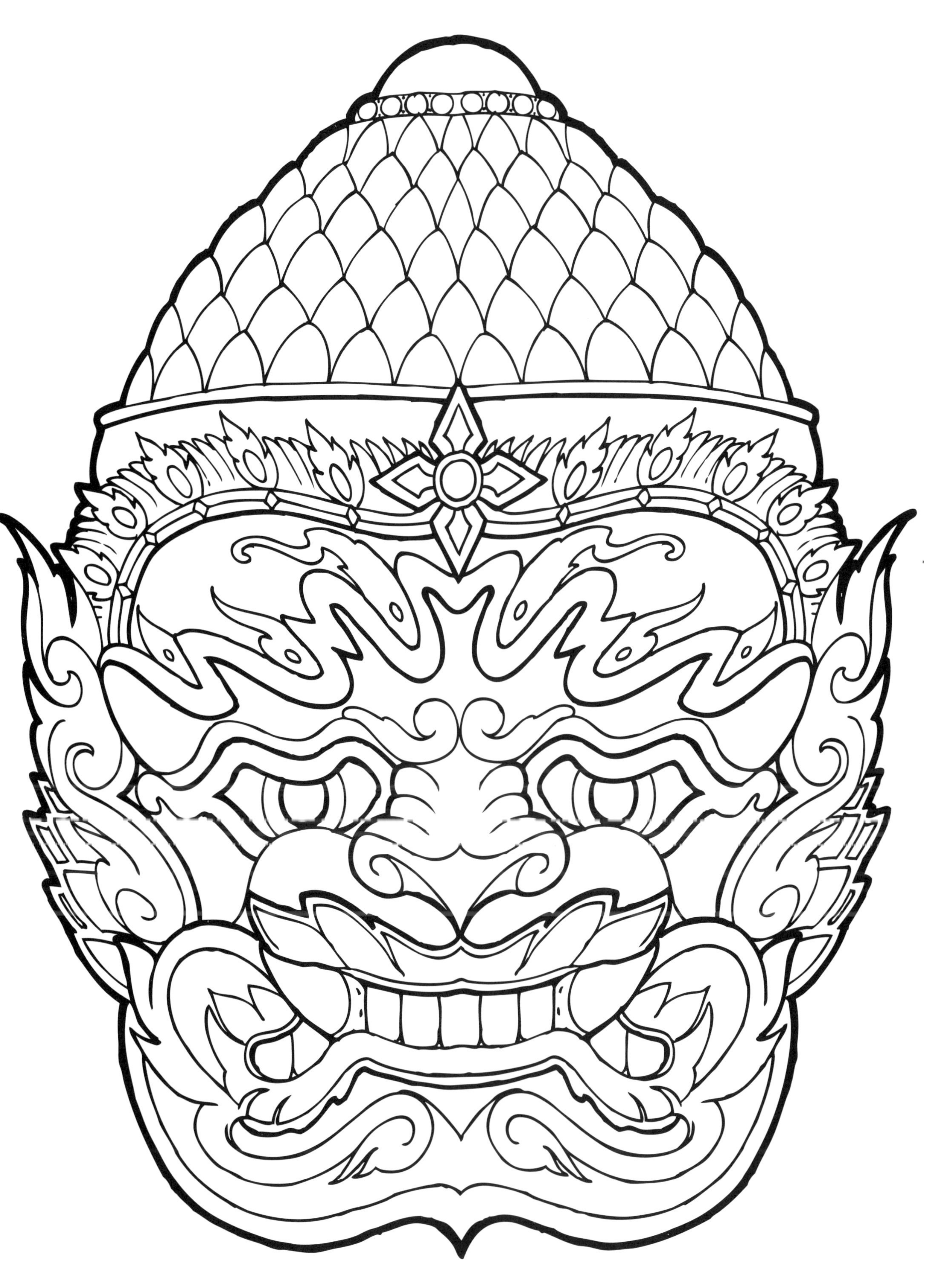

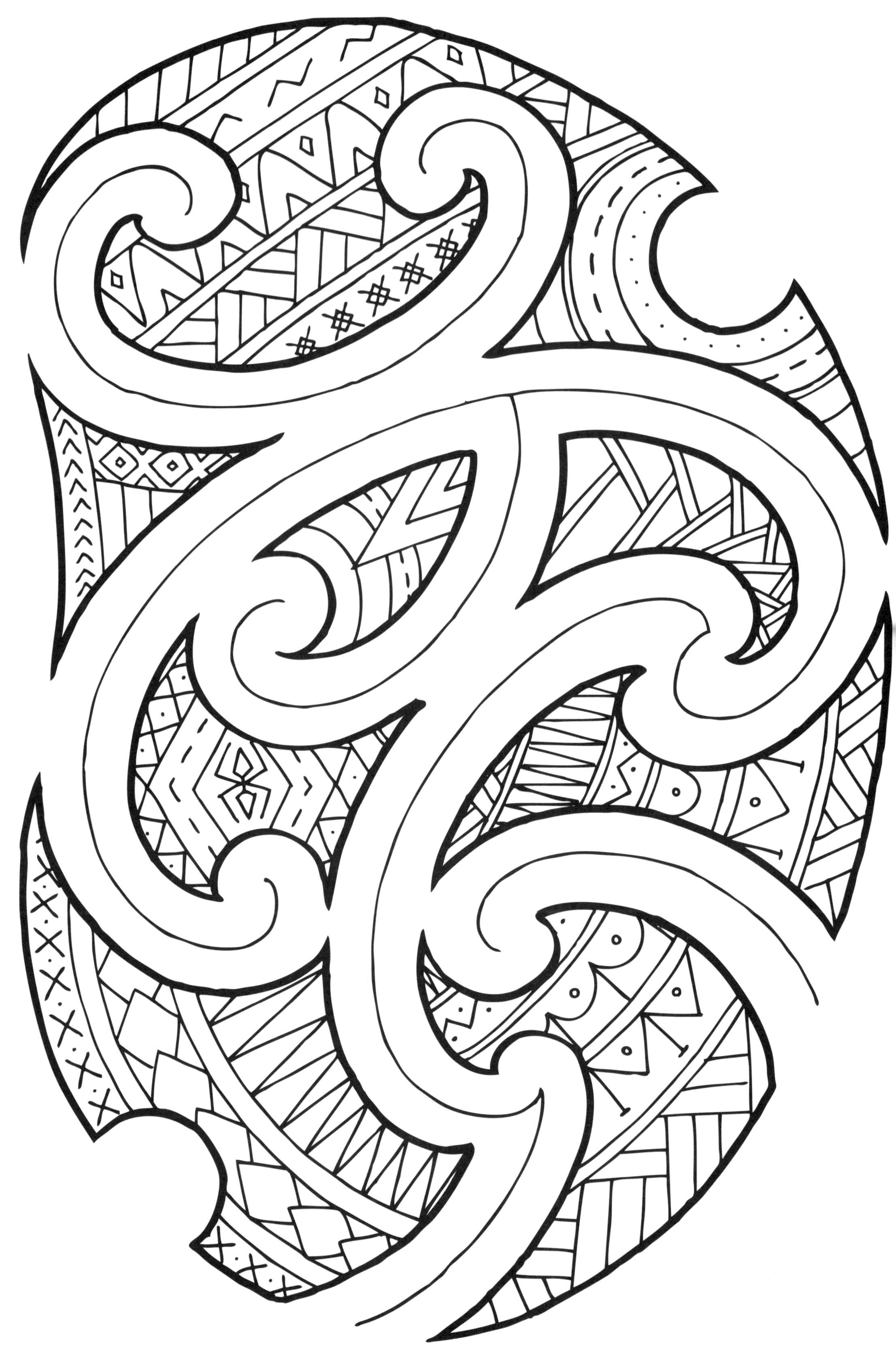

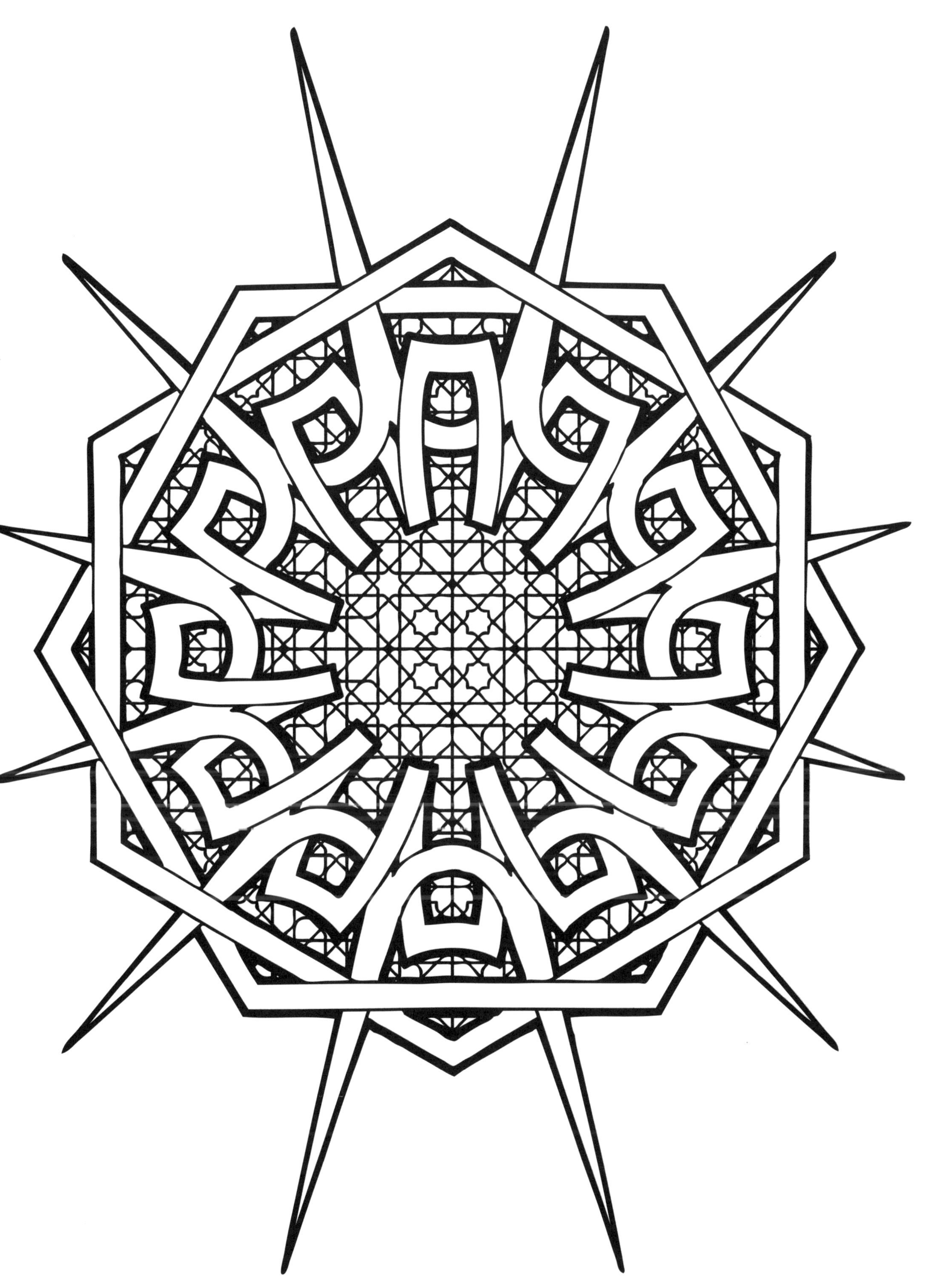

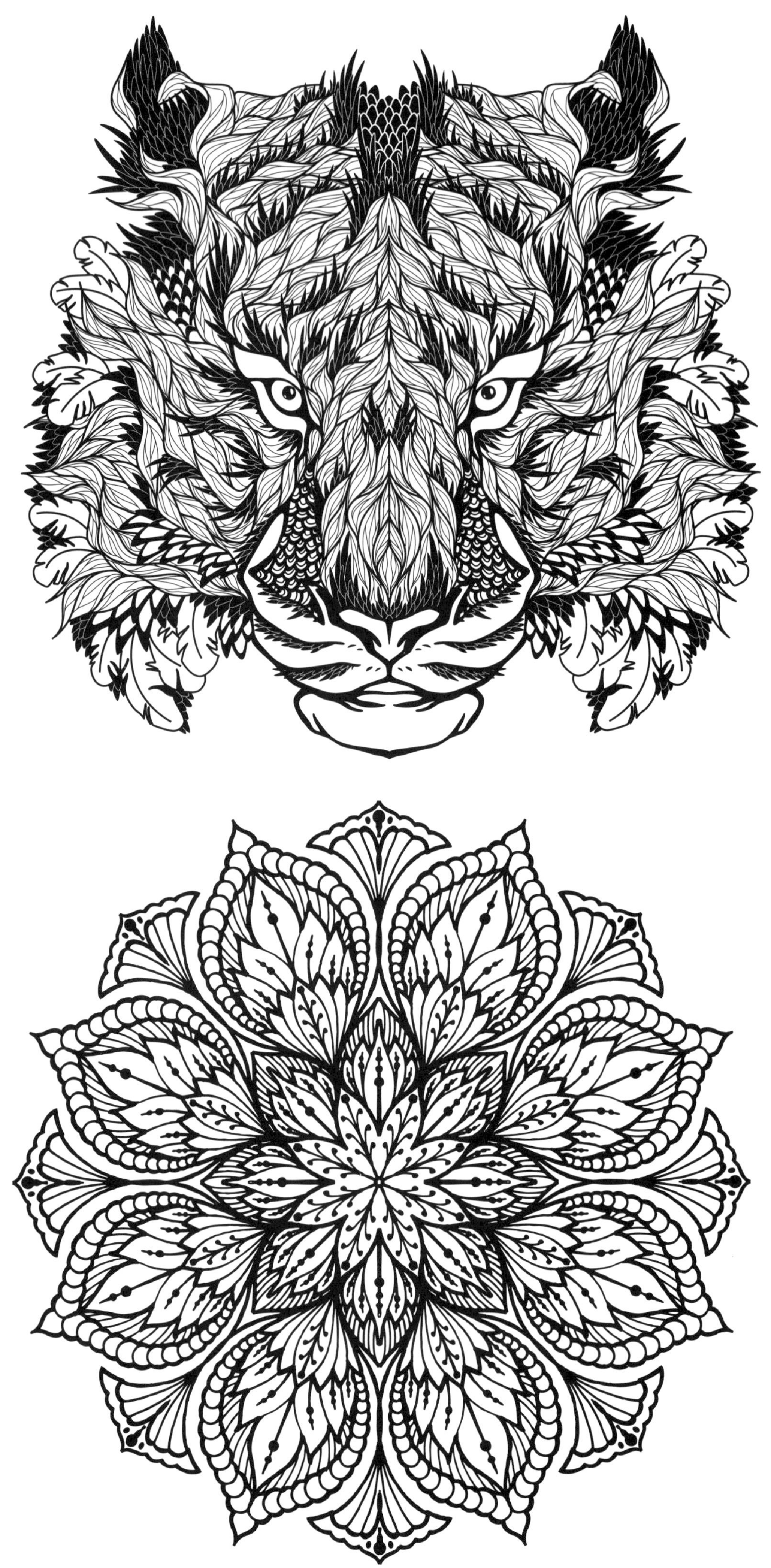

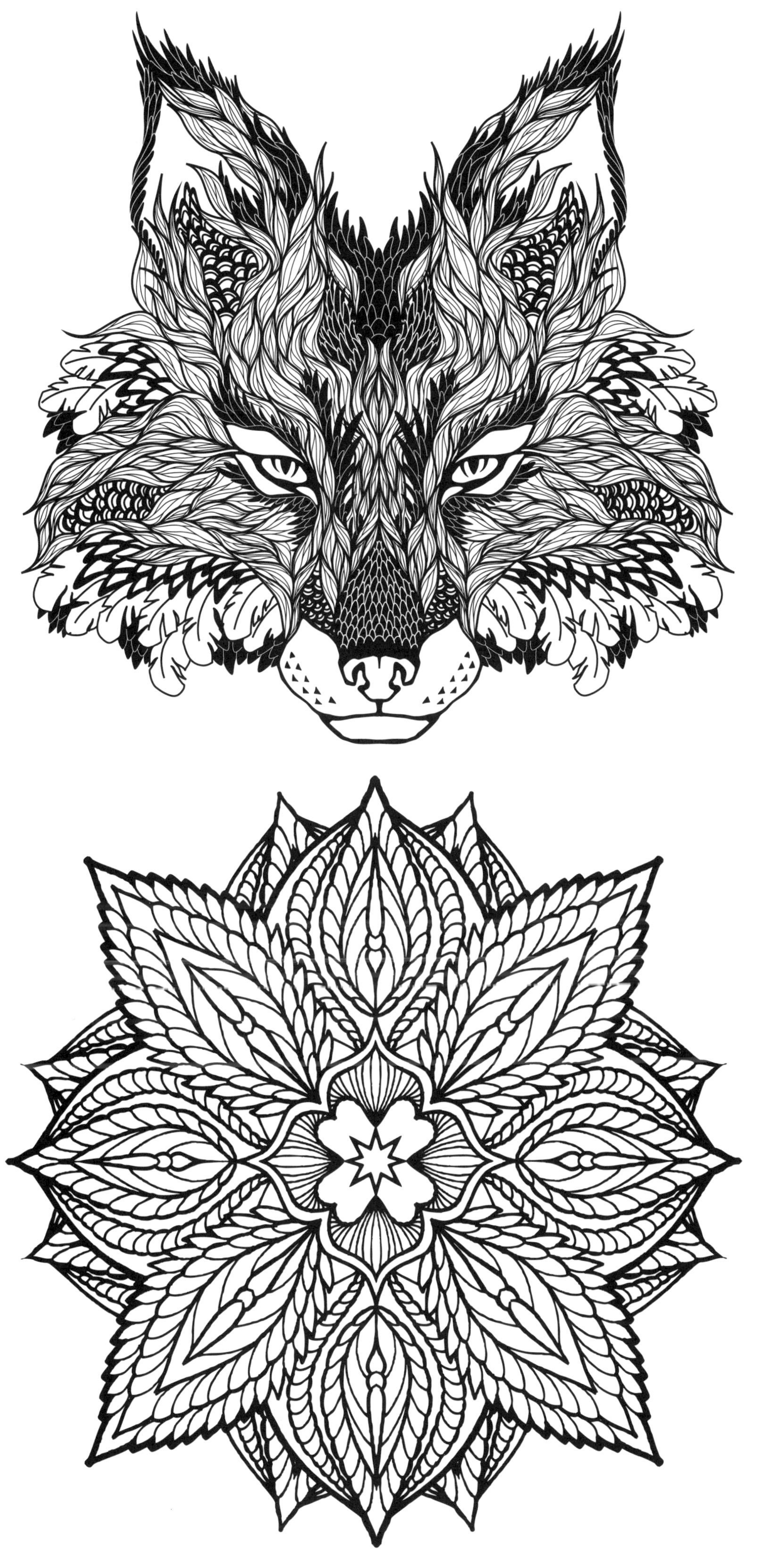

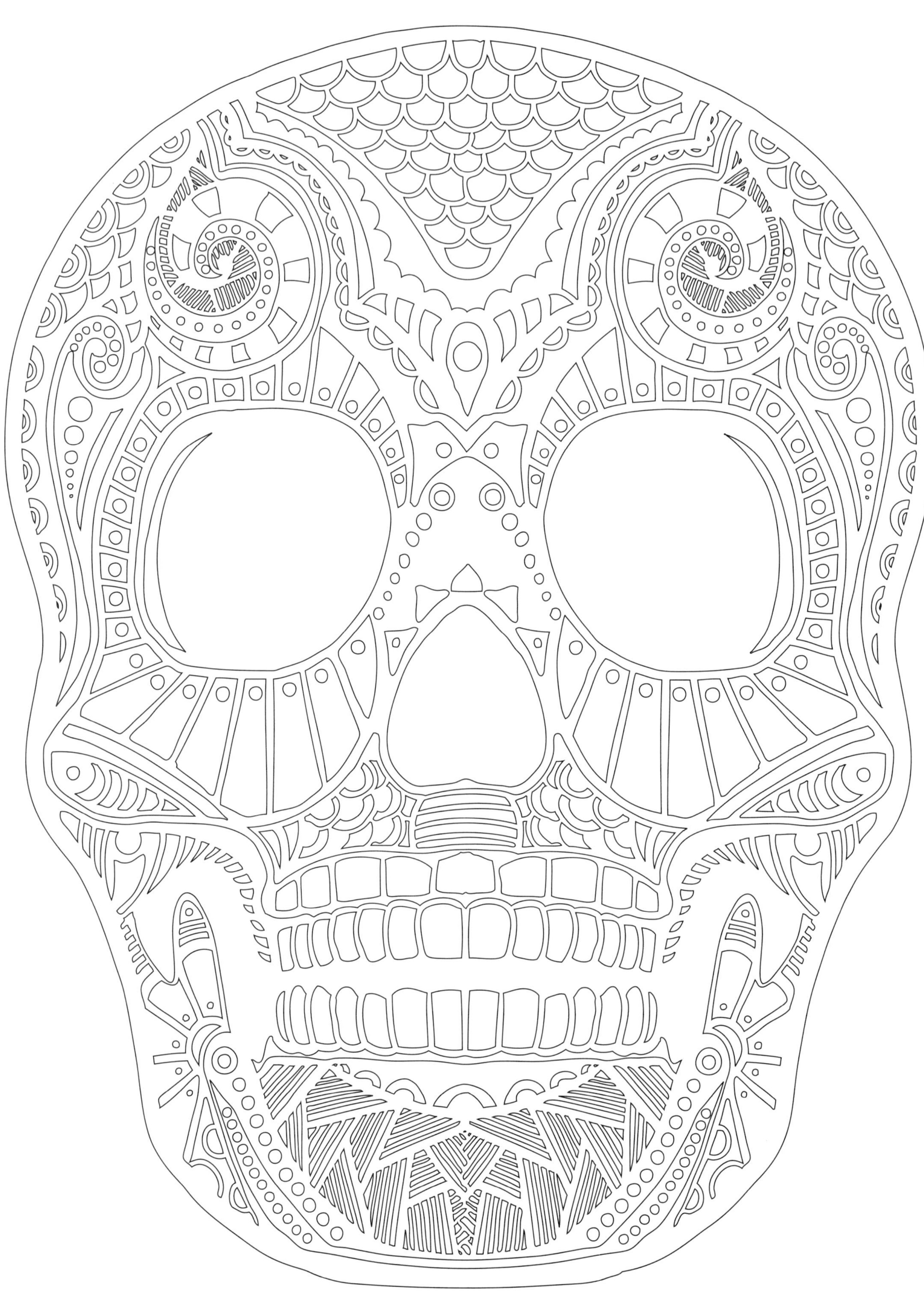

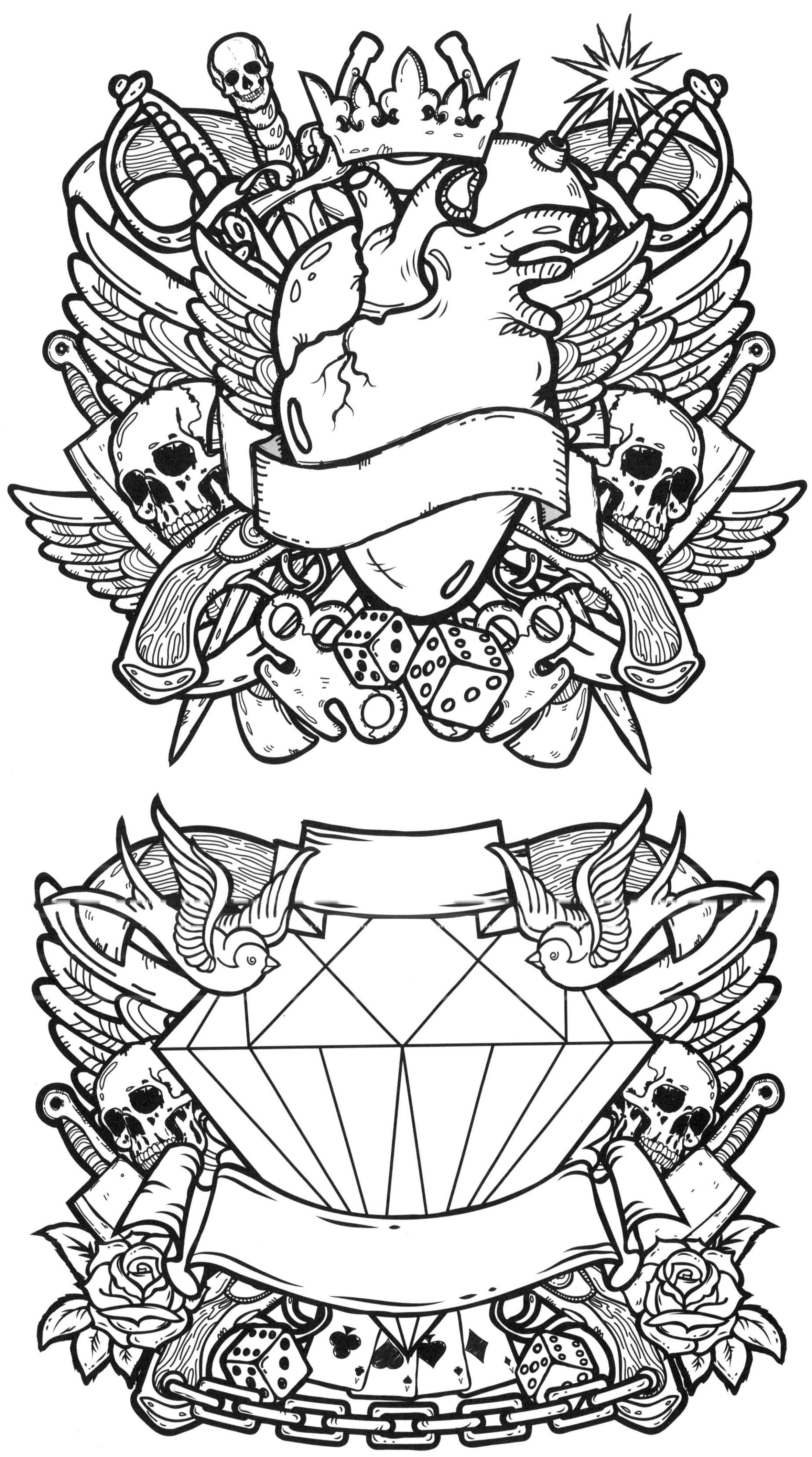

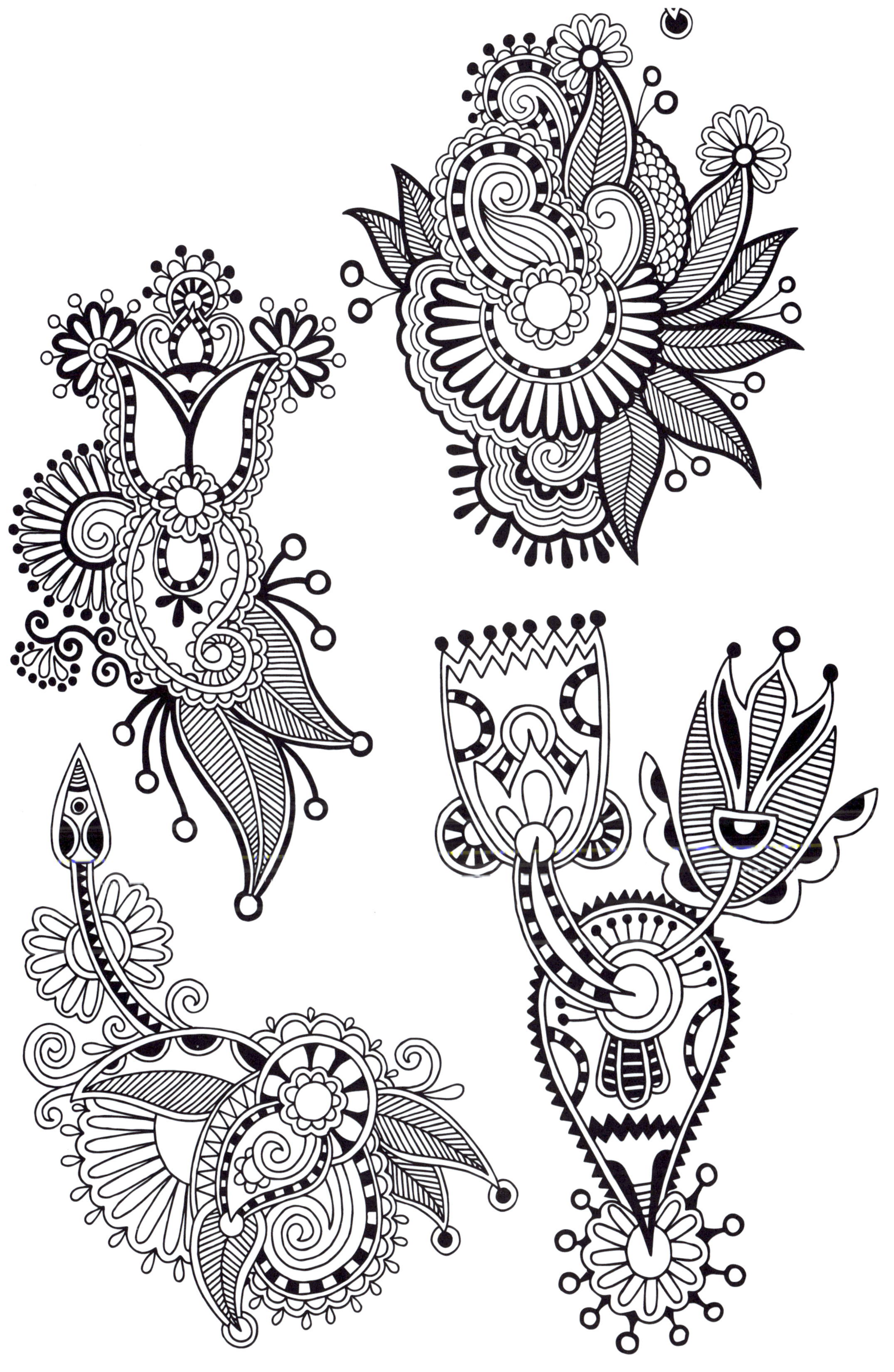

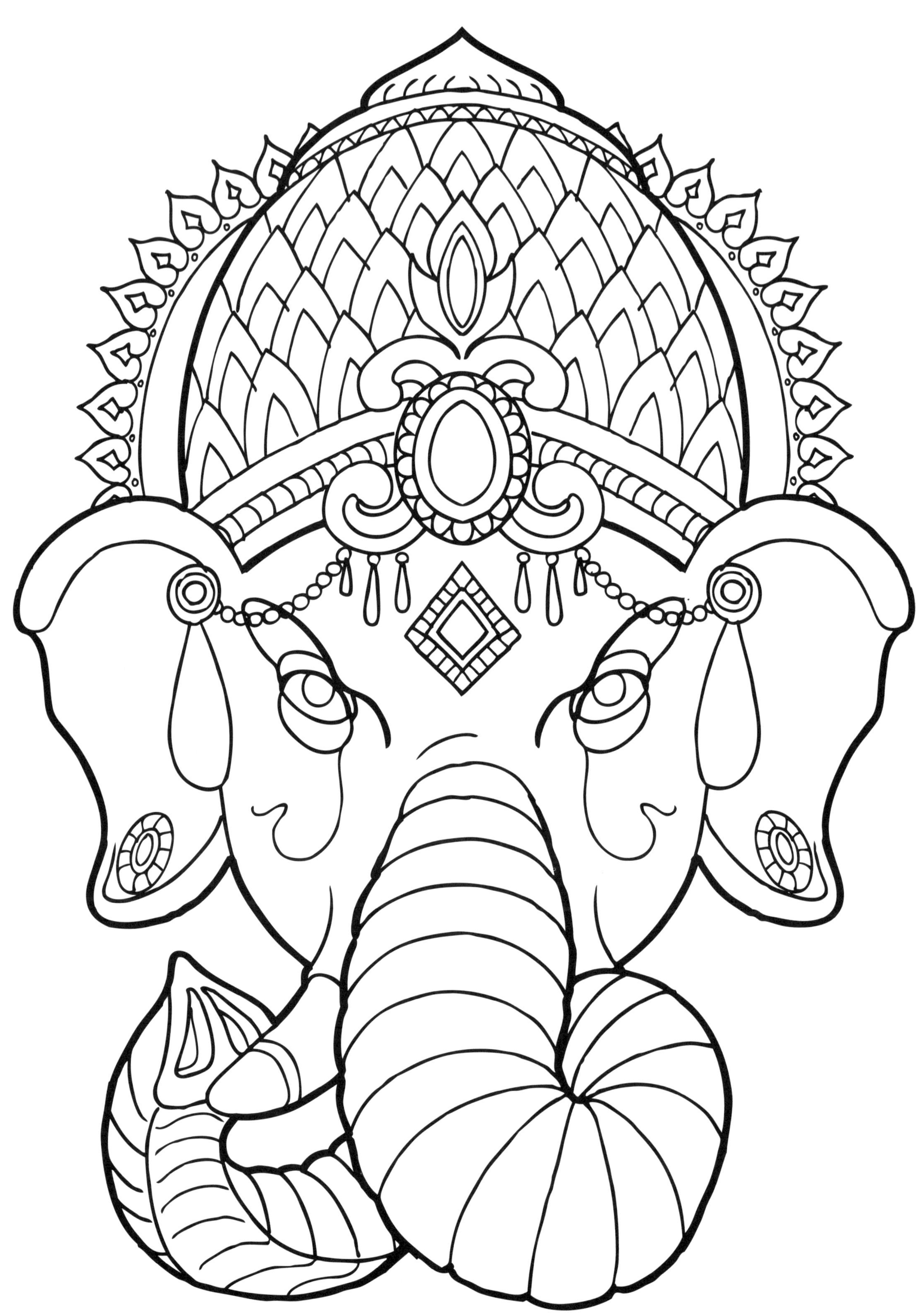

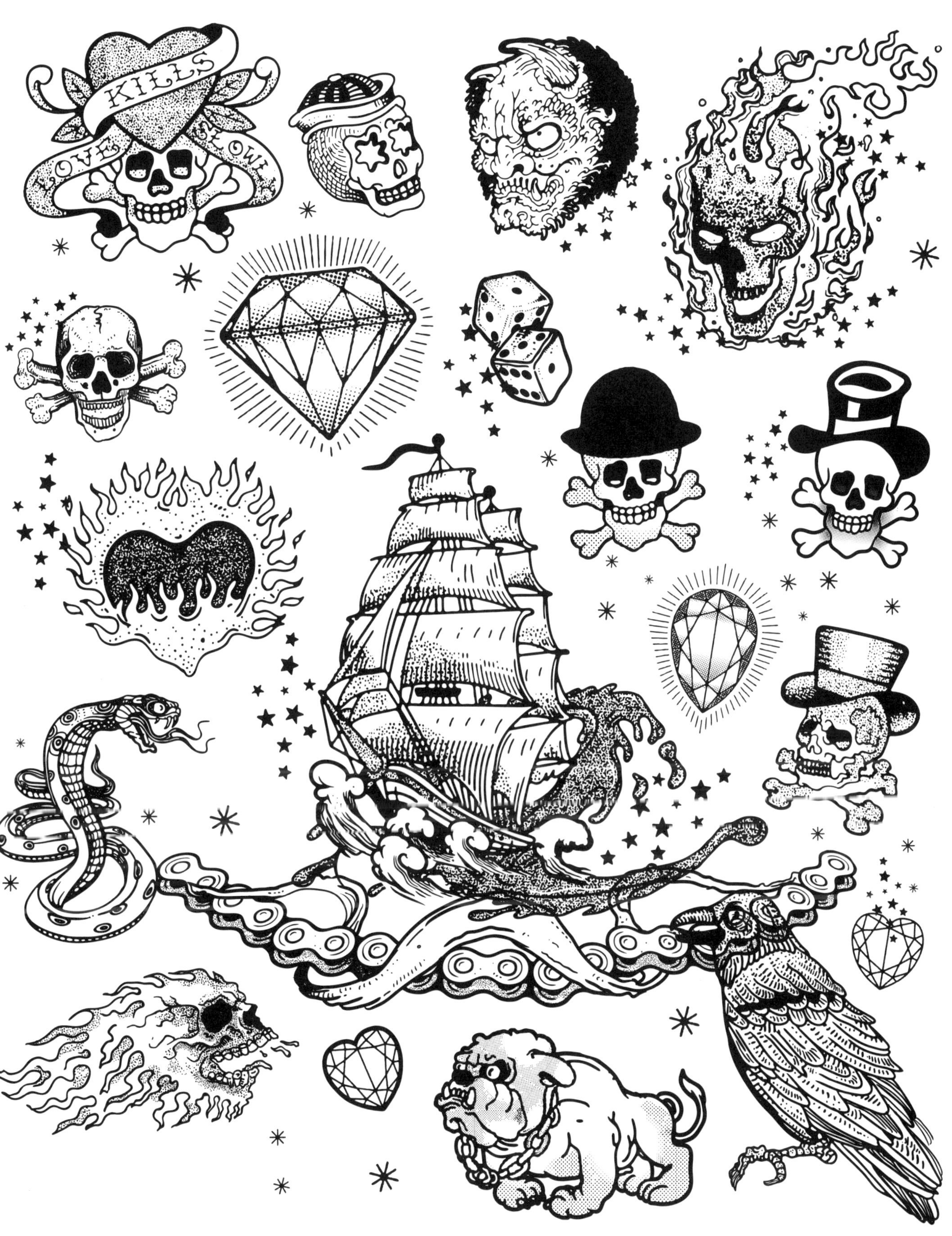
KILLS
LOVE
SLOWLY

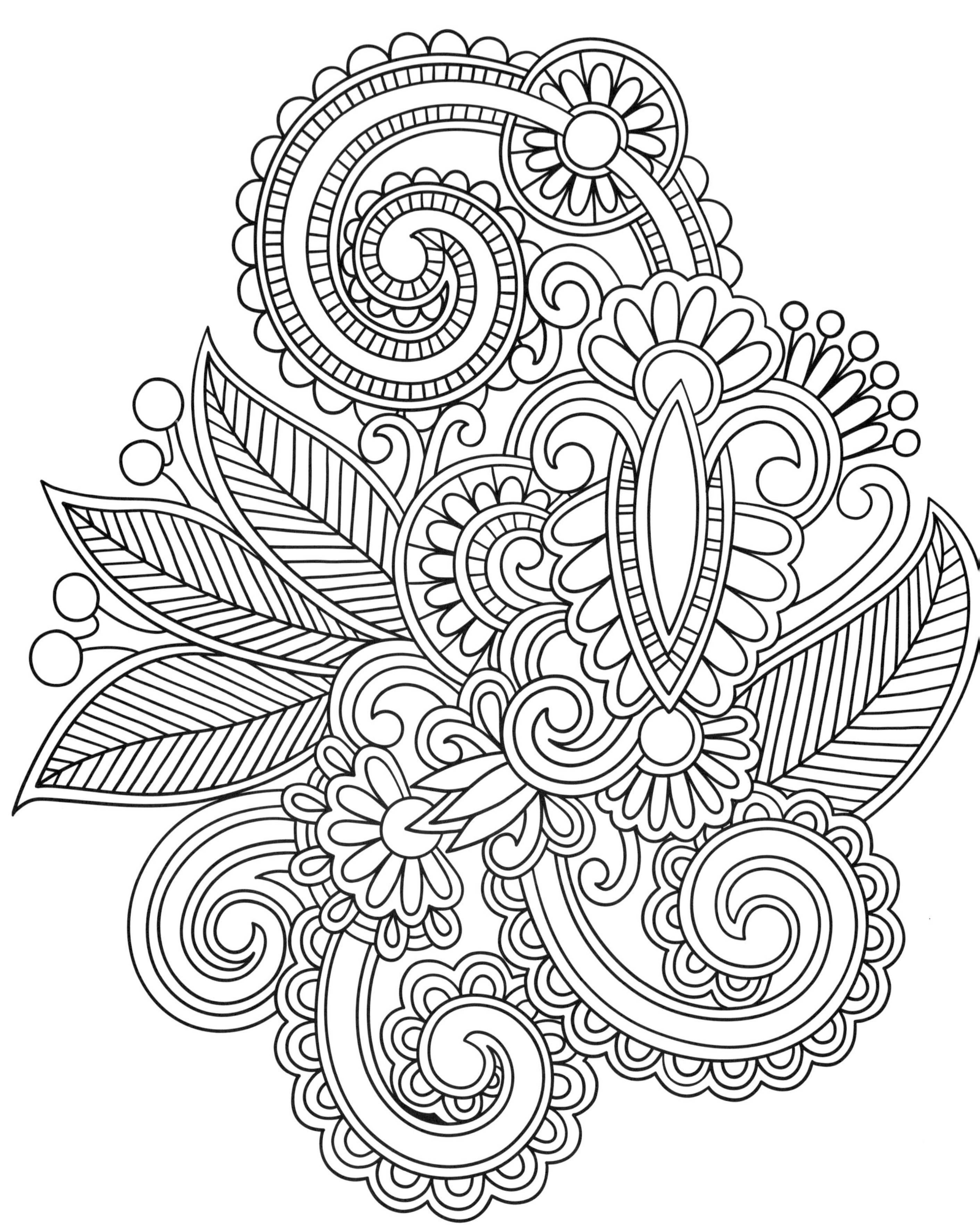

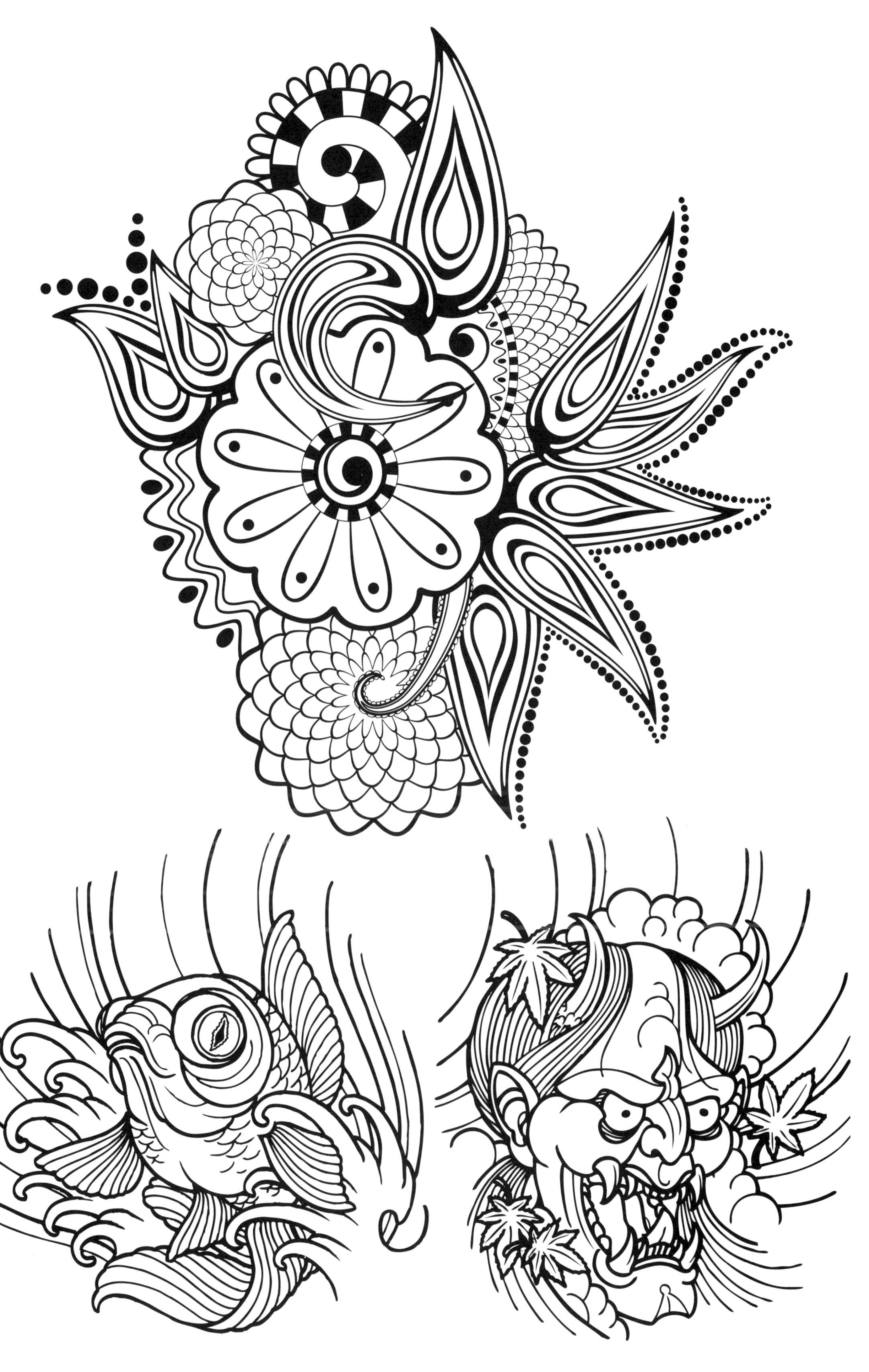

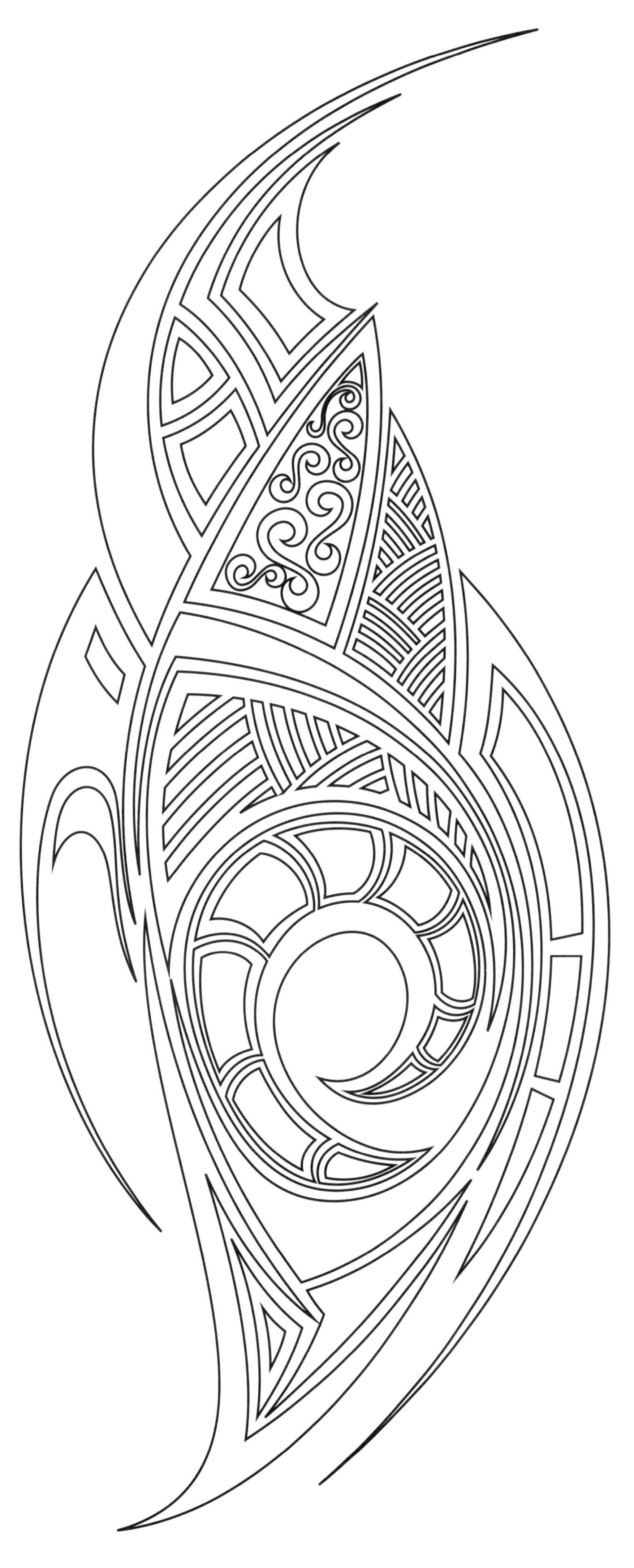

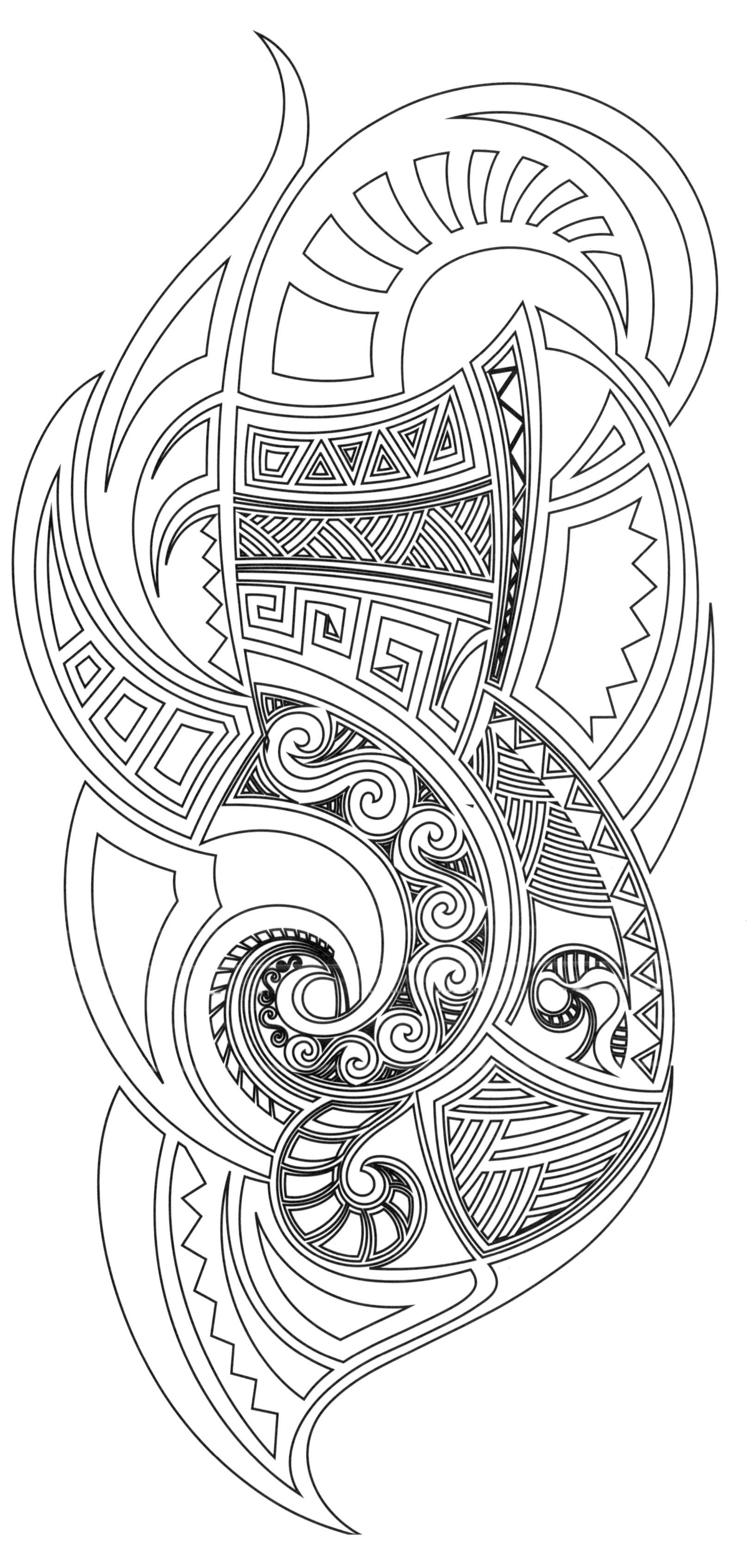

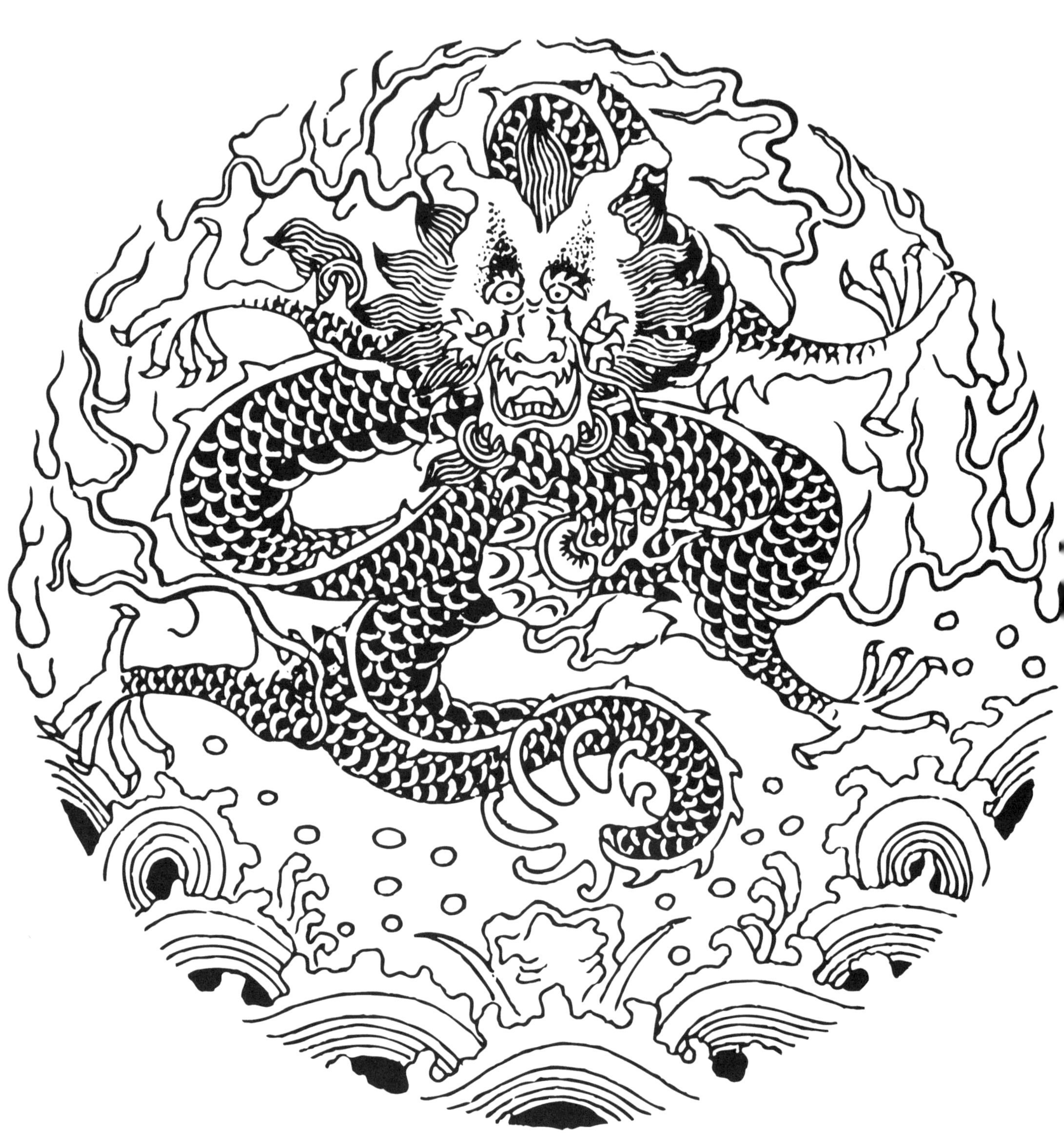

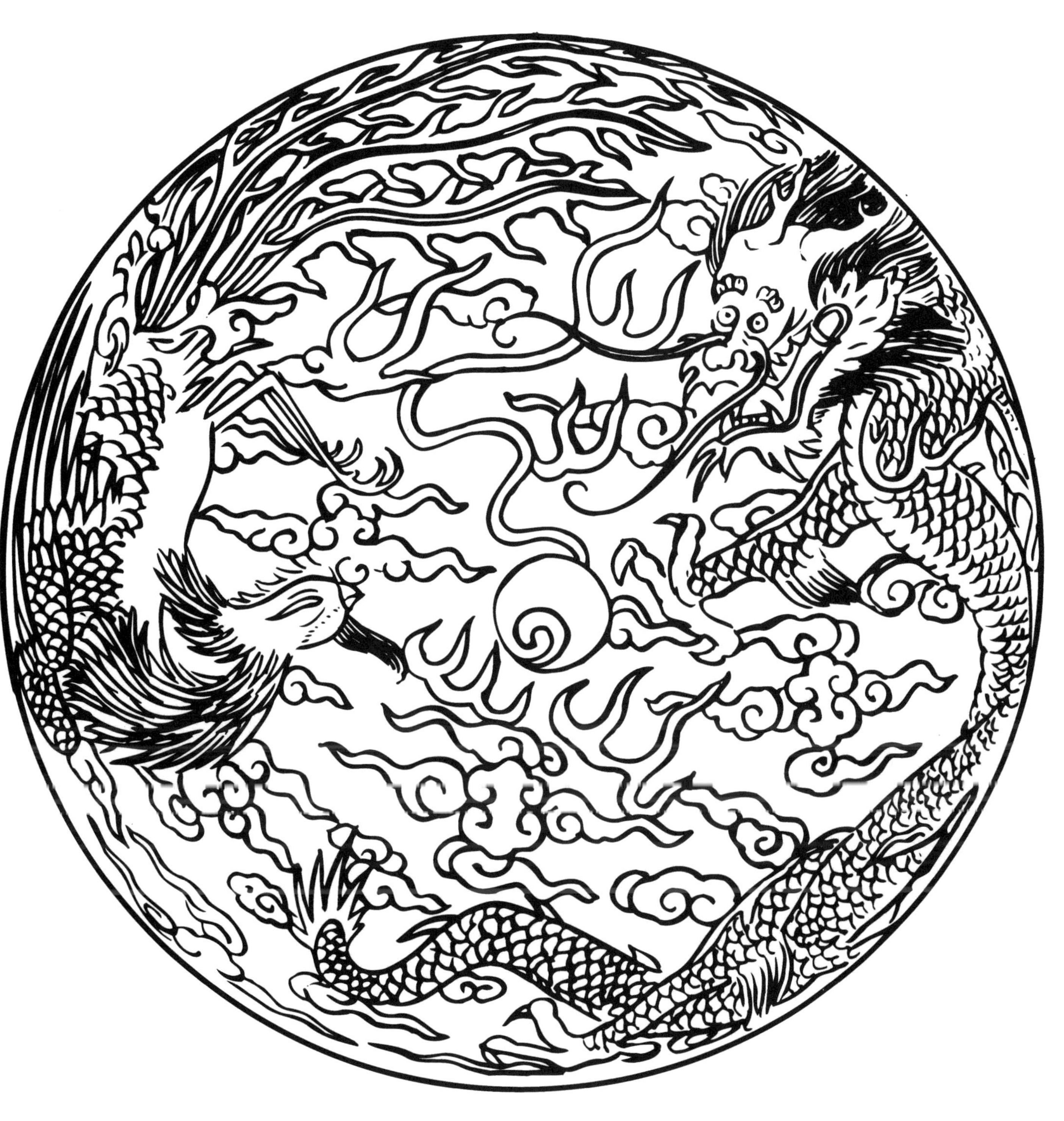

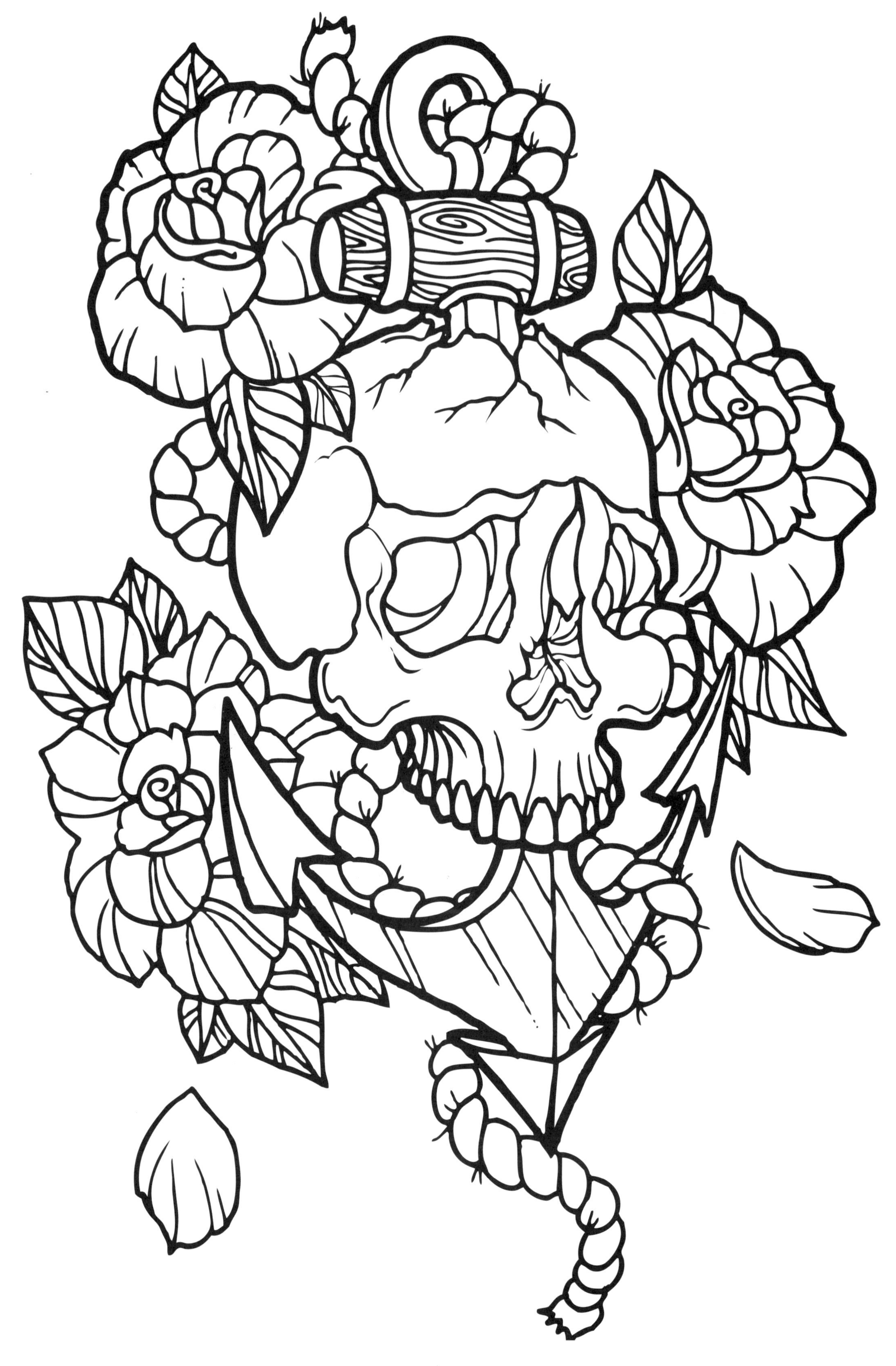

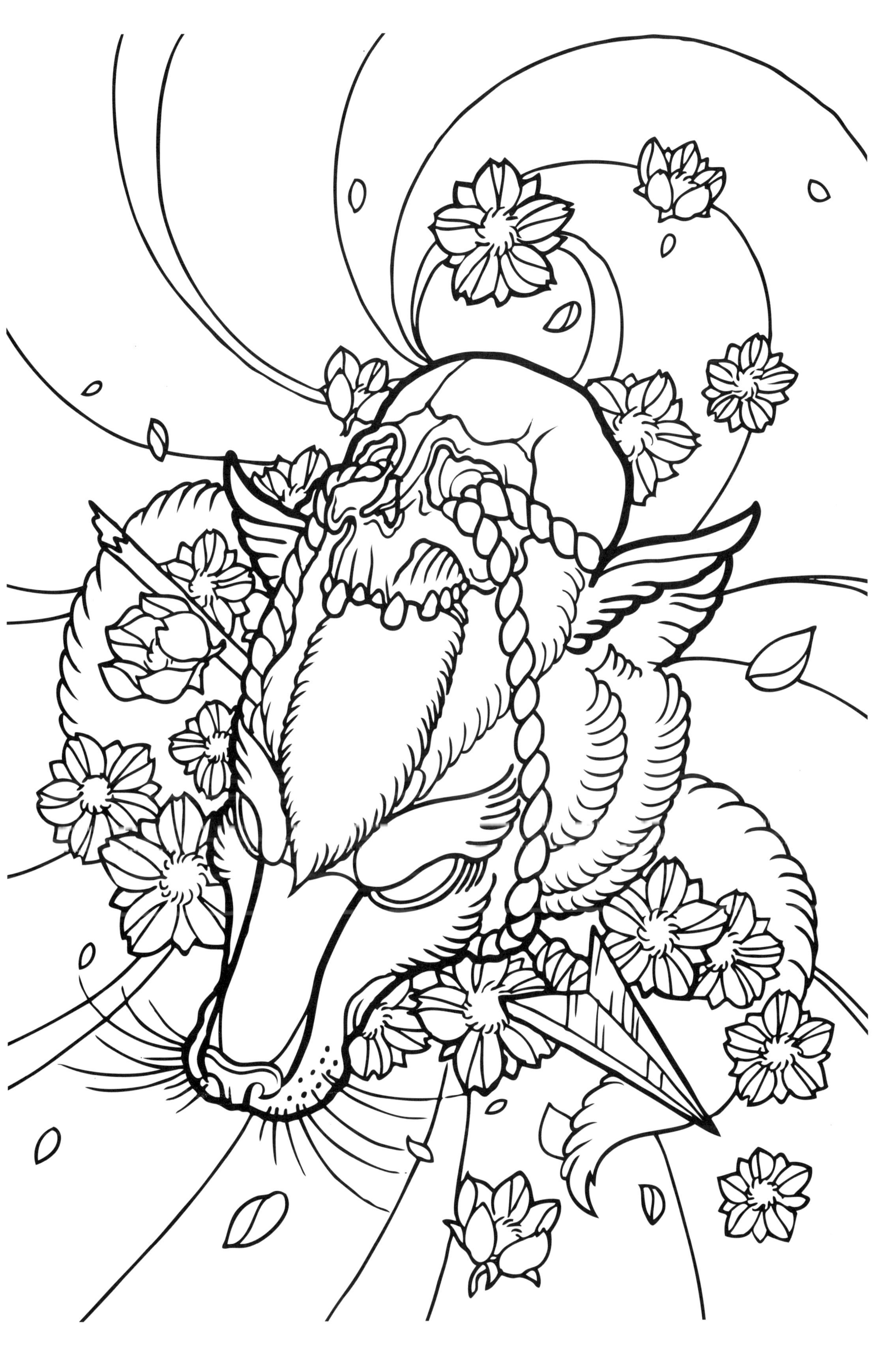

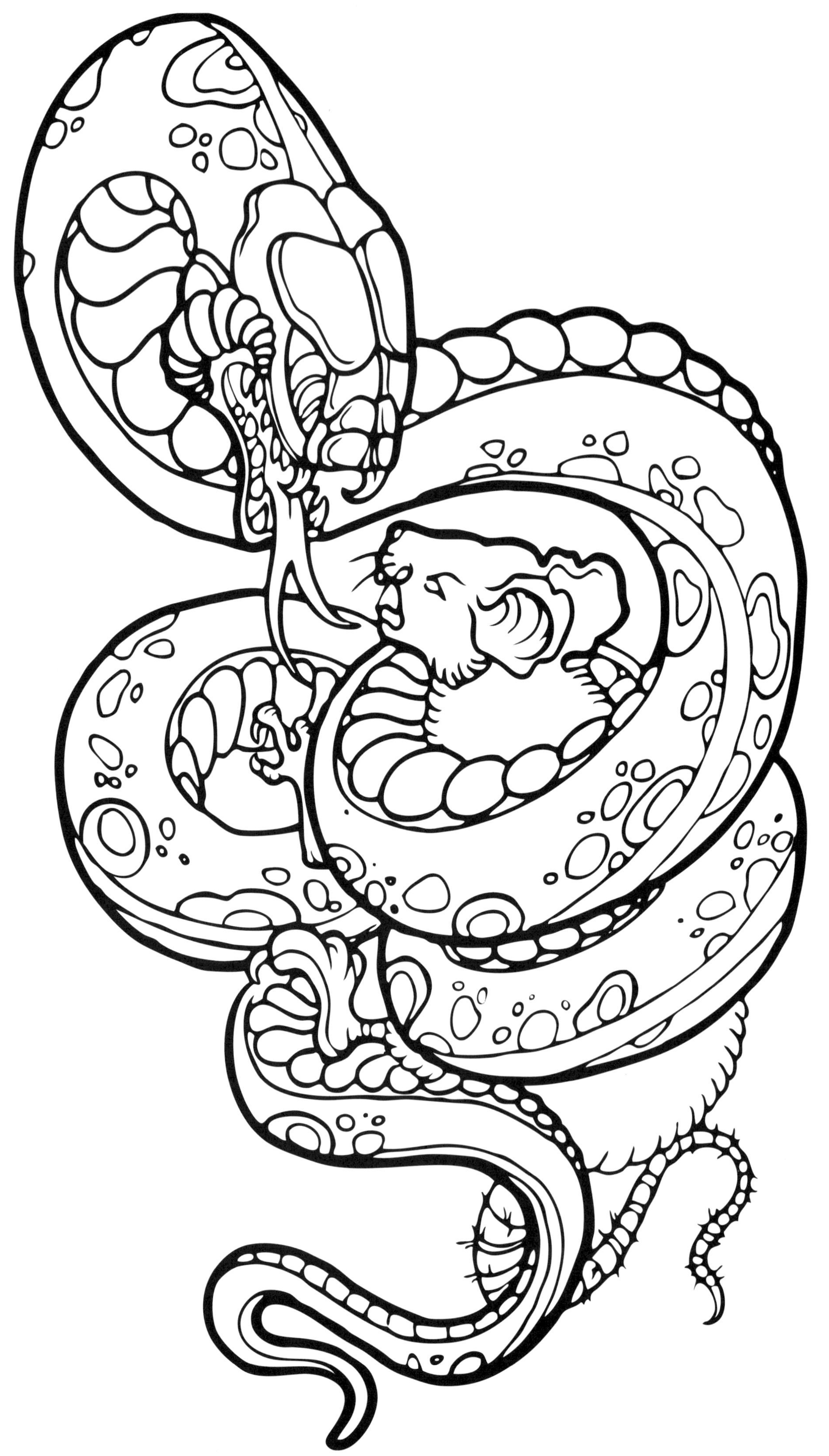

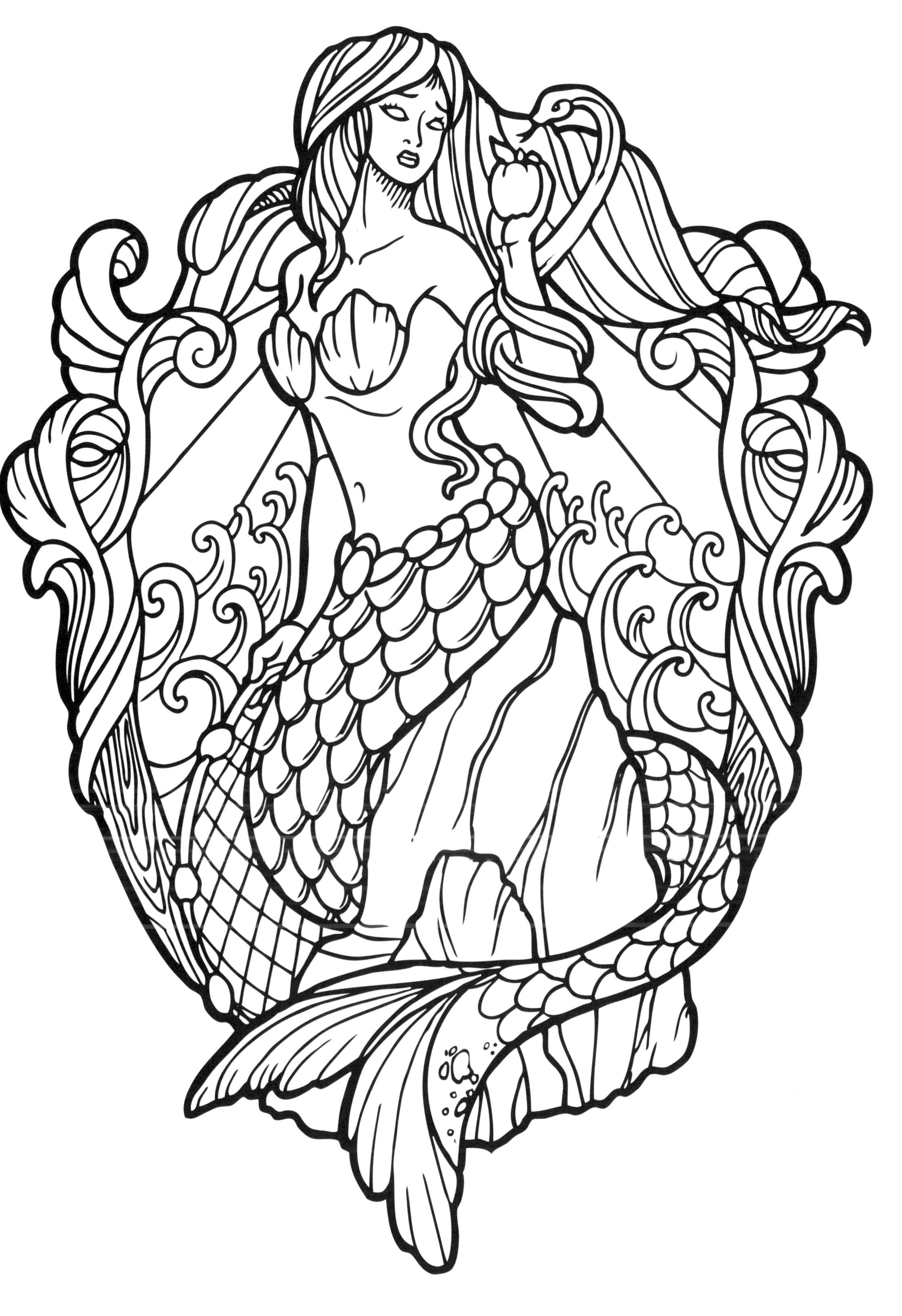

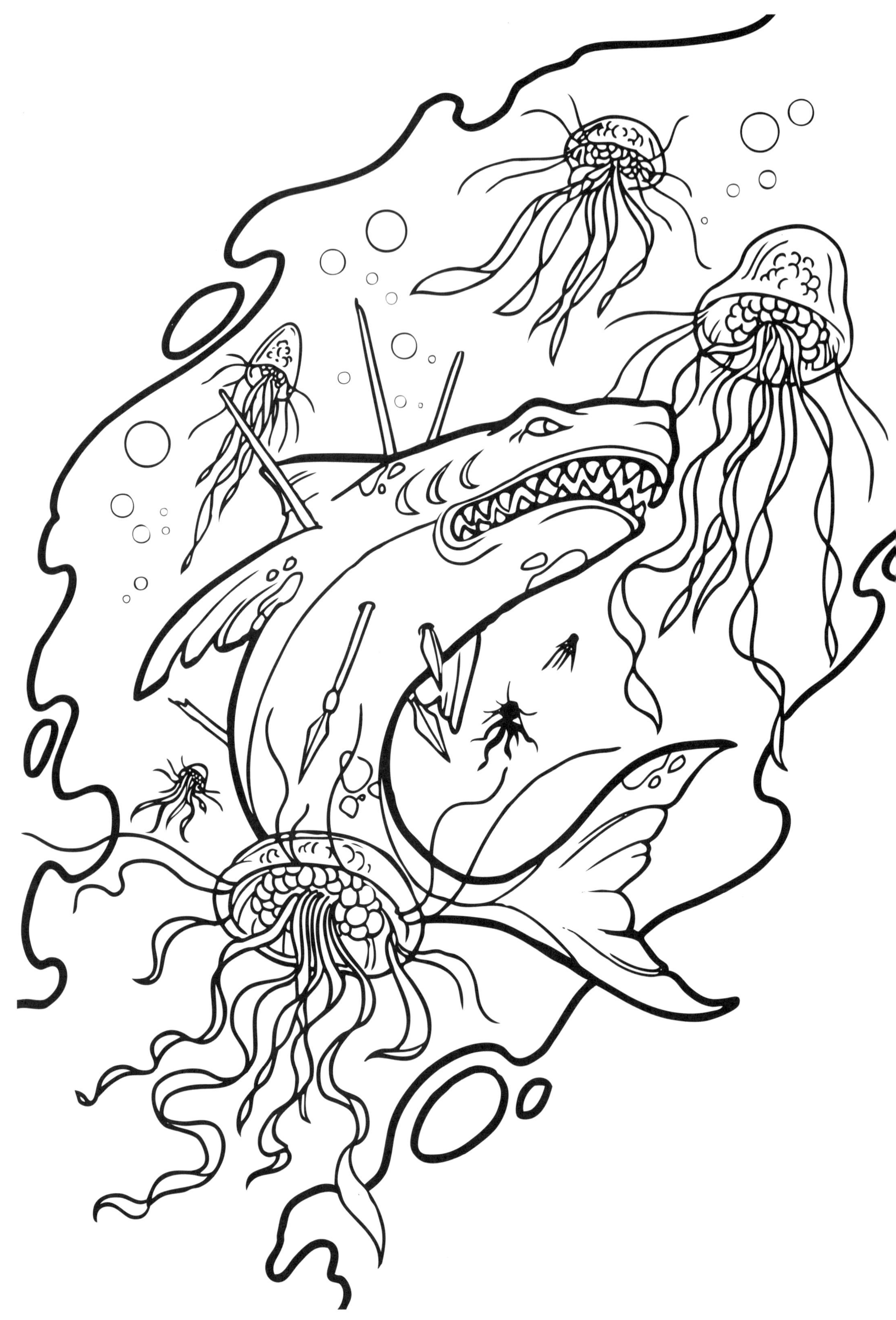

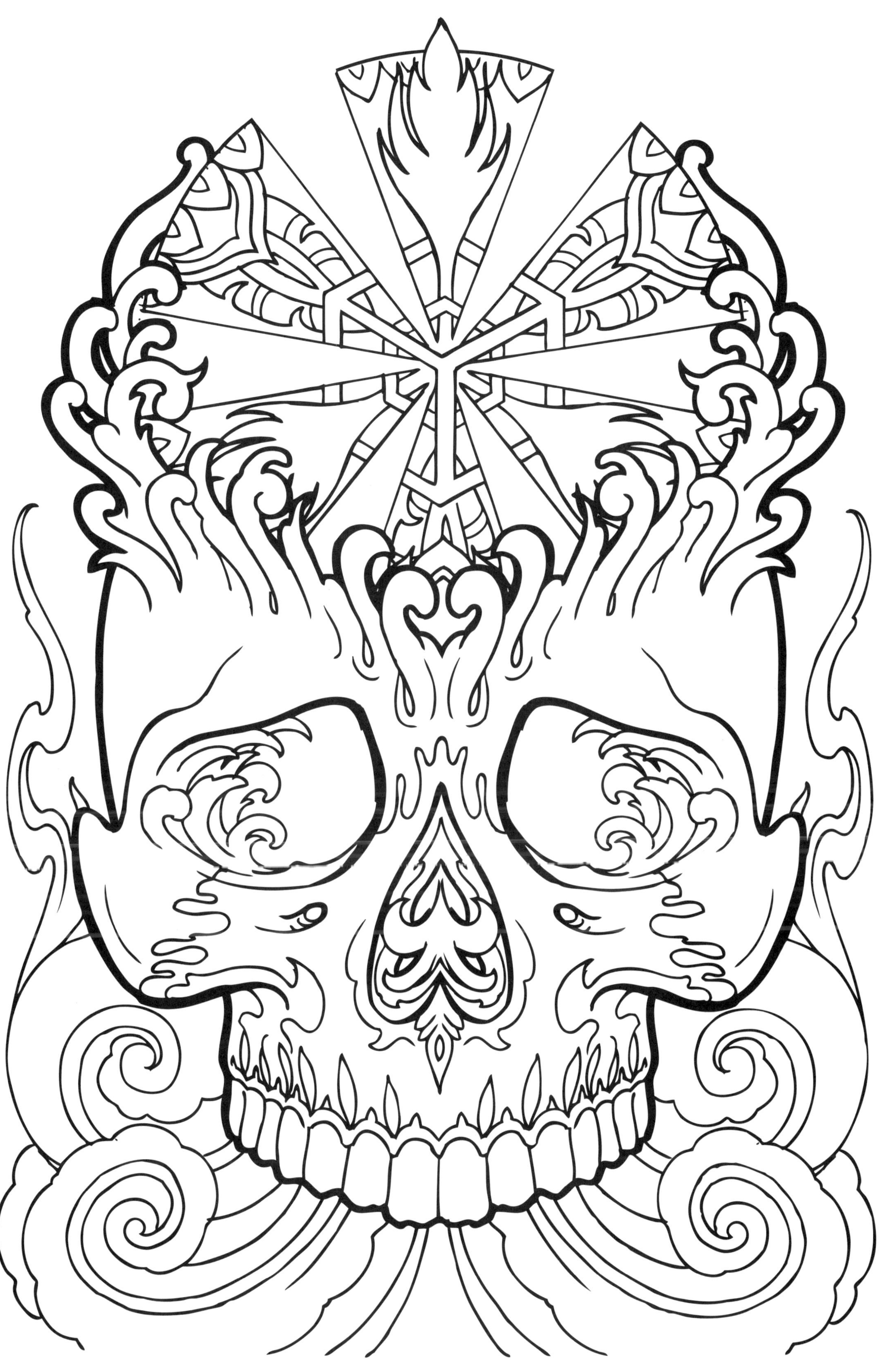

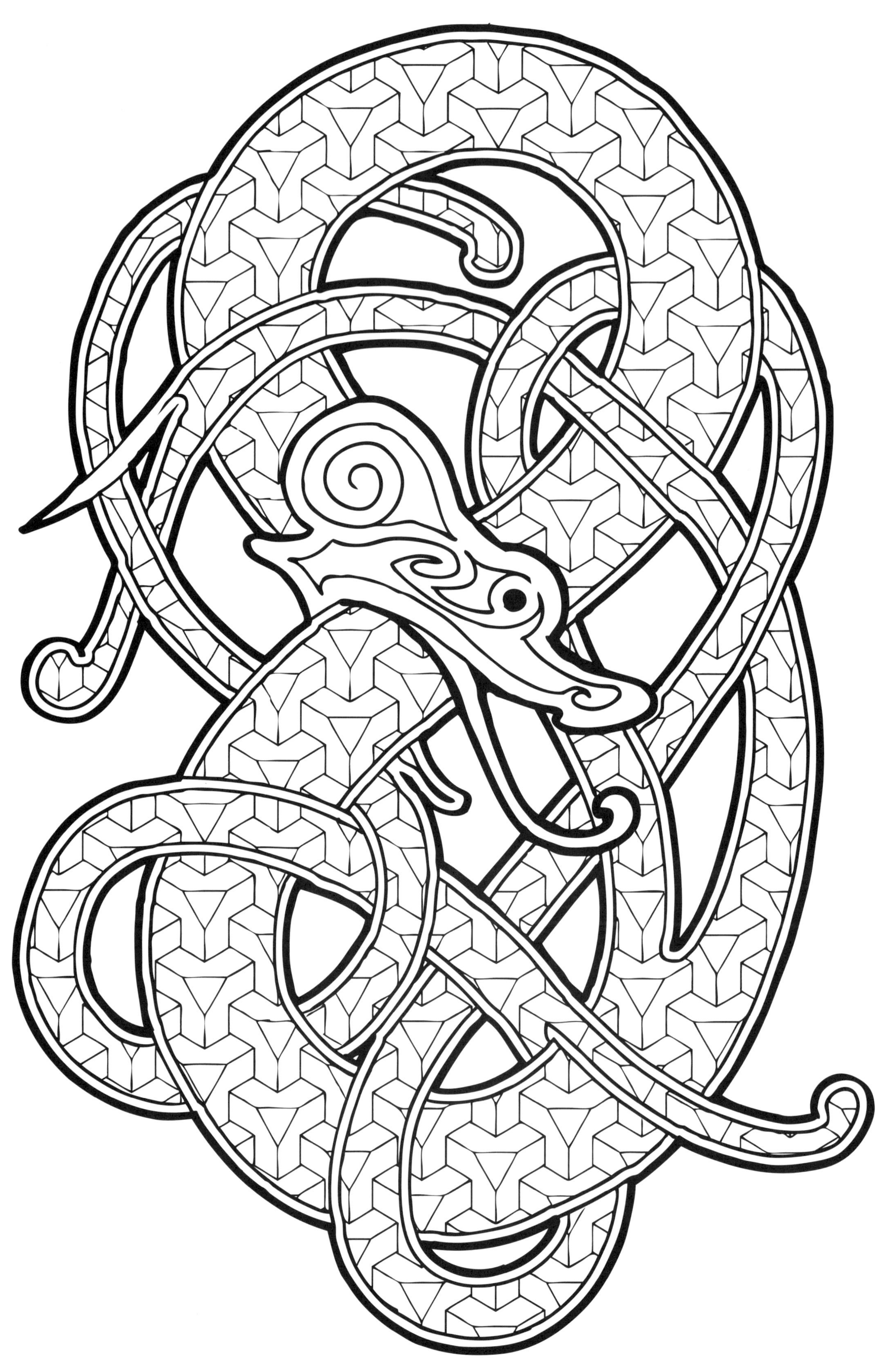

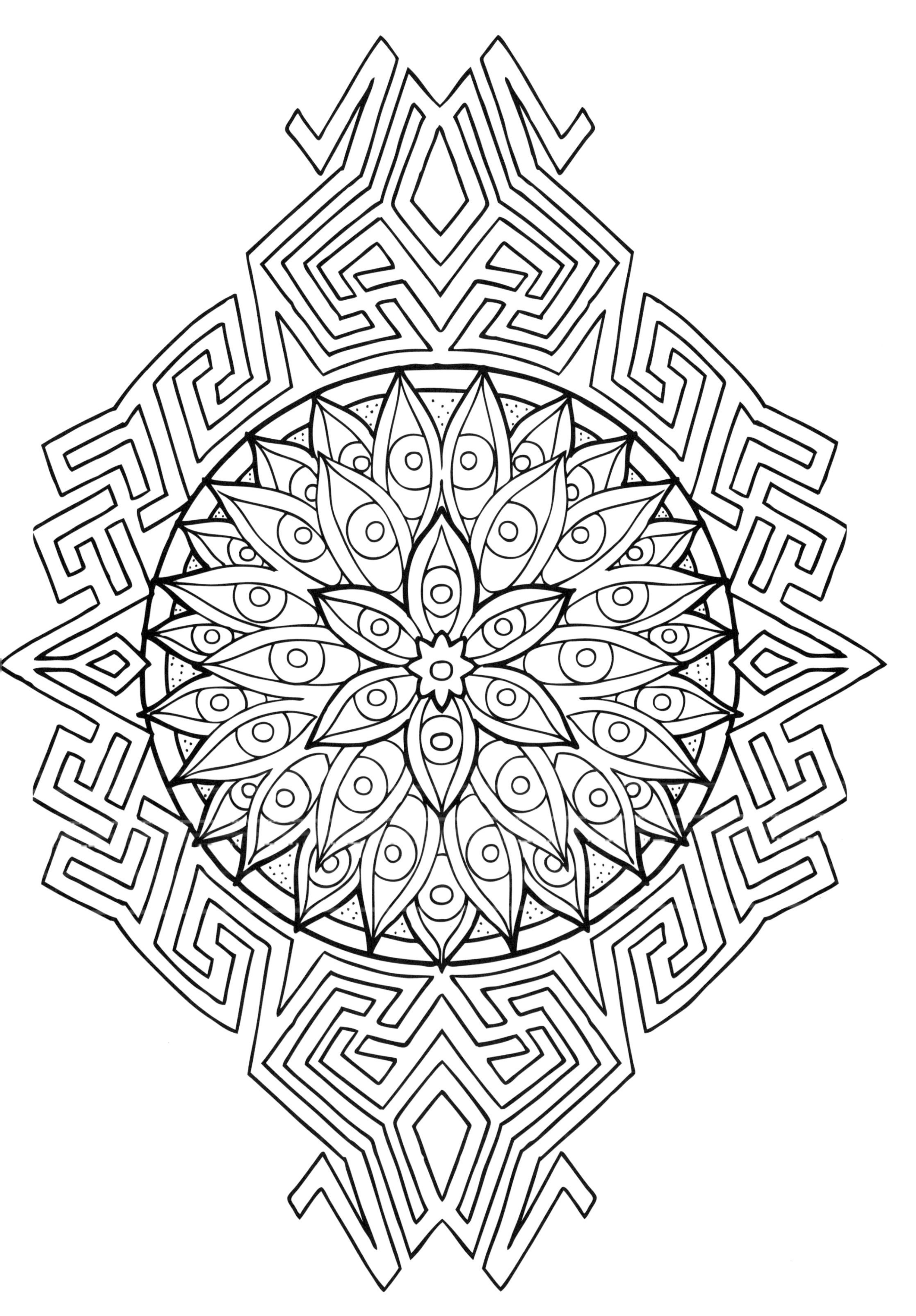

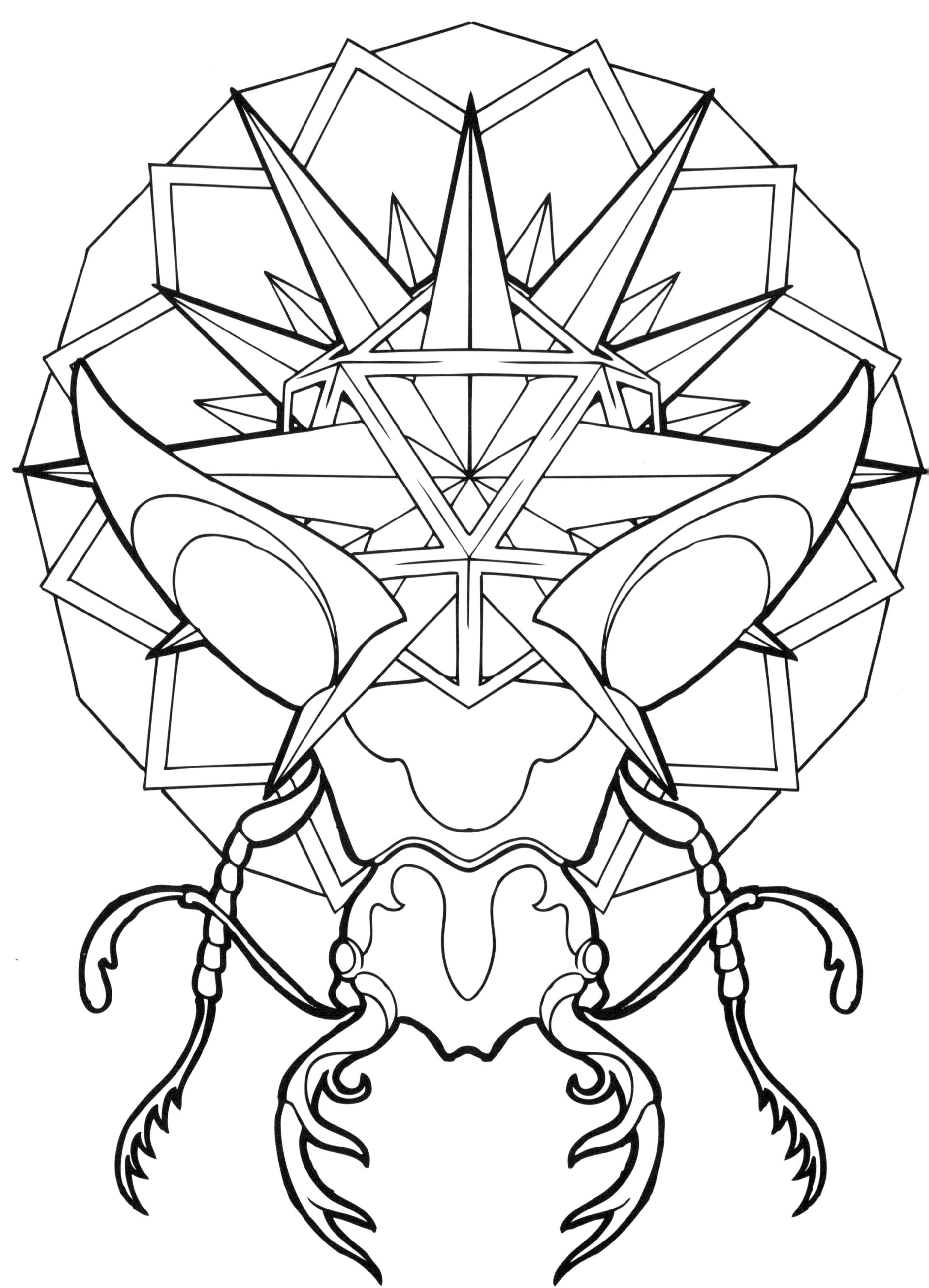

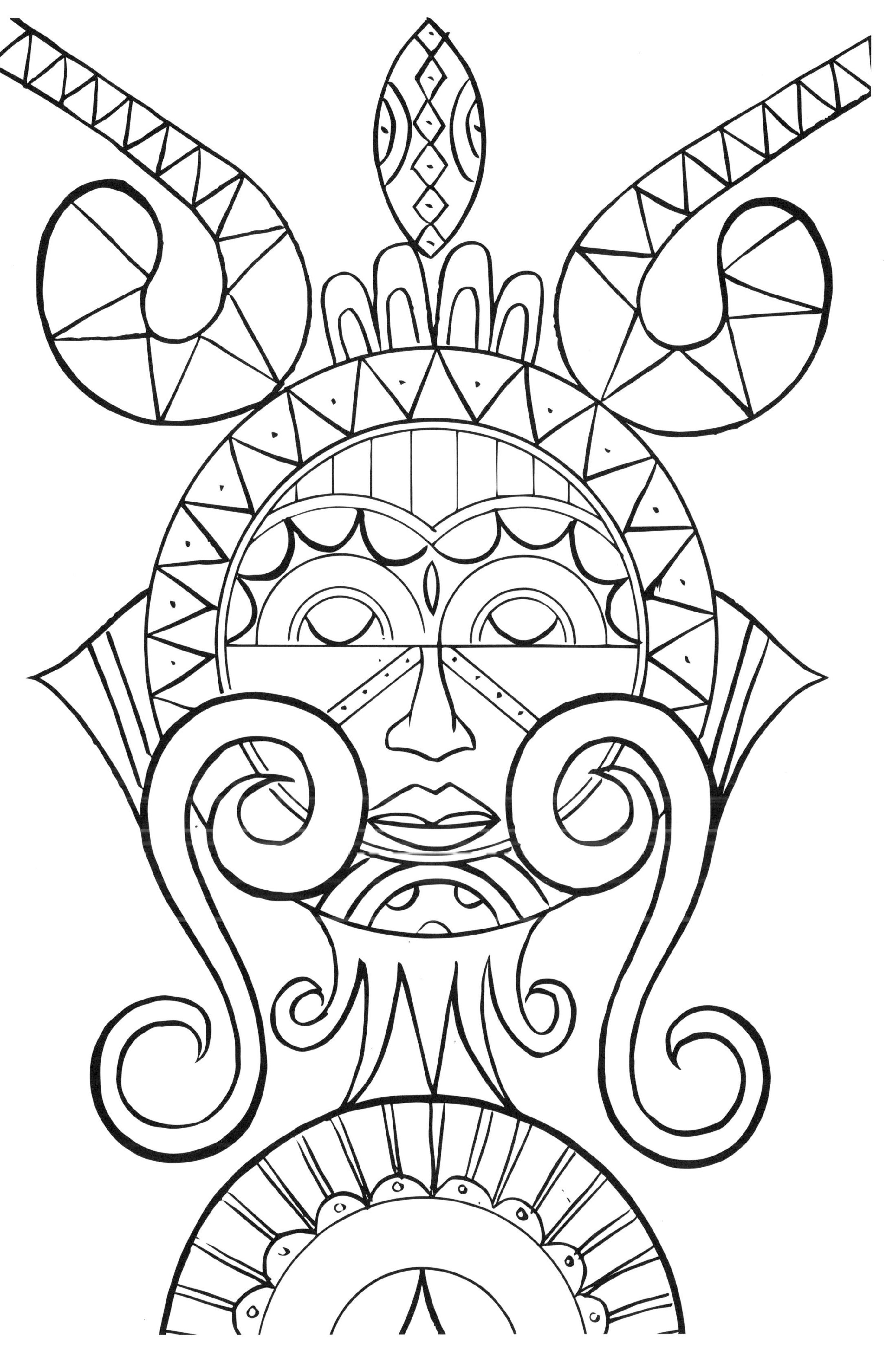

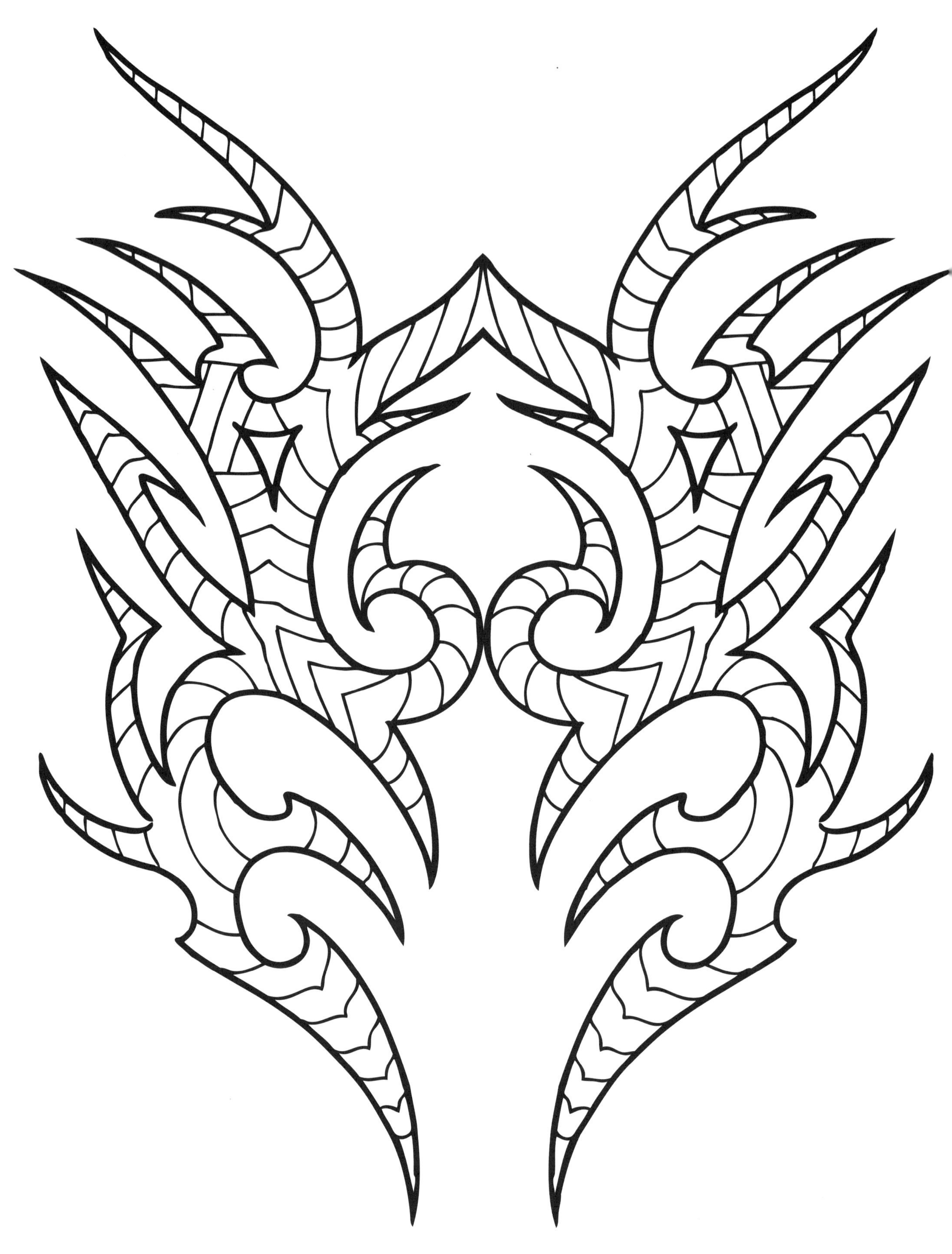

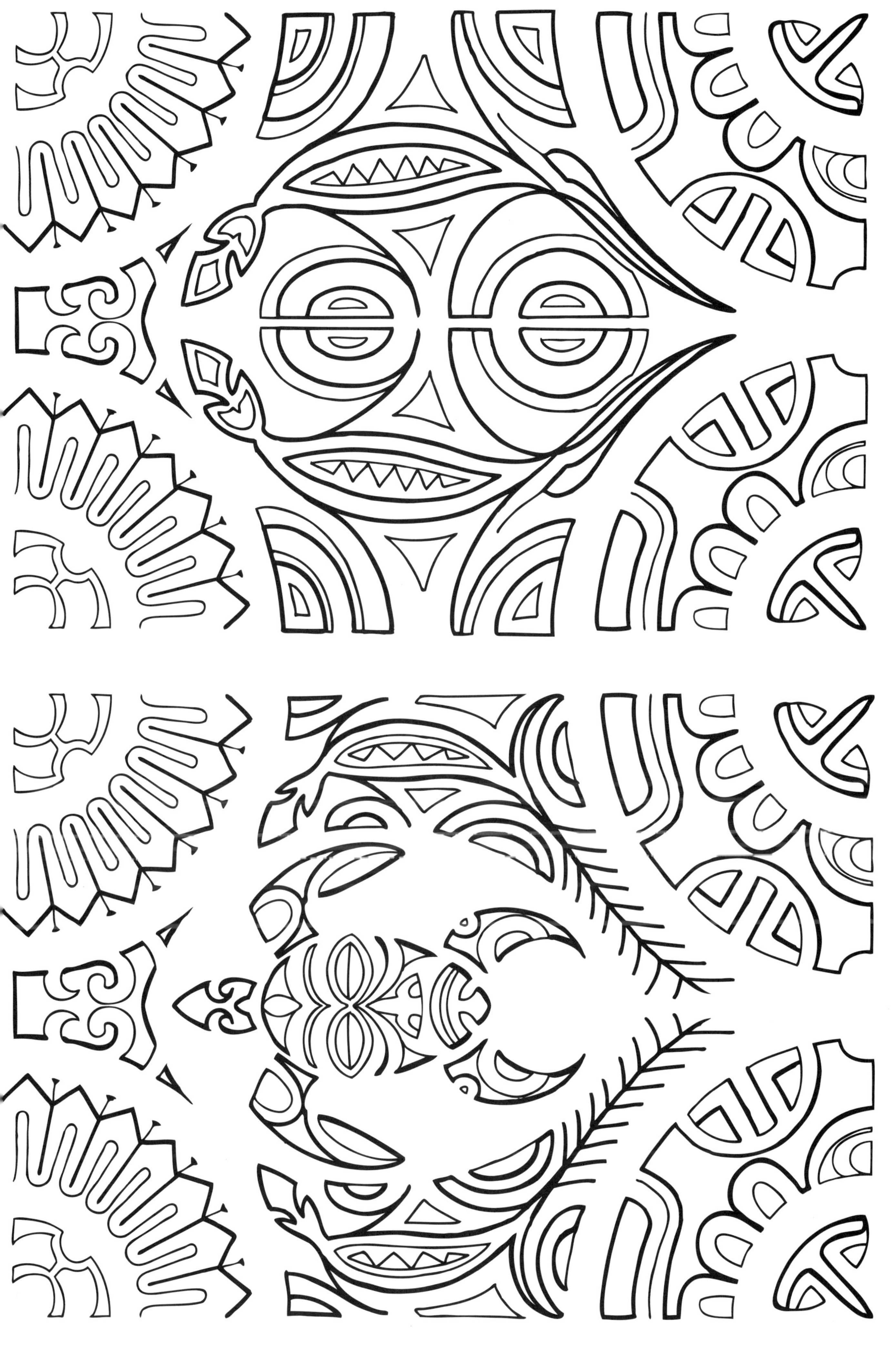

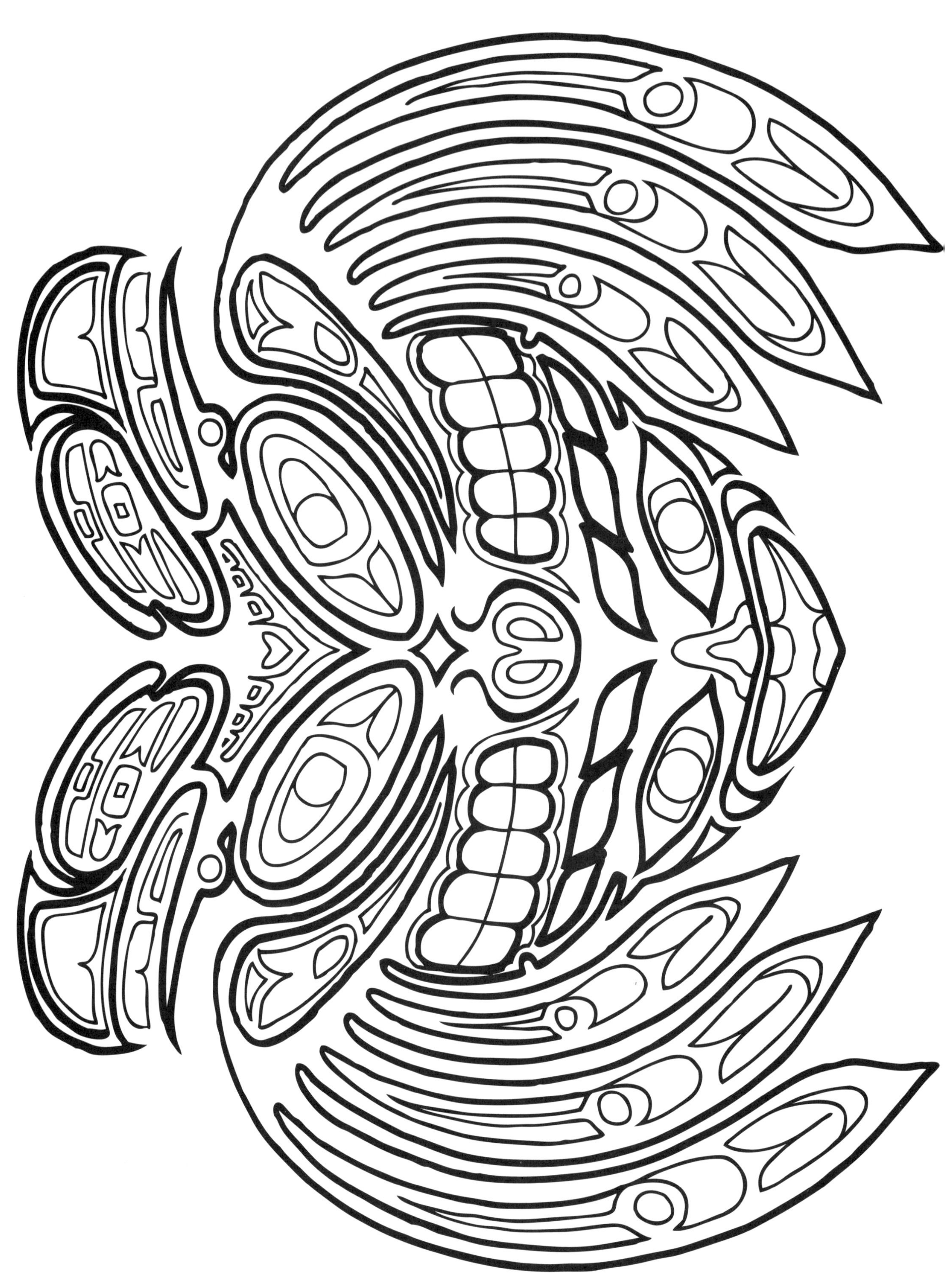

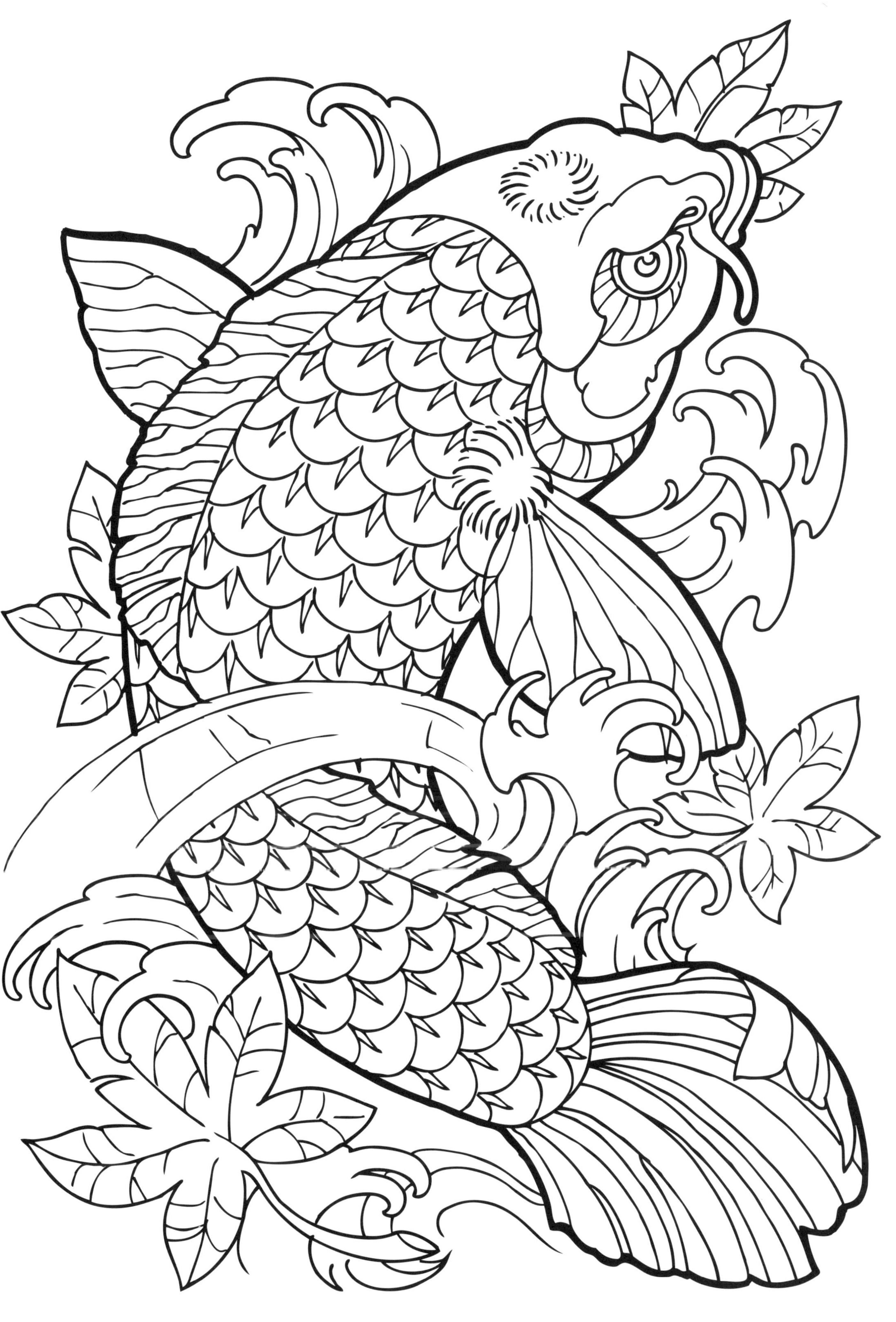

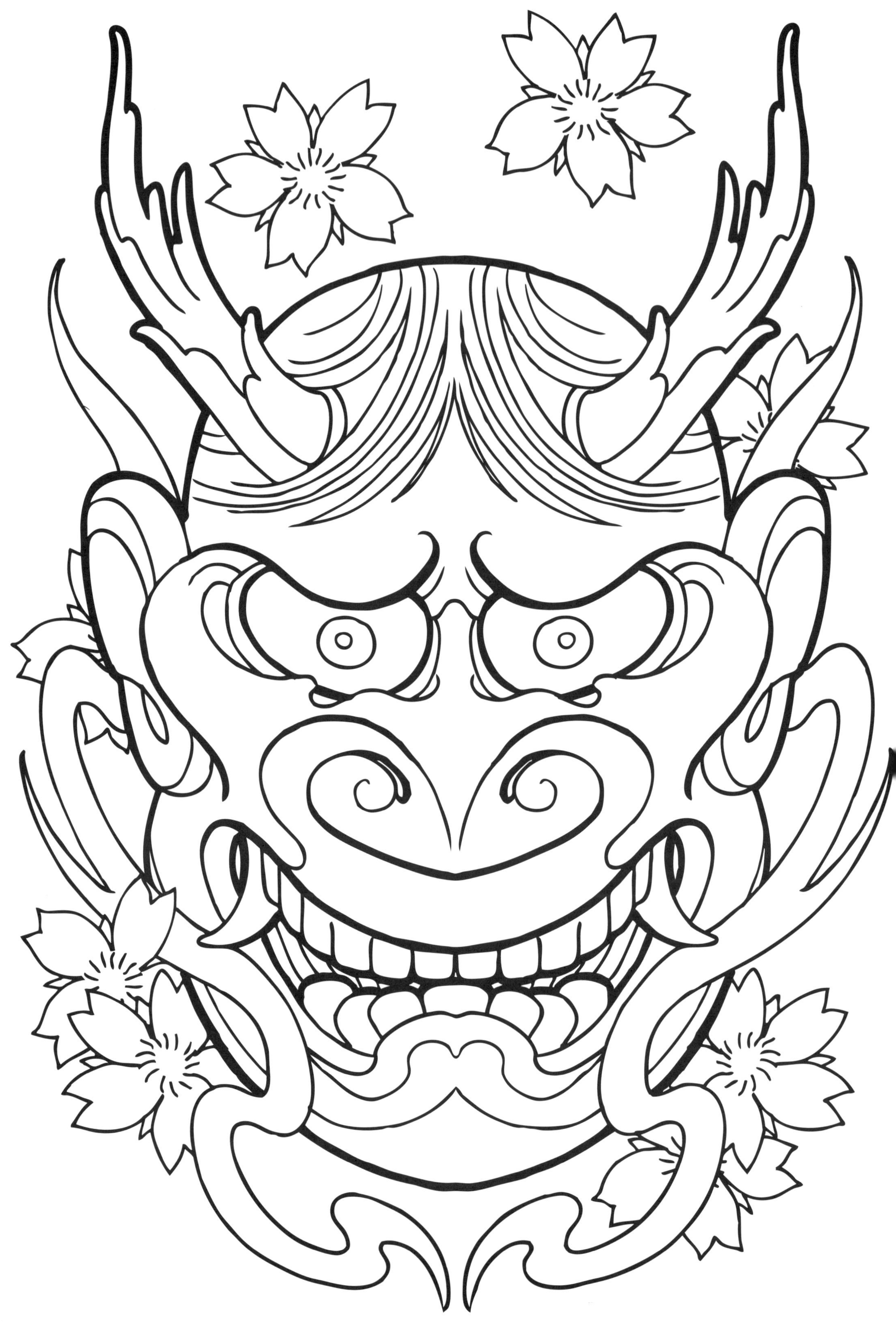

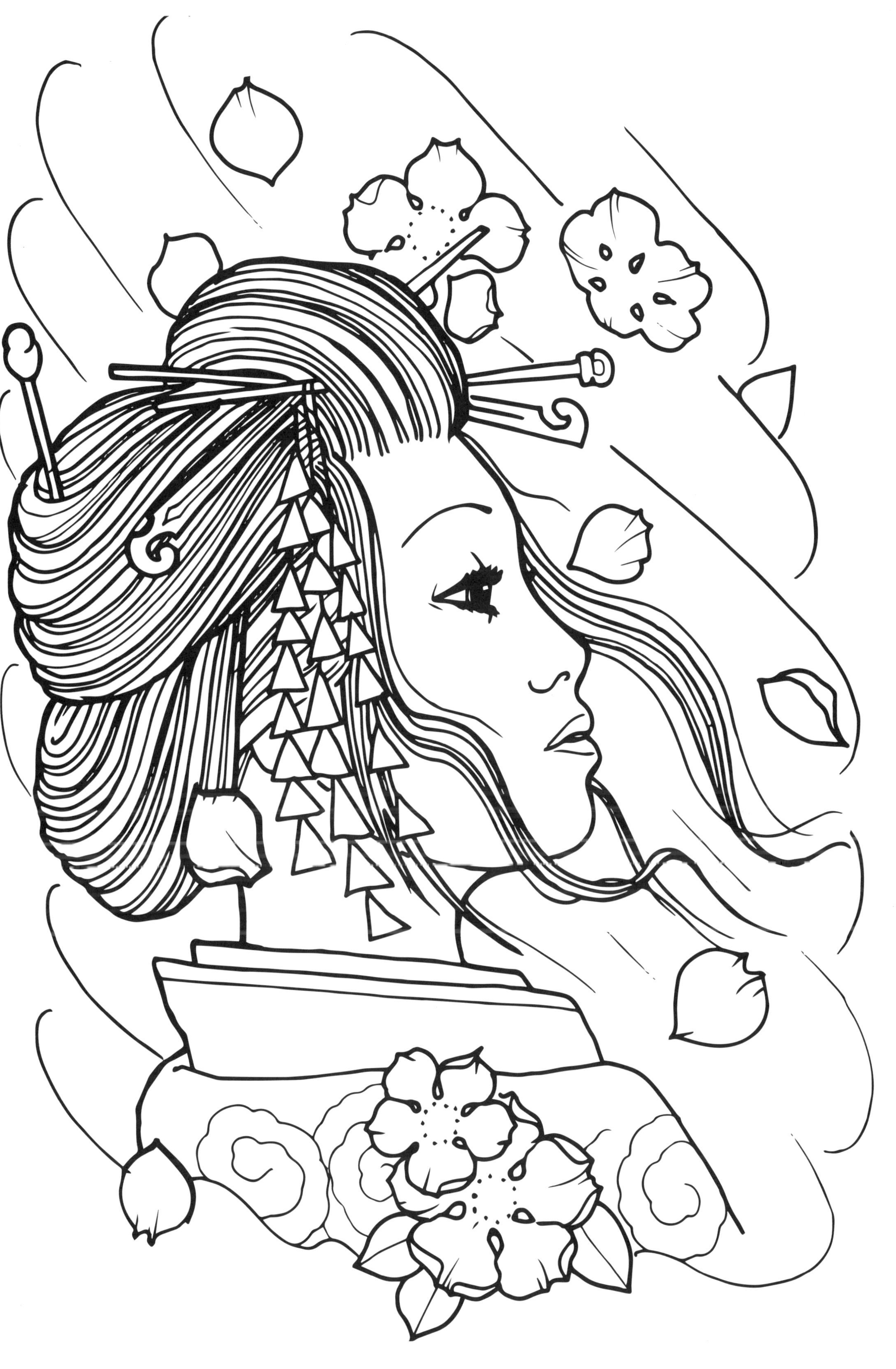

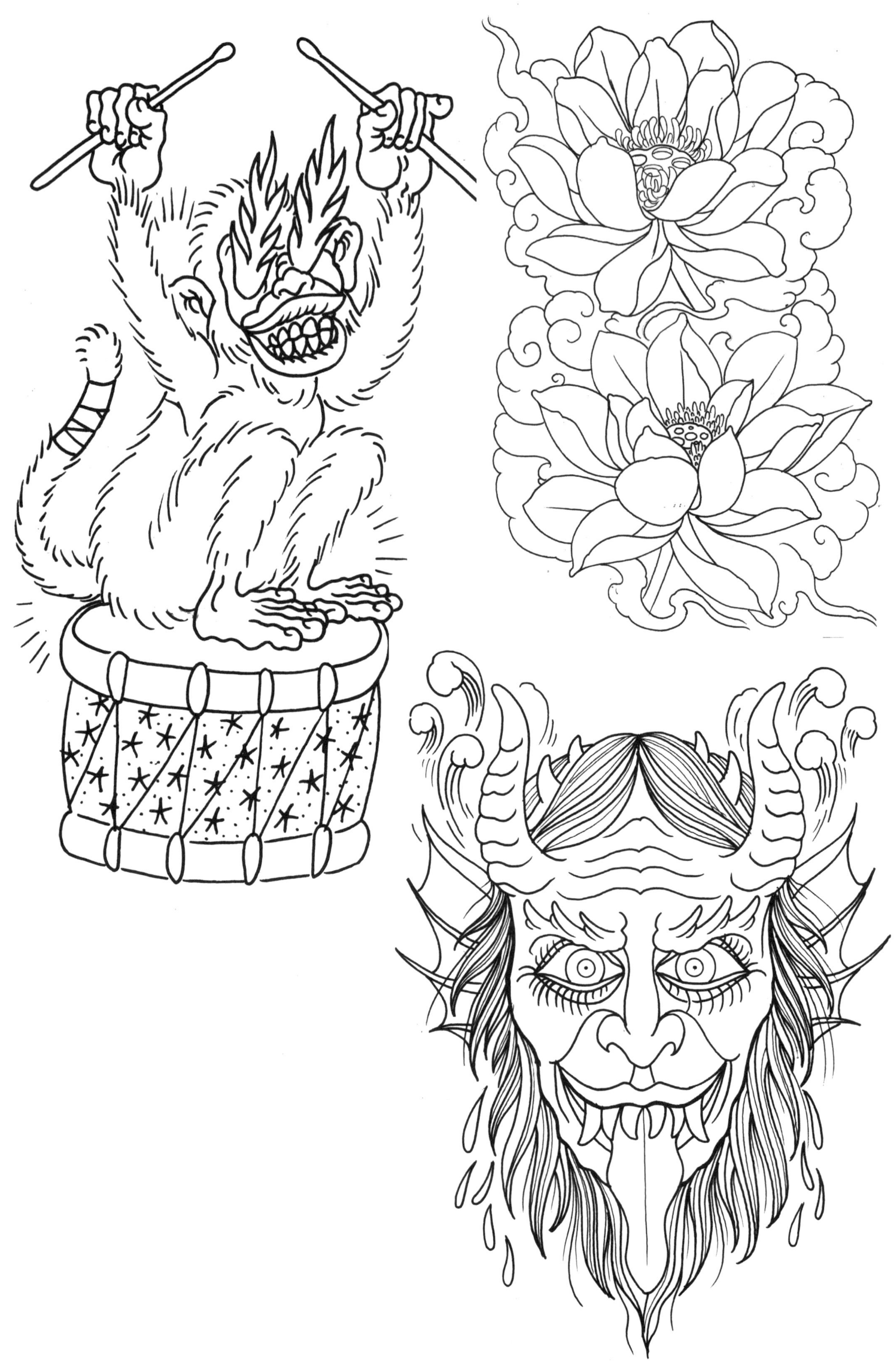

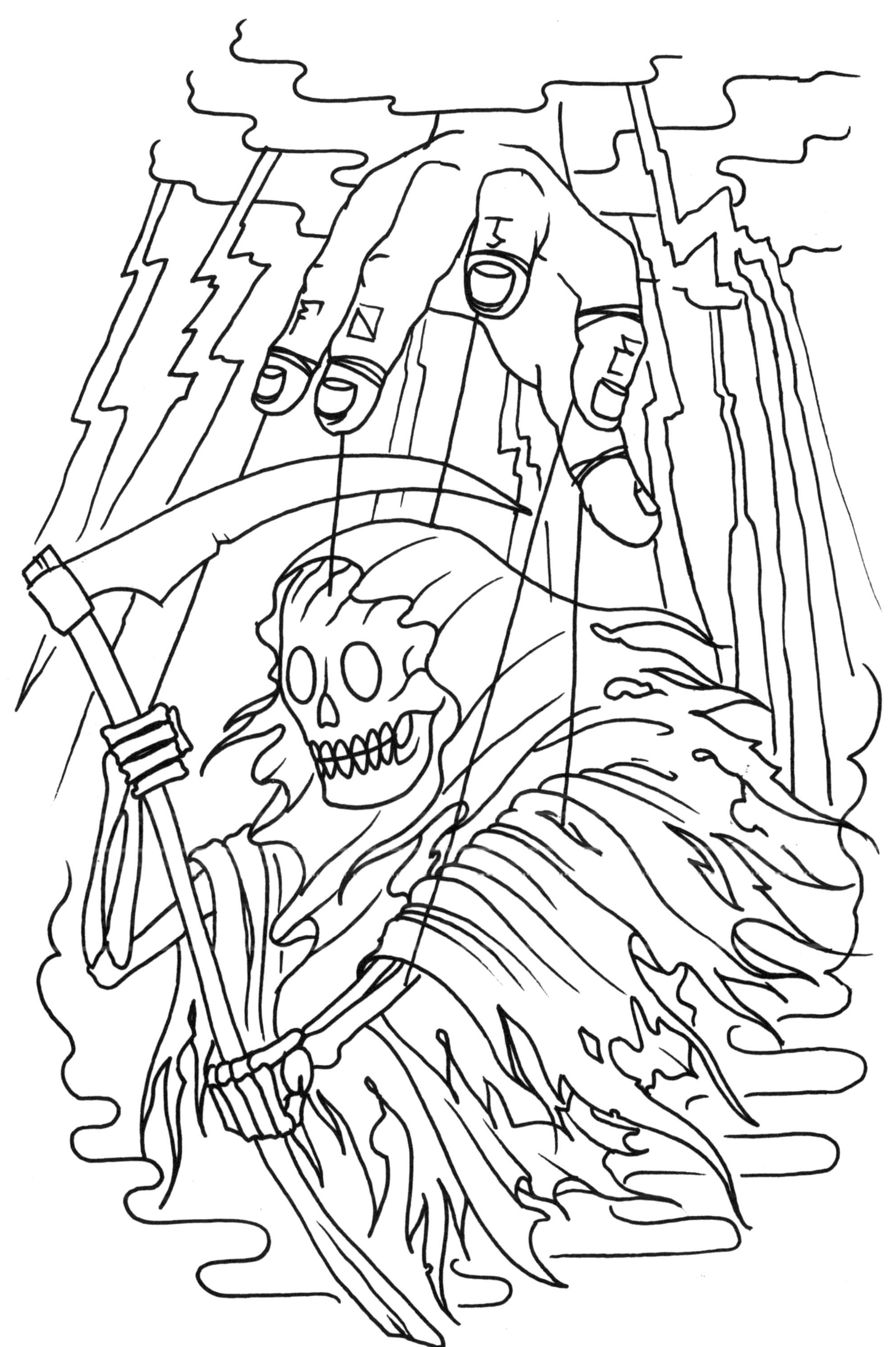

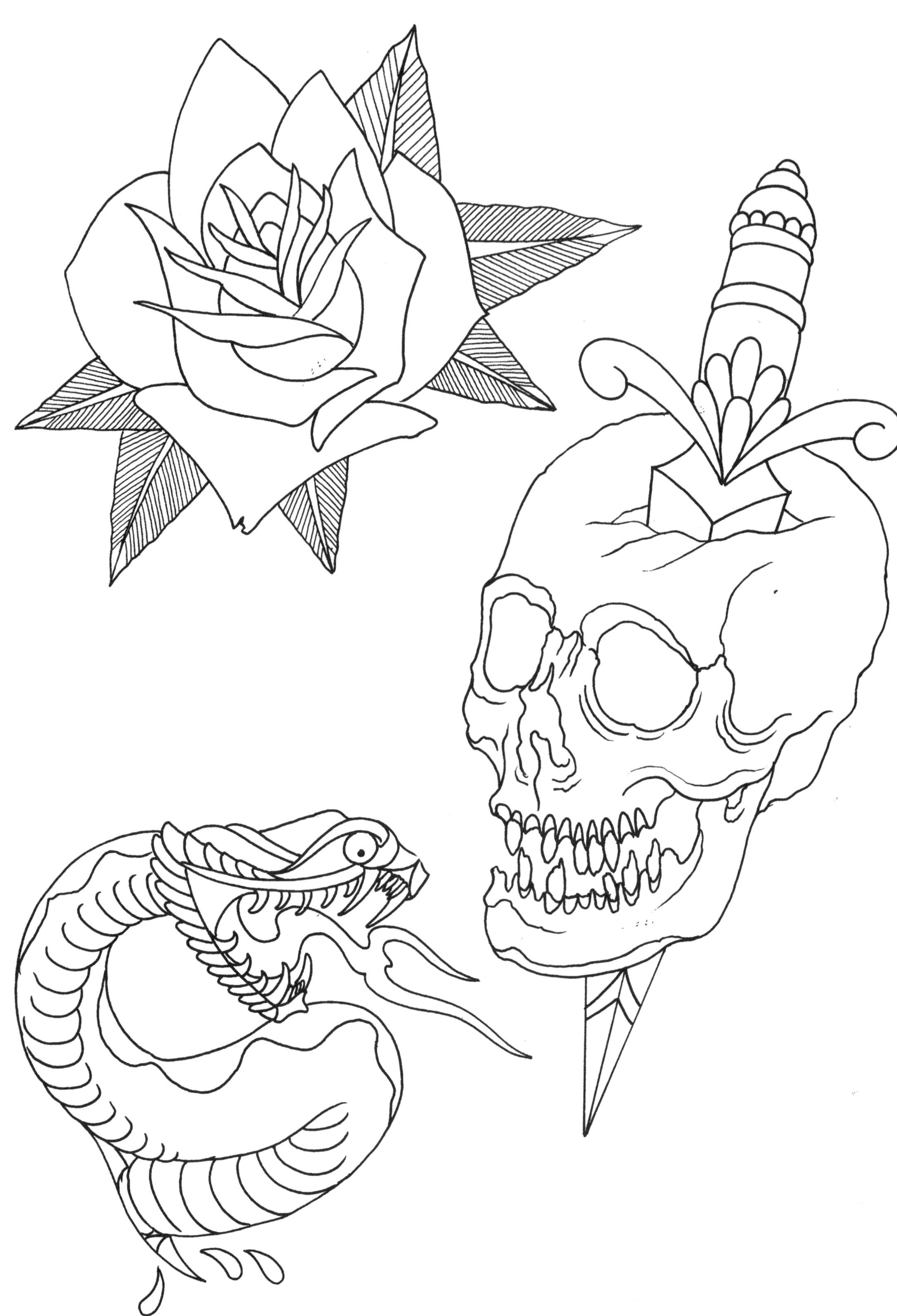

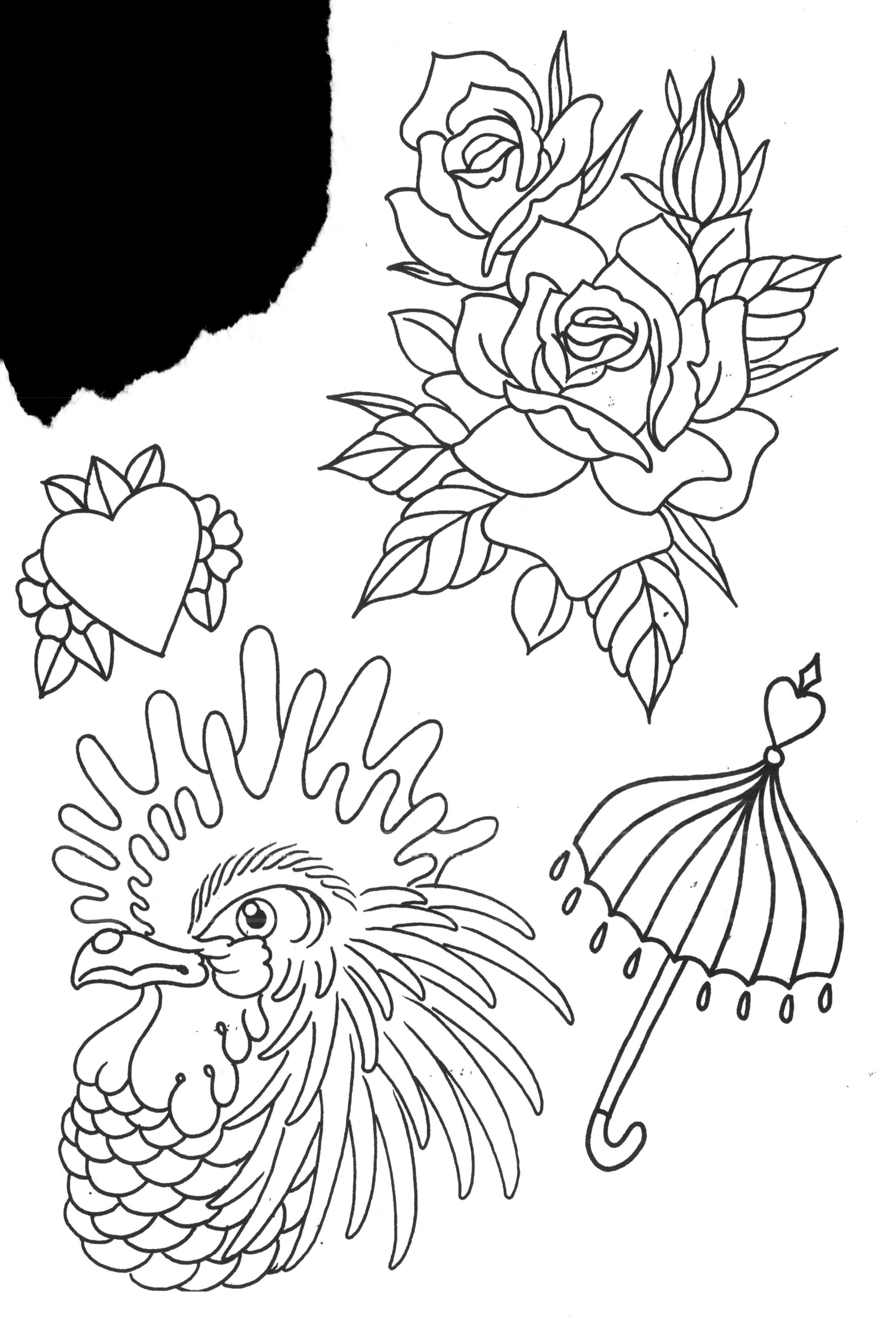

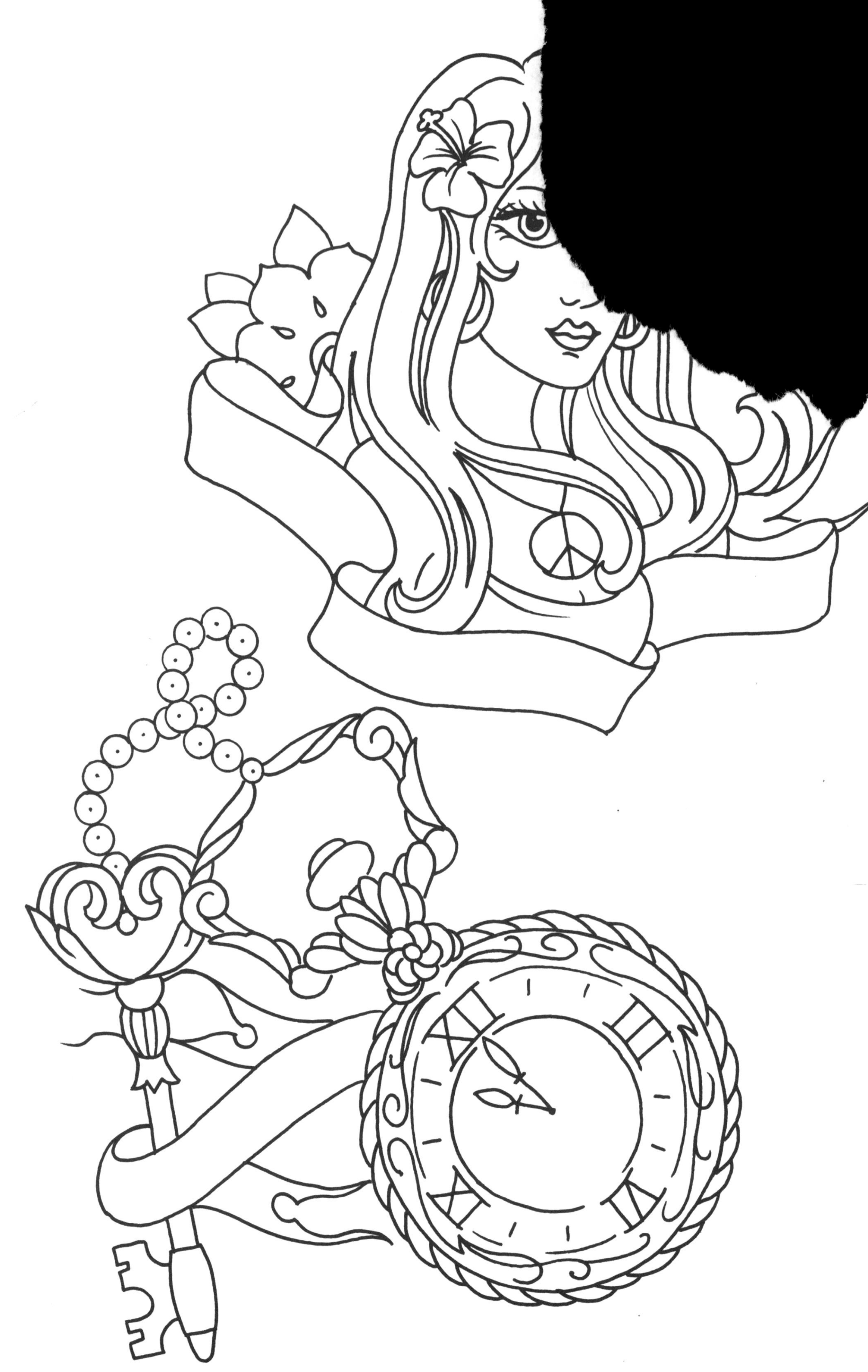

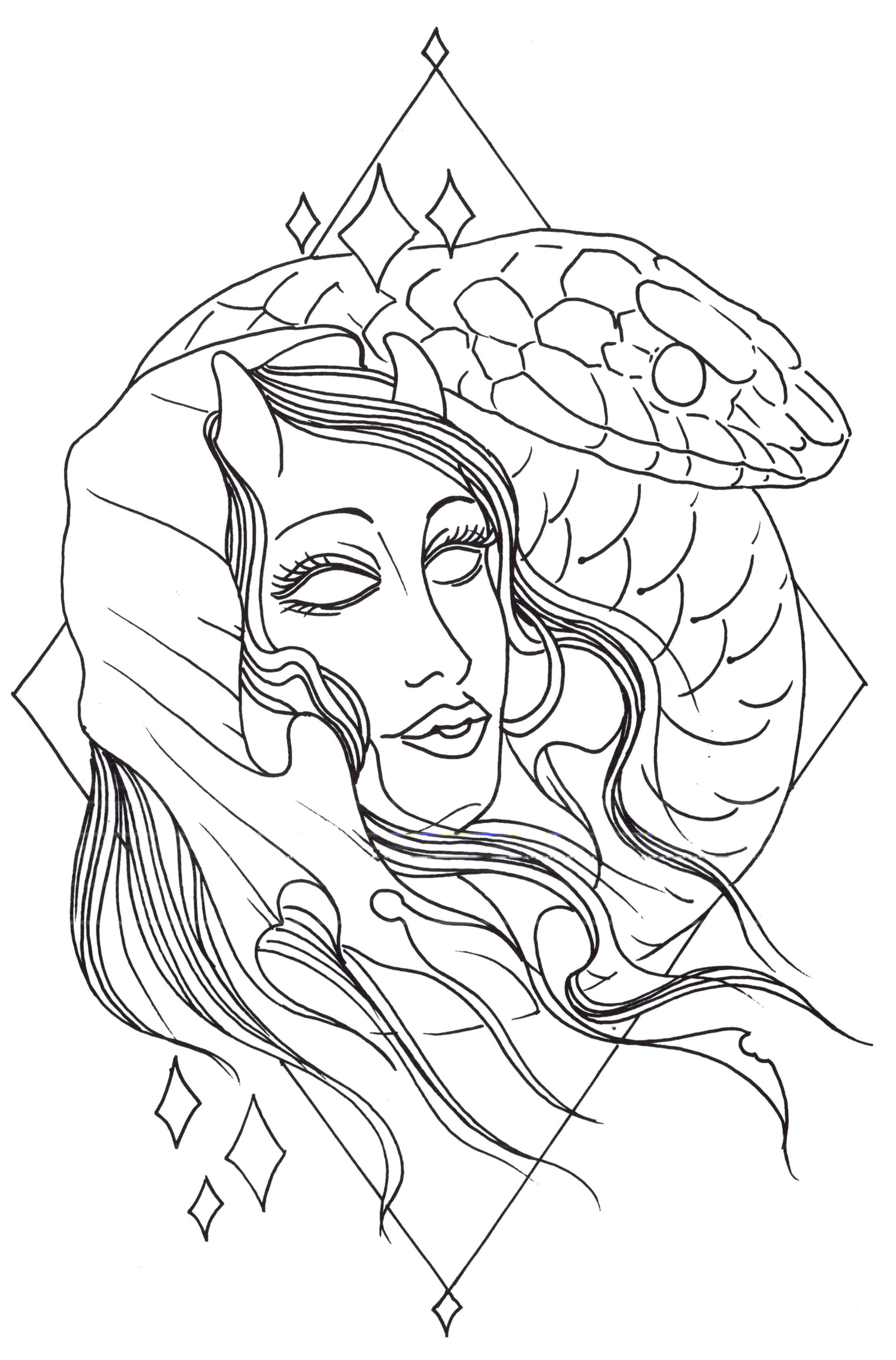

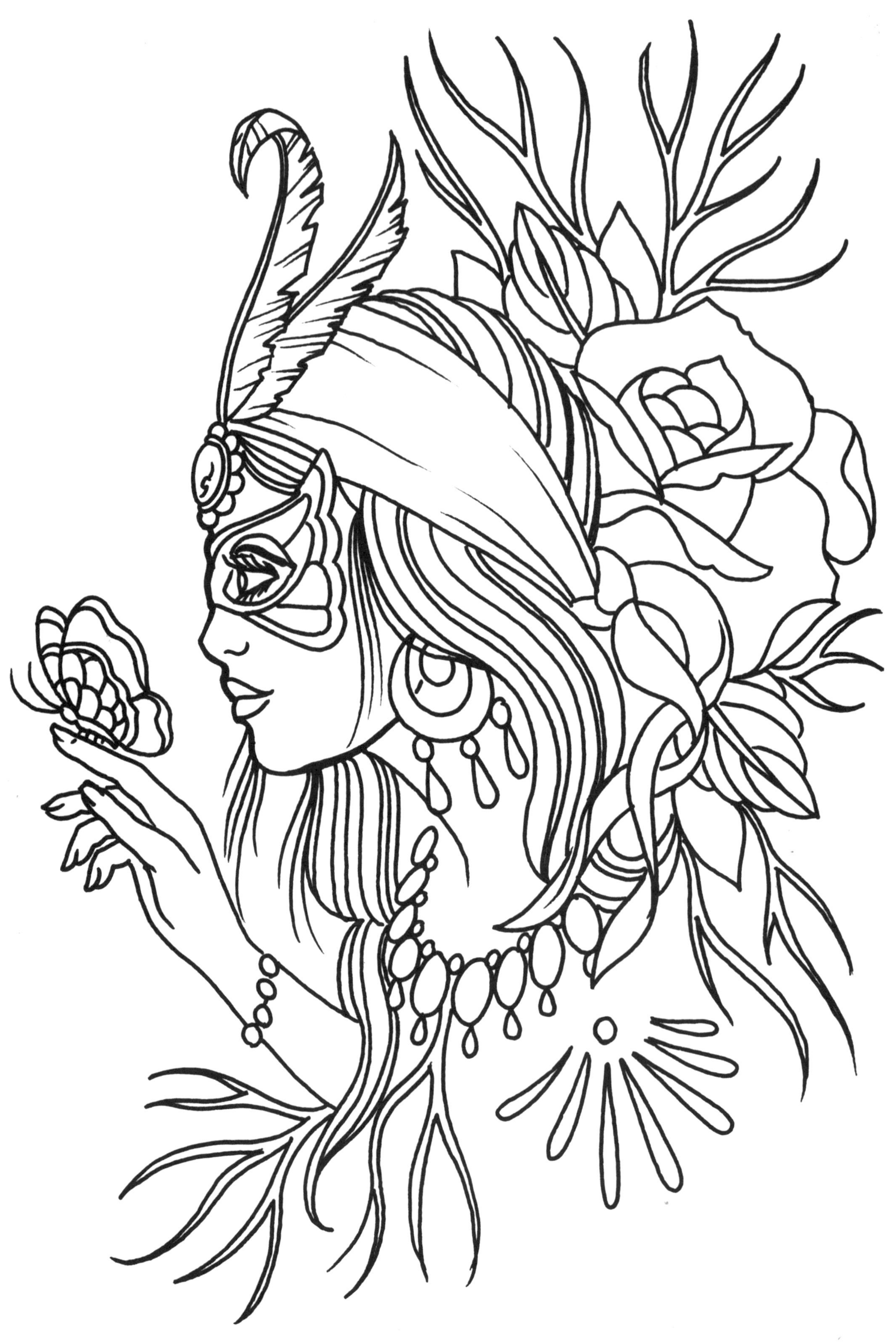

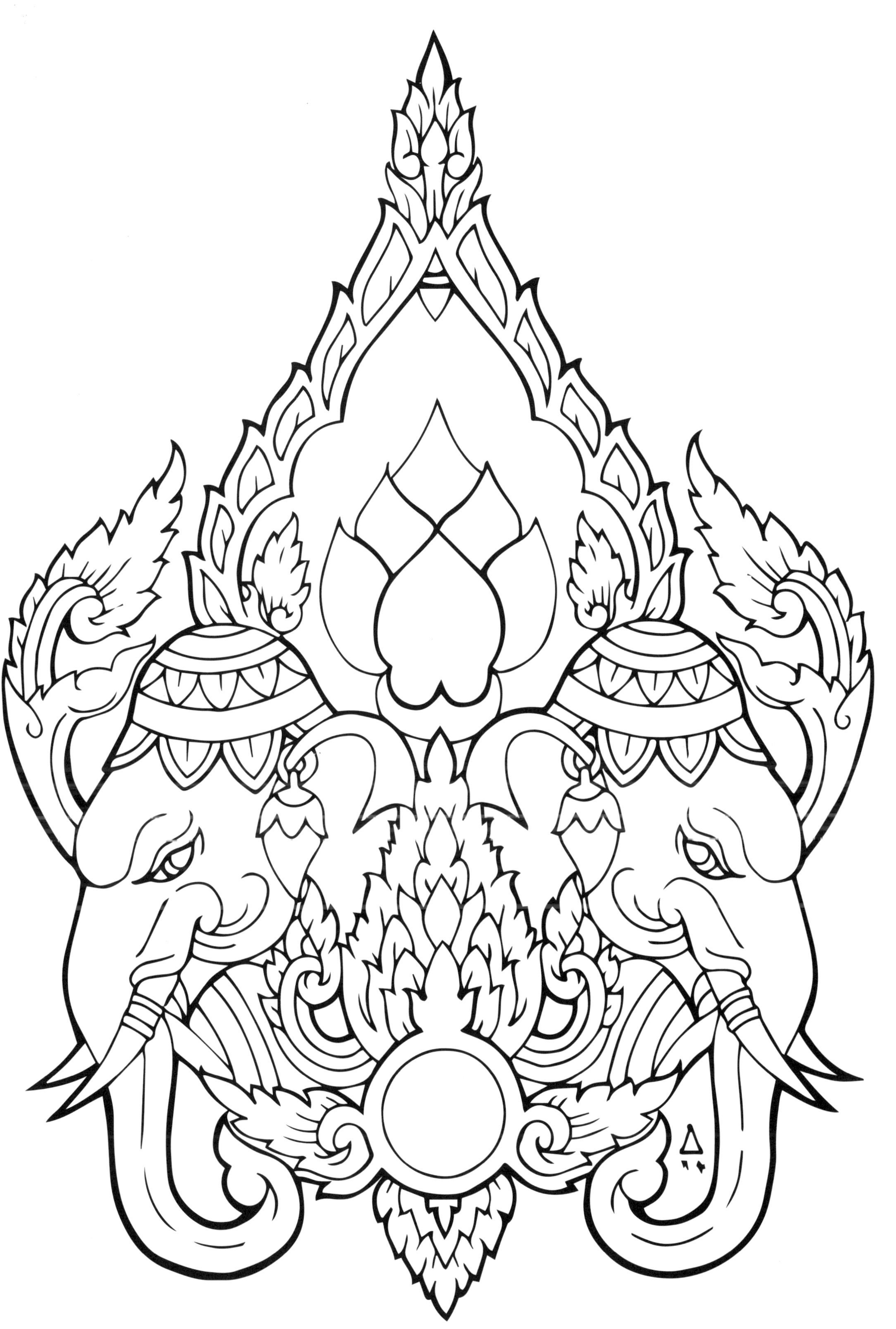

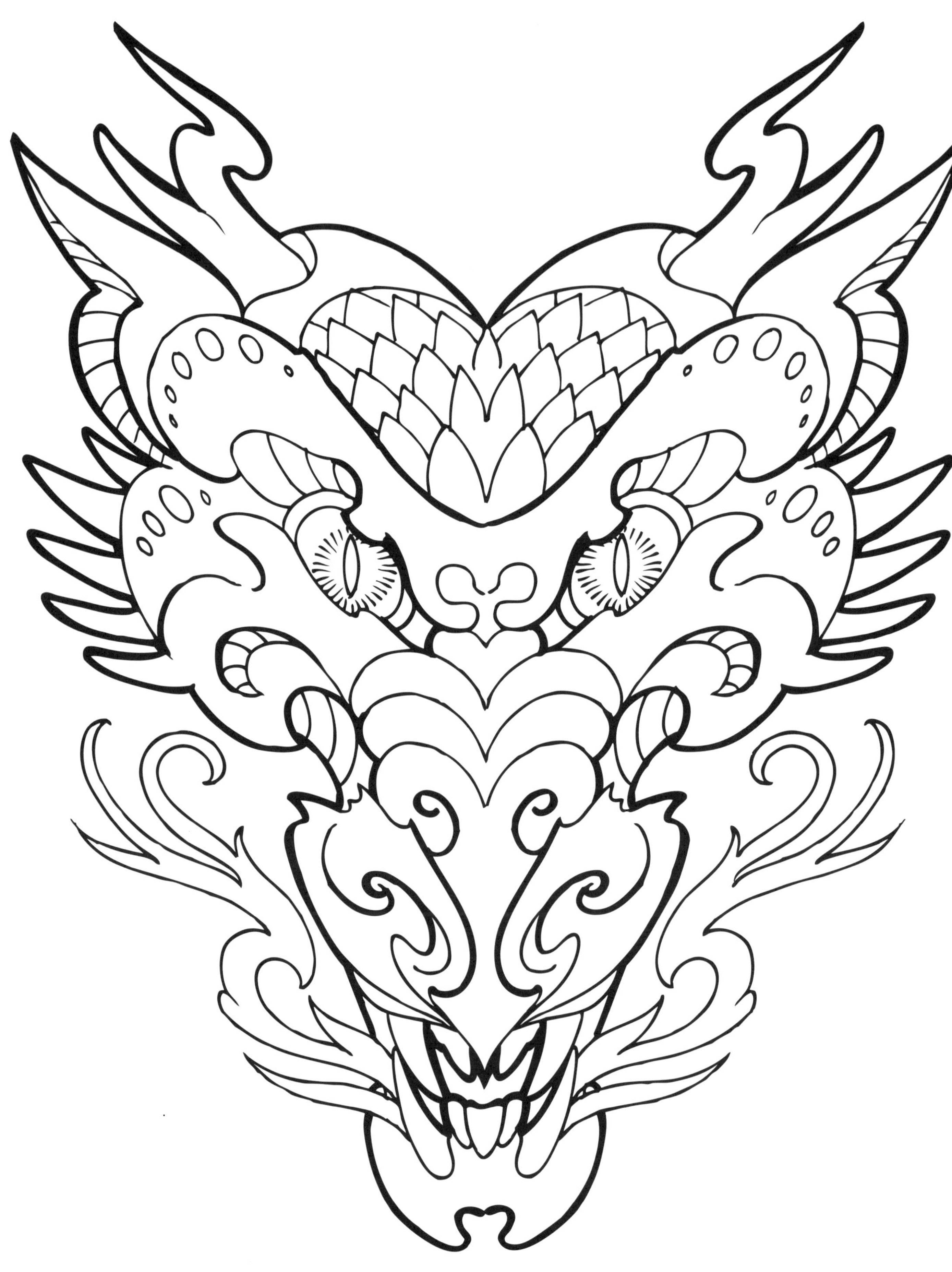

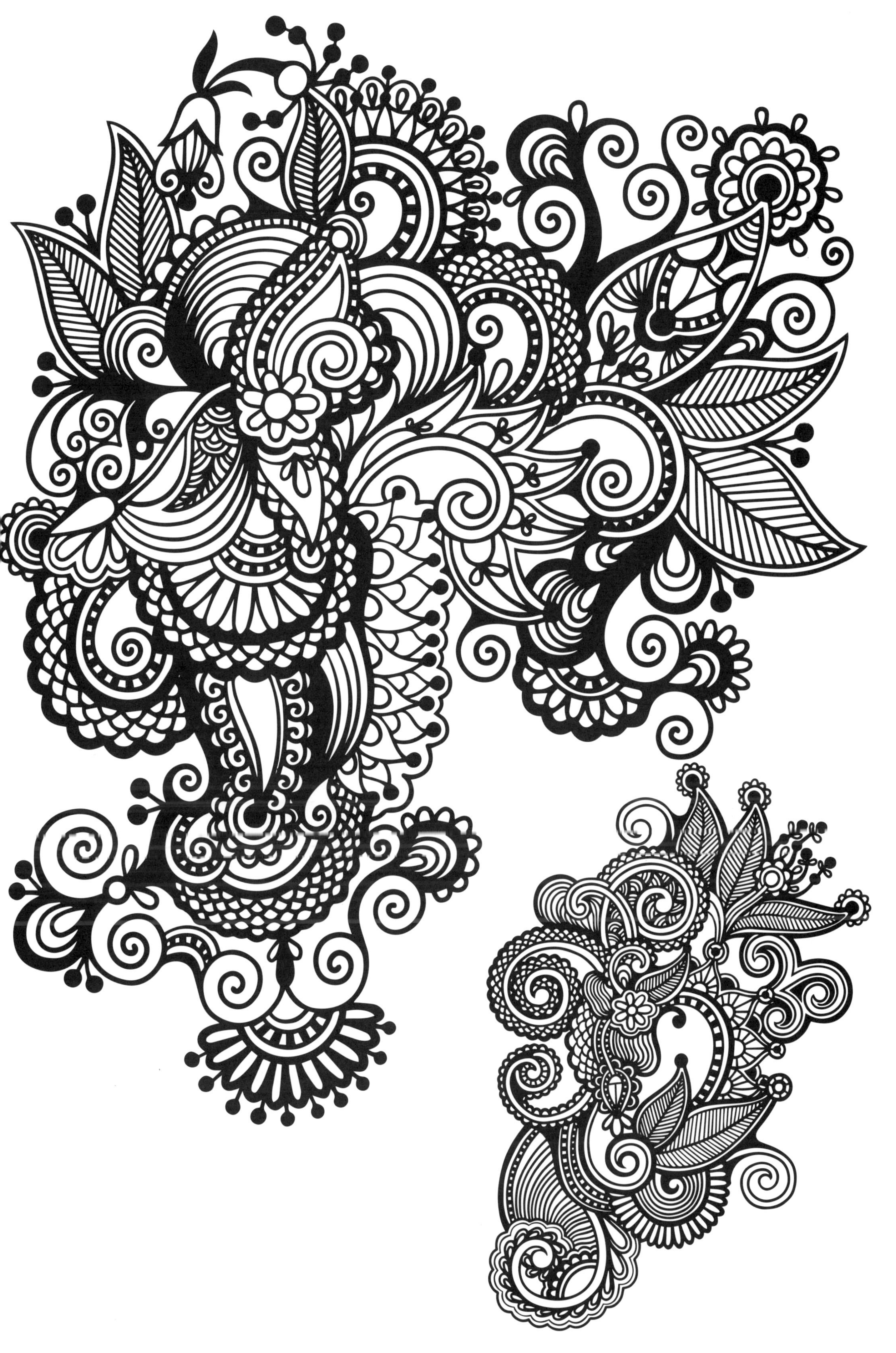

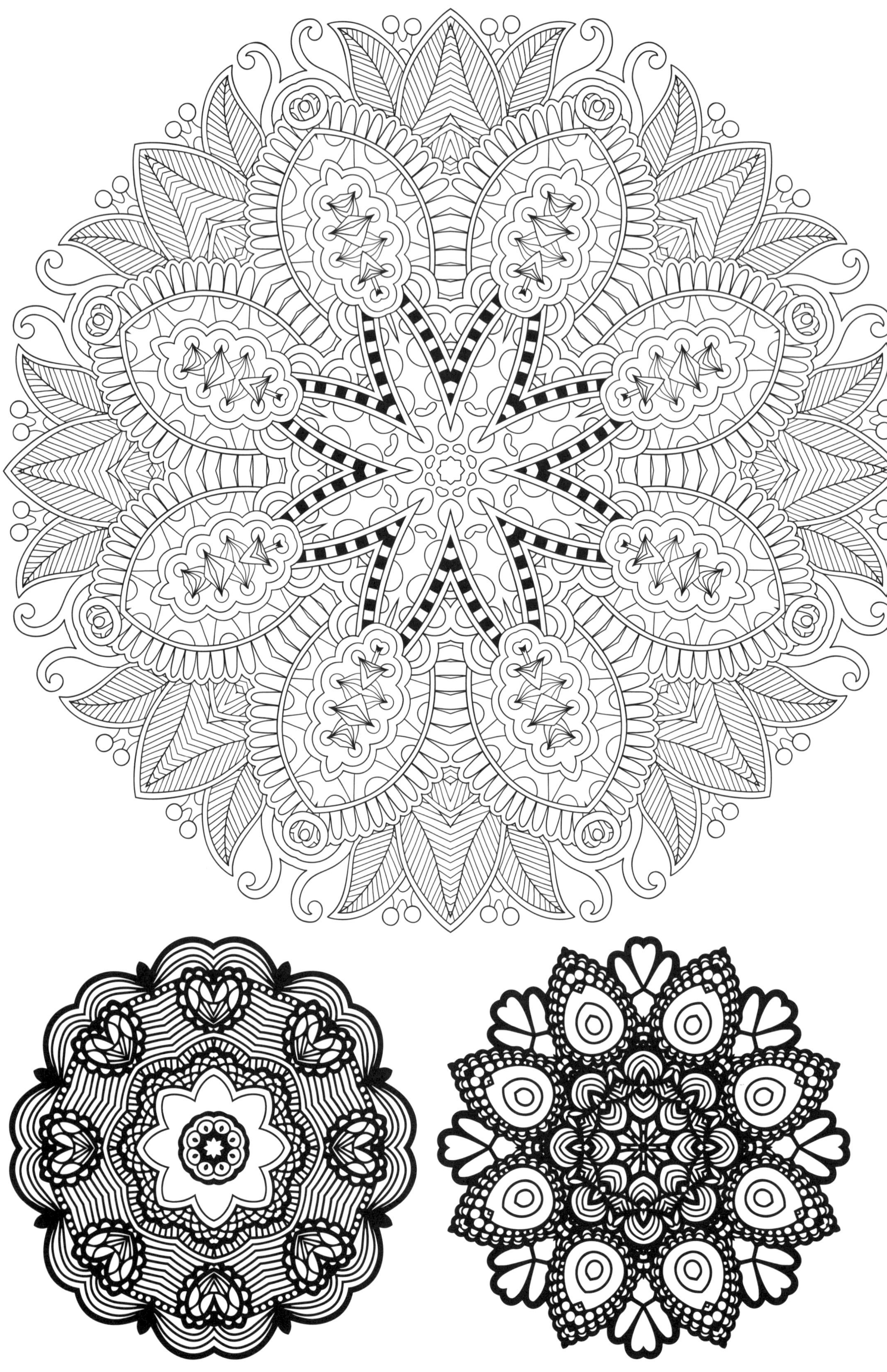

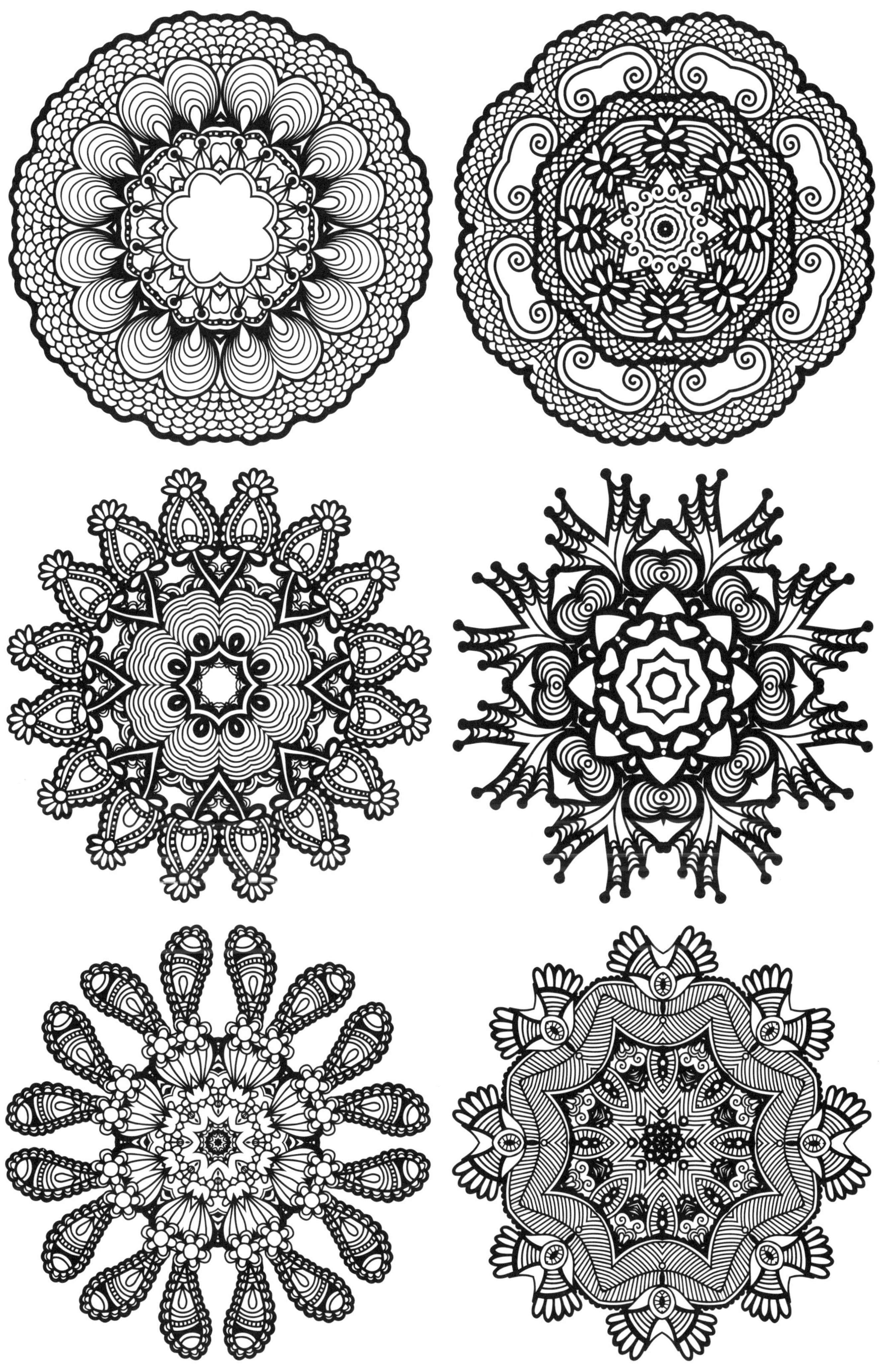

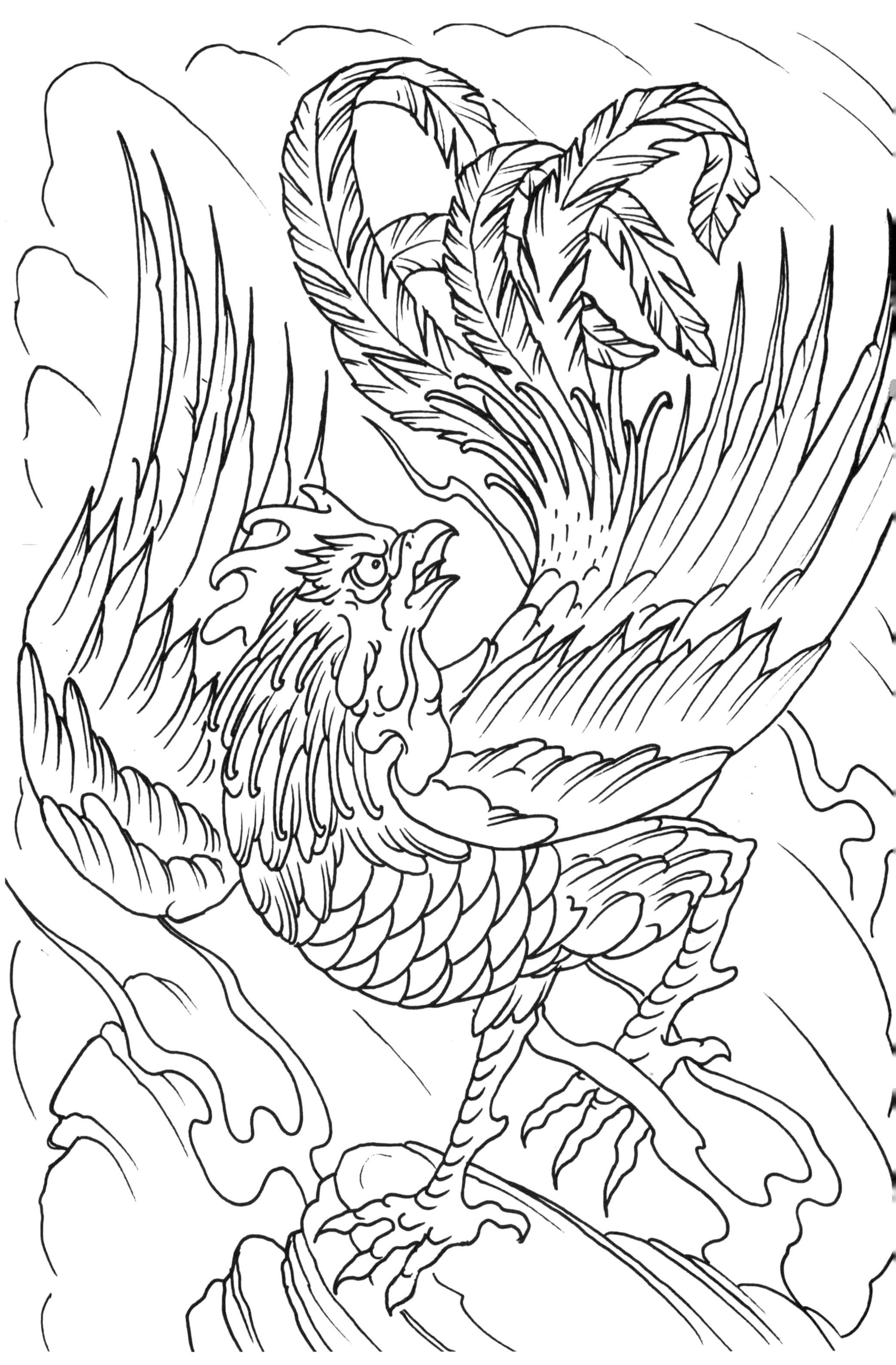

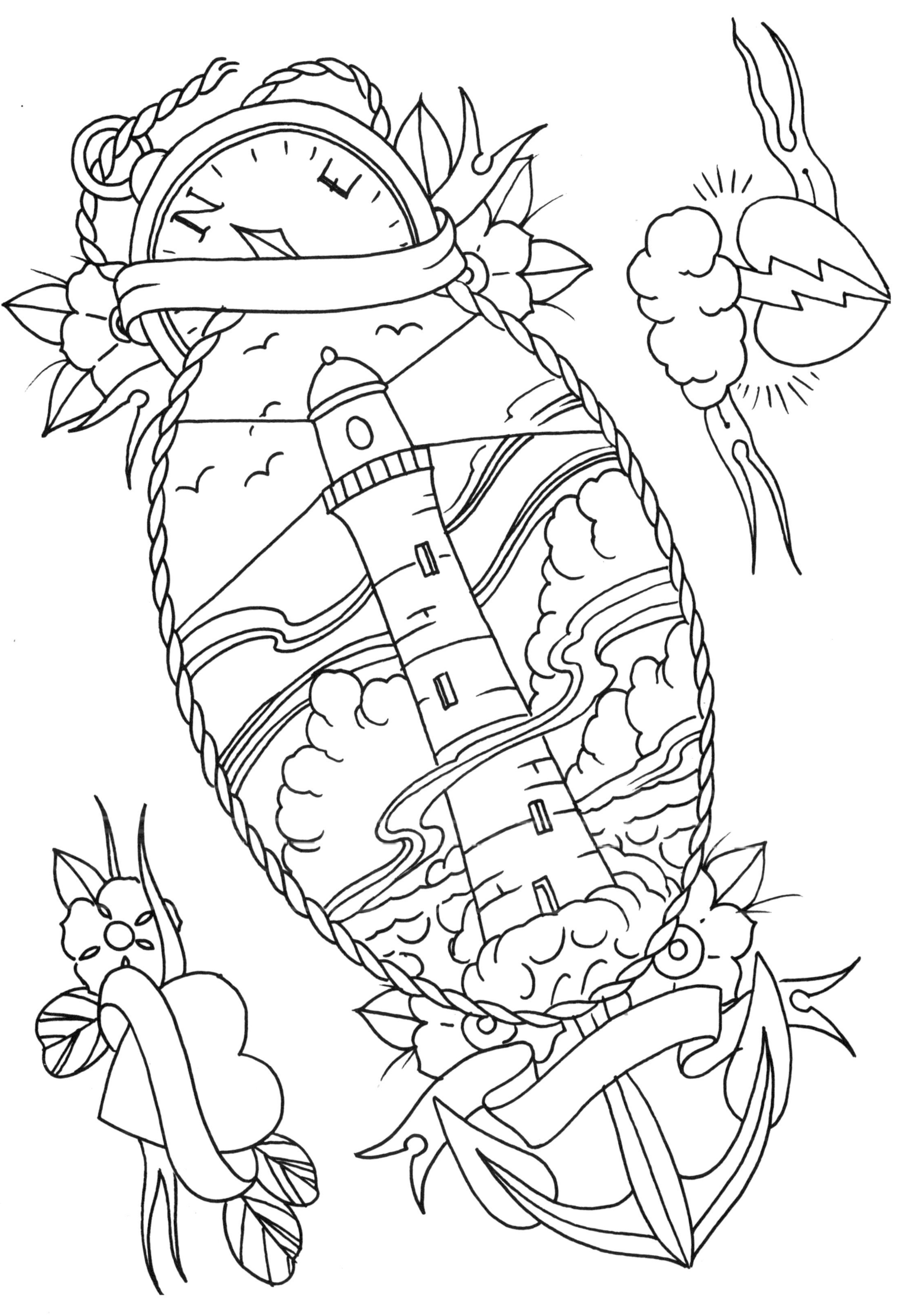
N
E

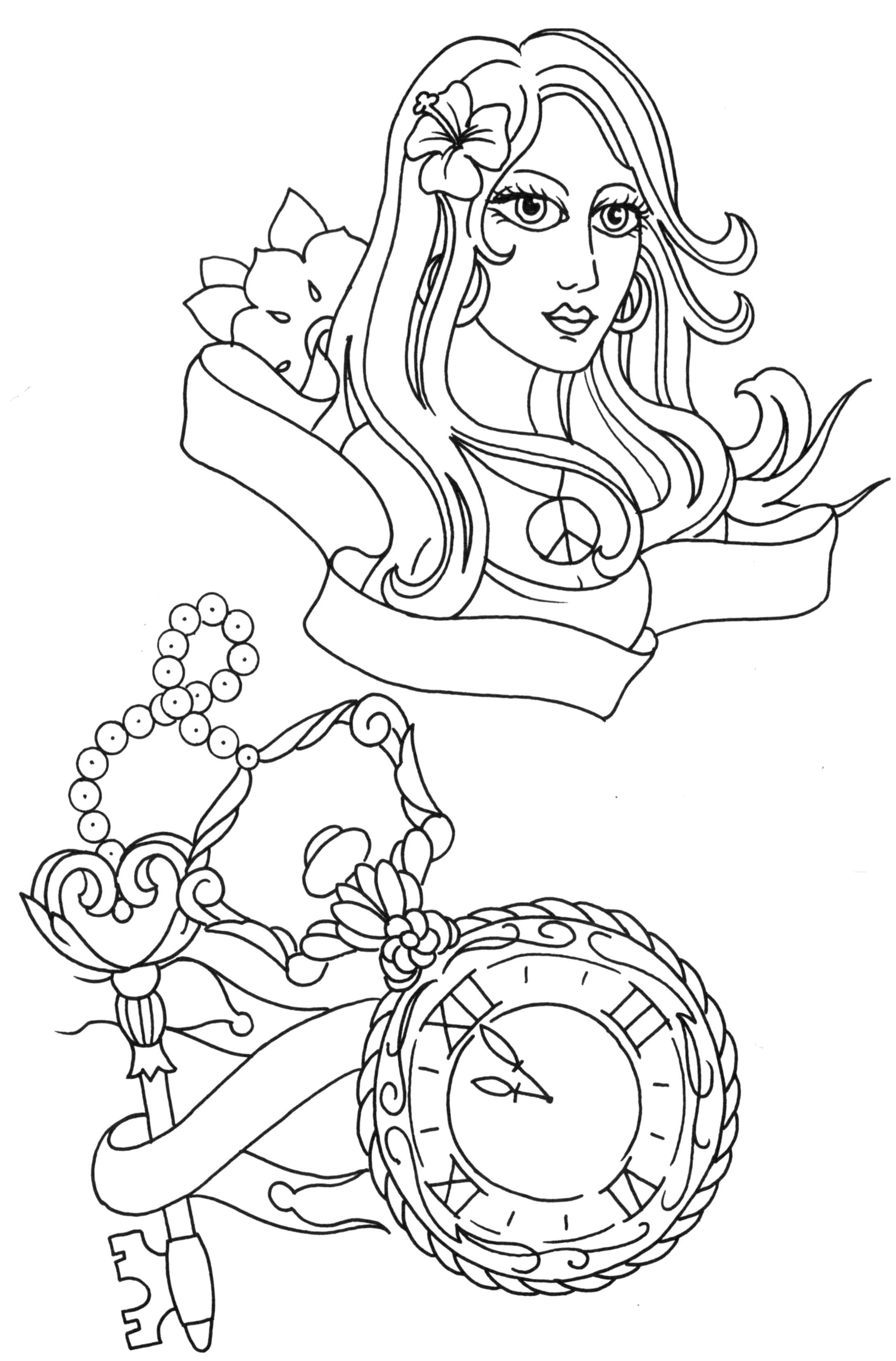

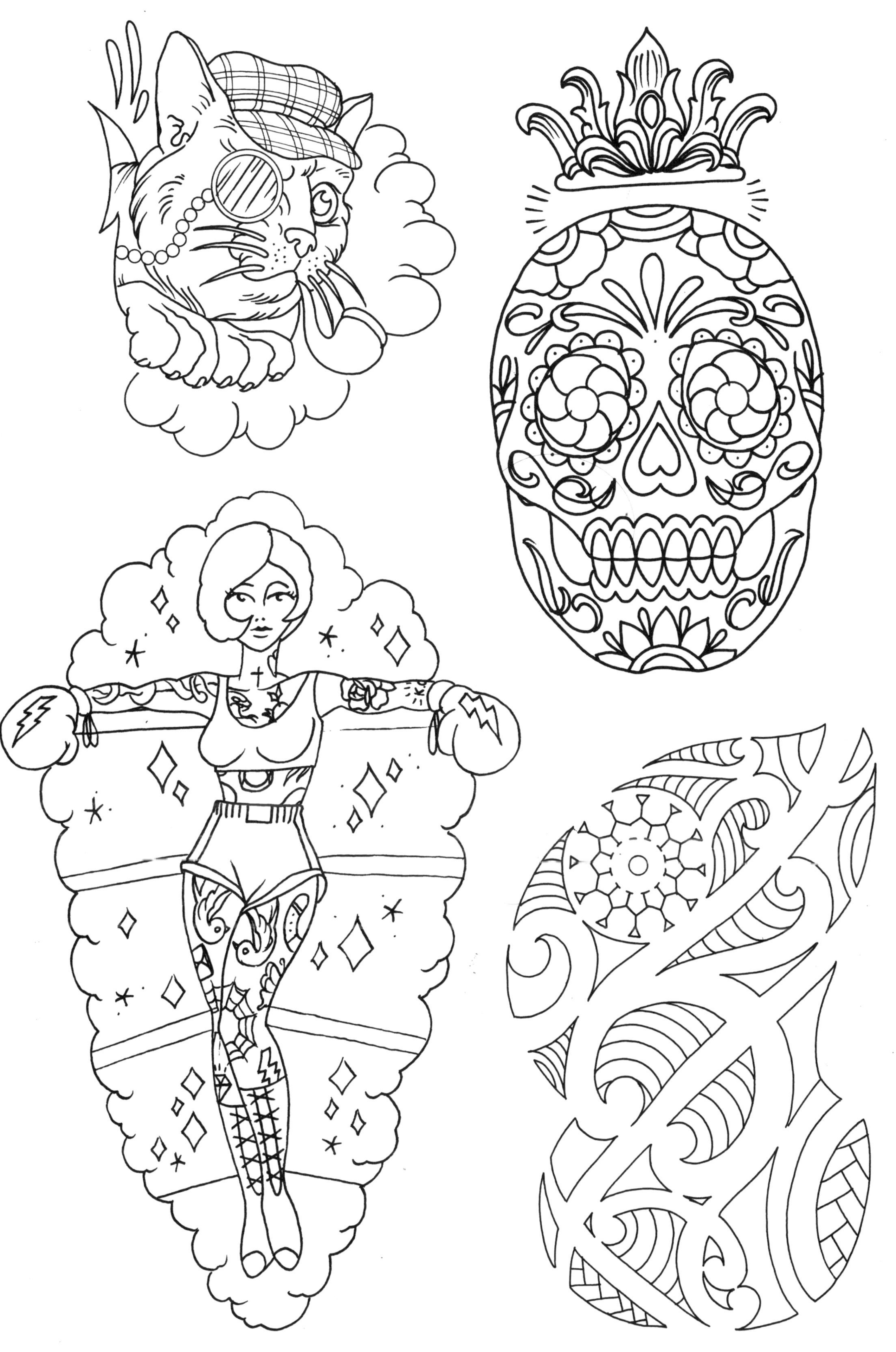

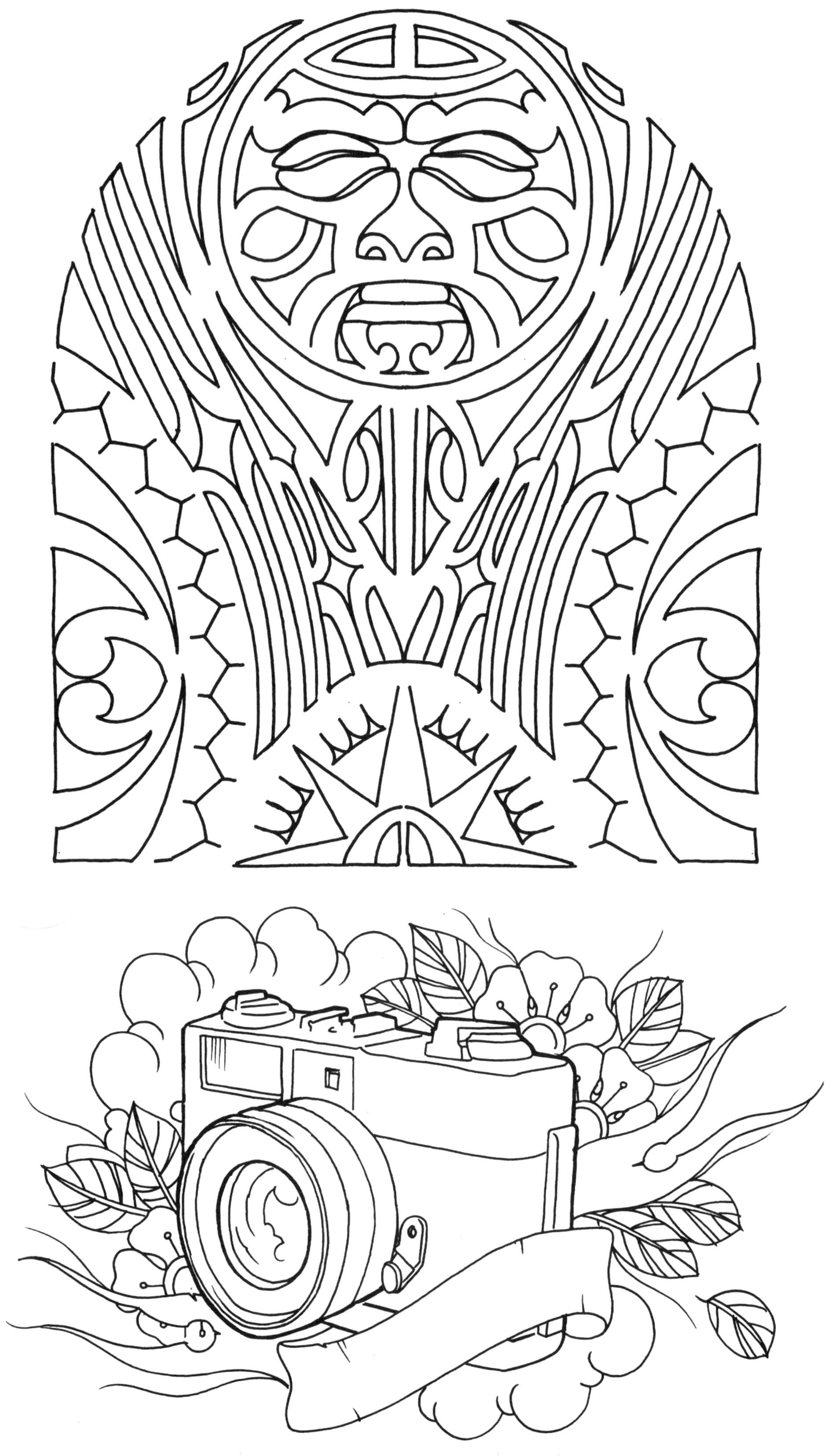

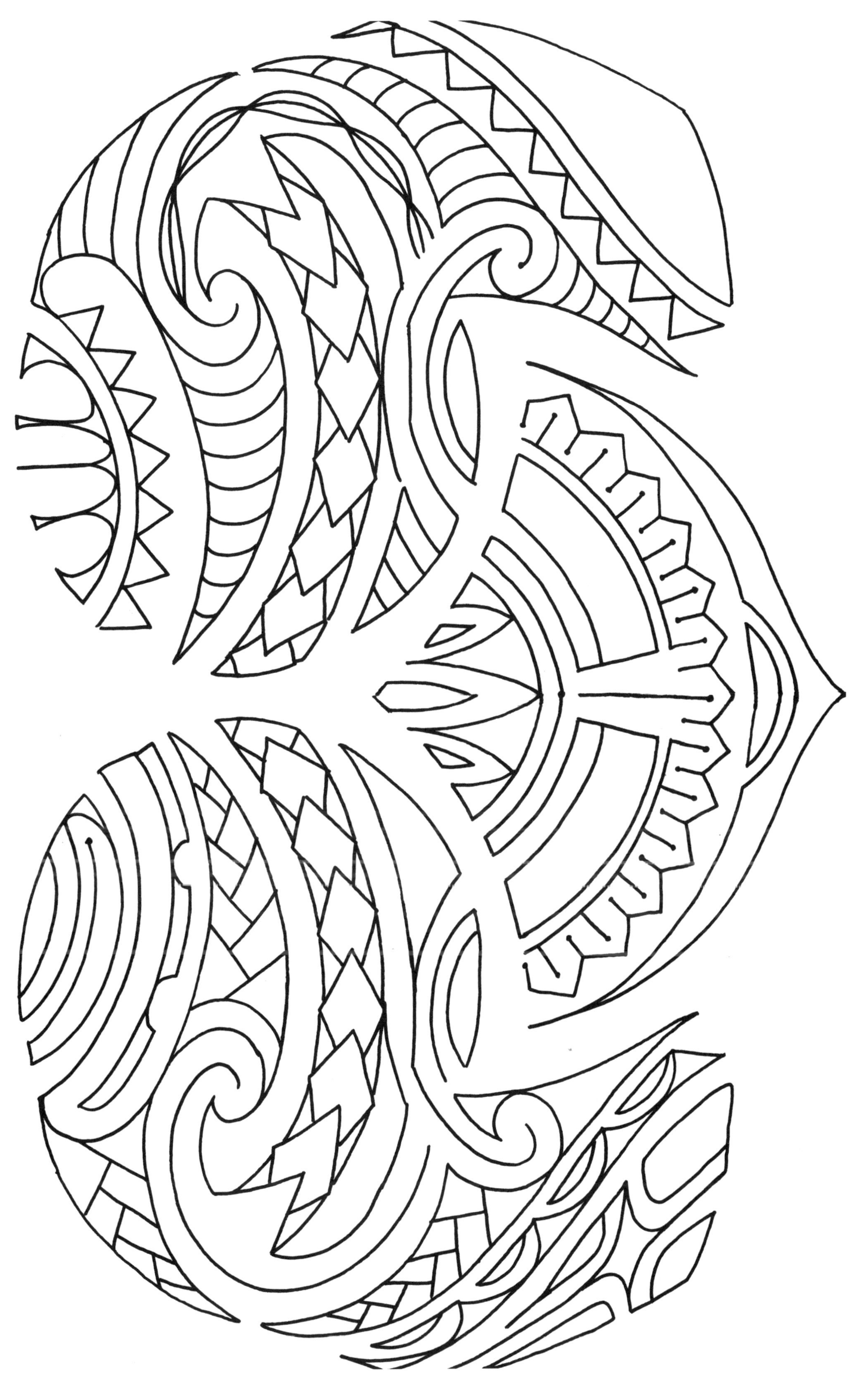

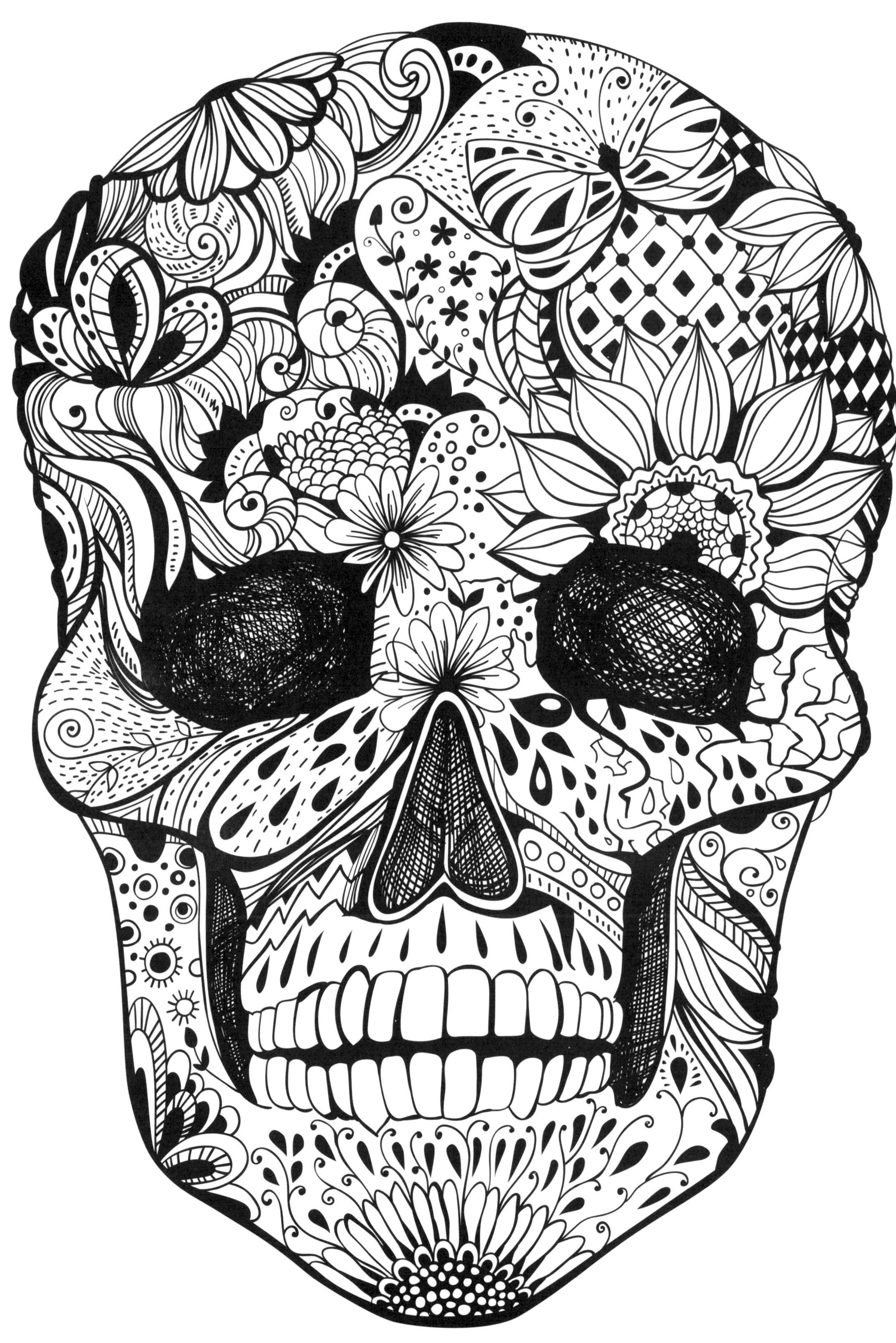

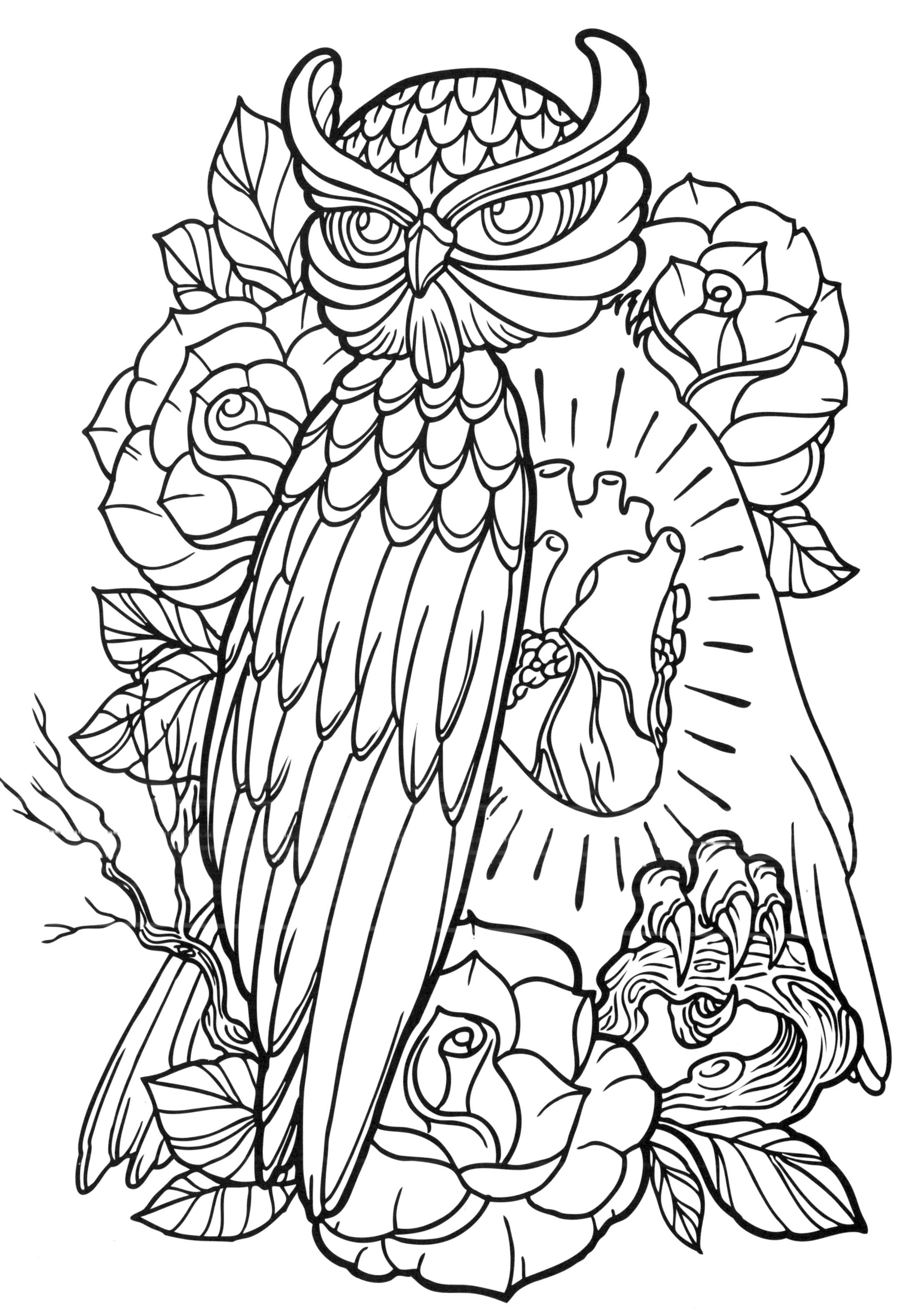

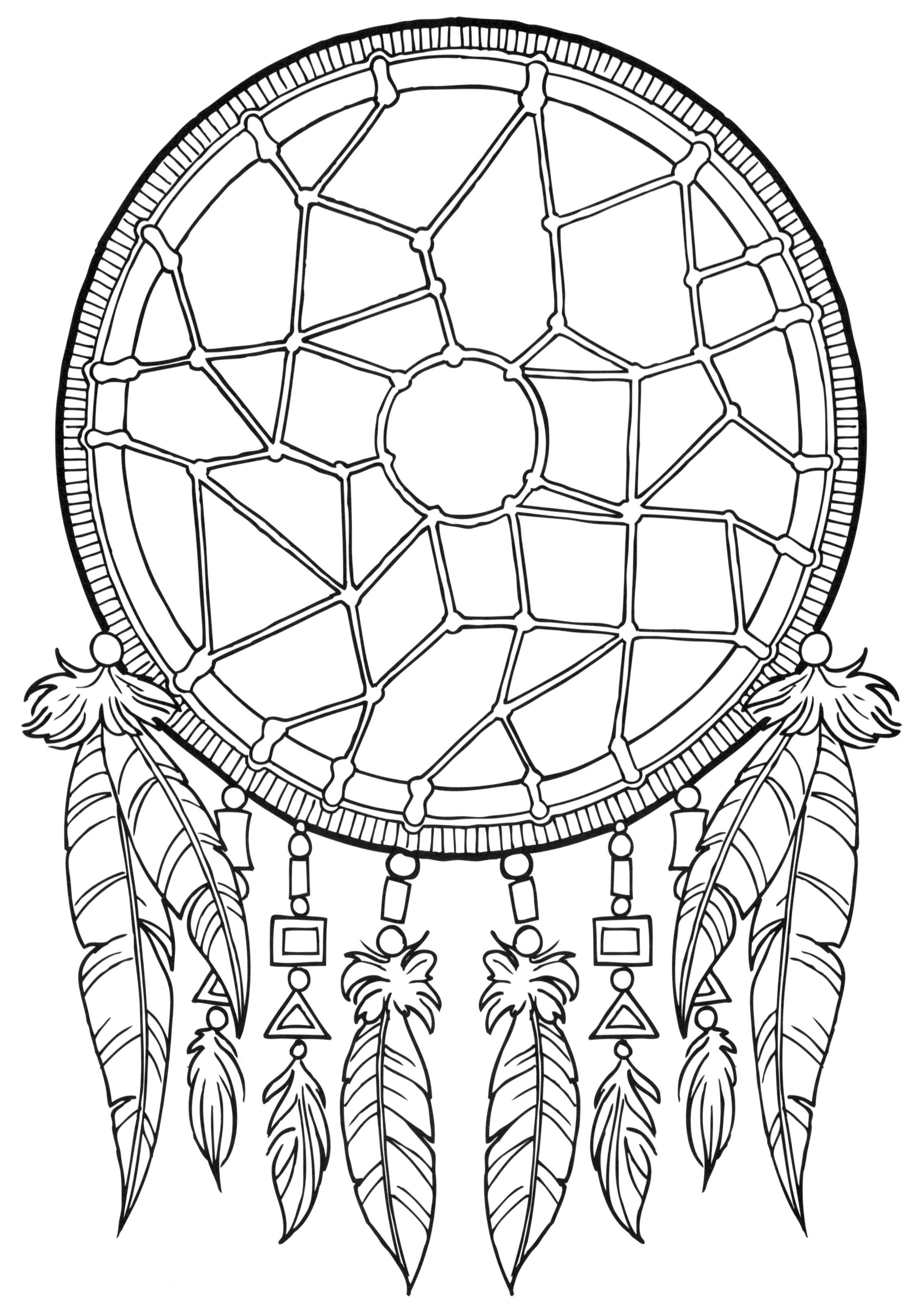

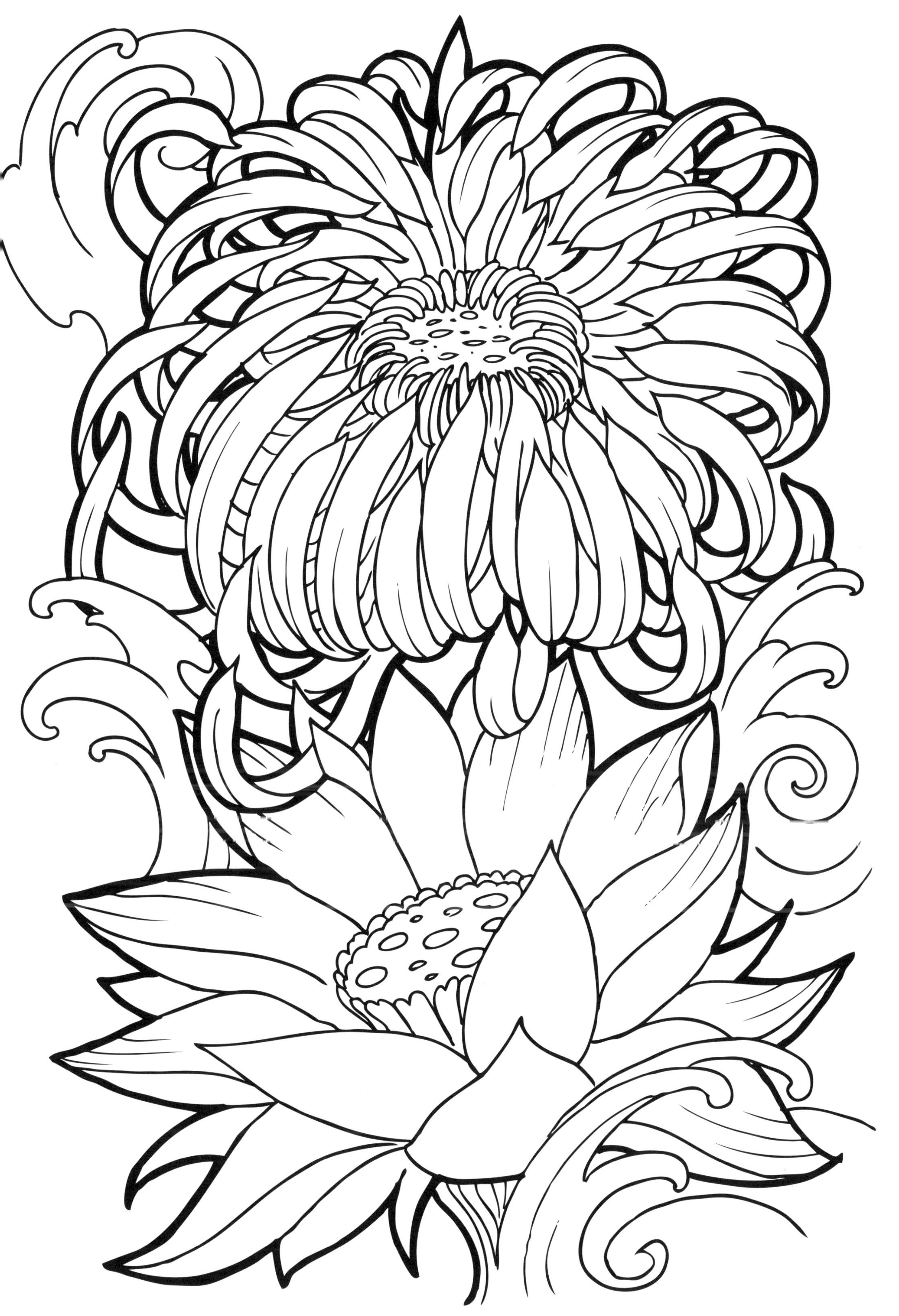

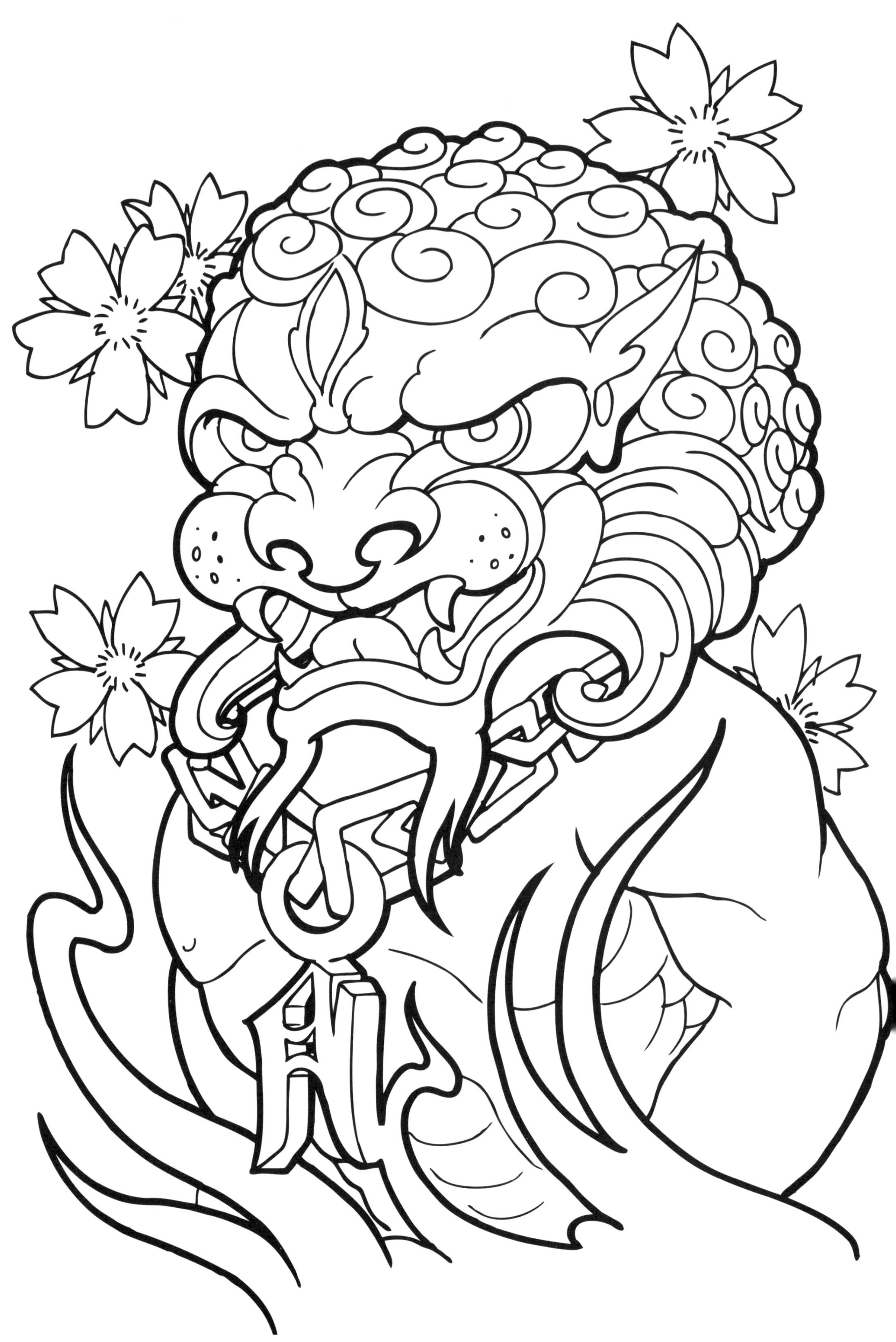

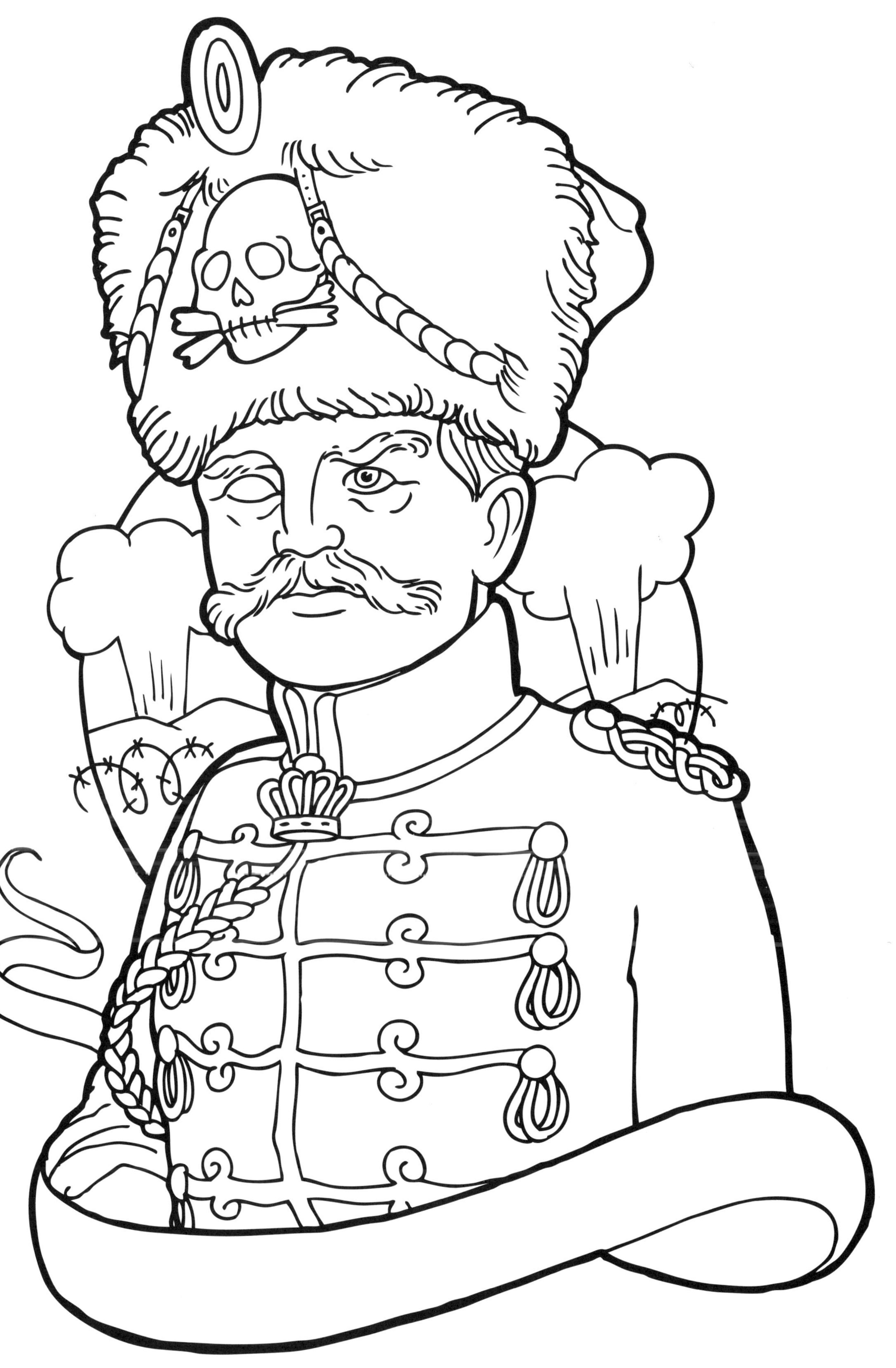

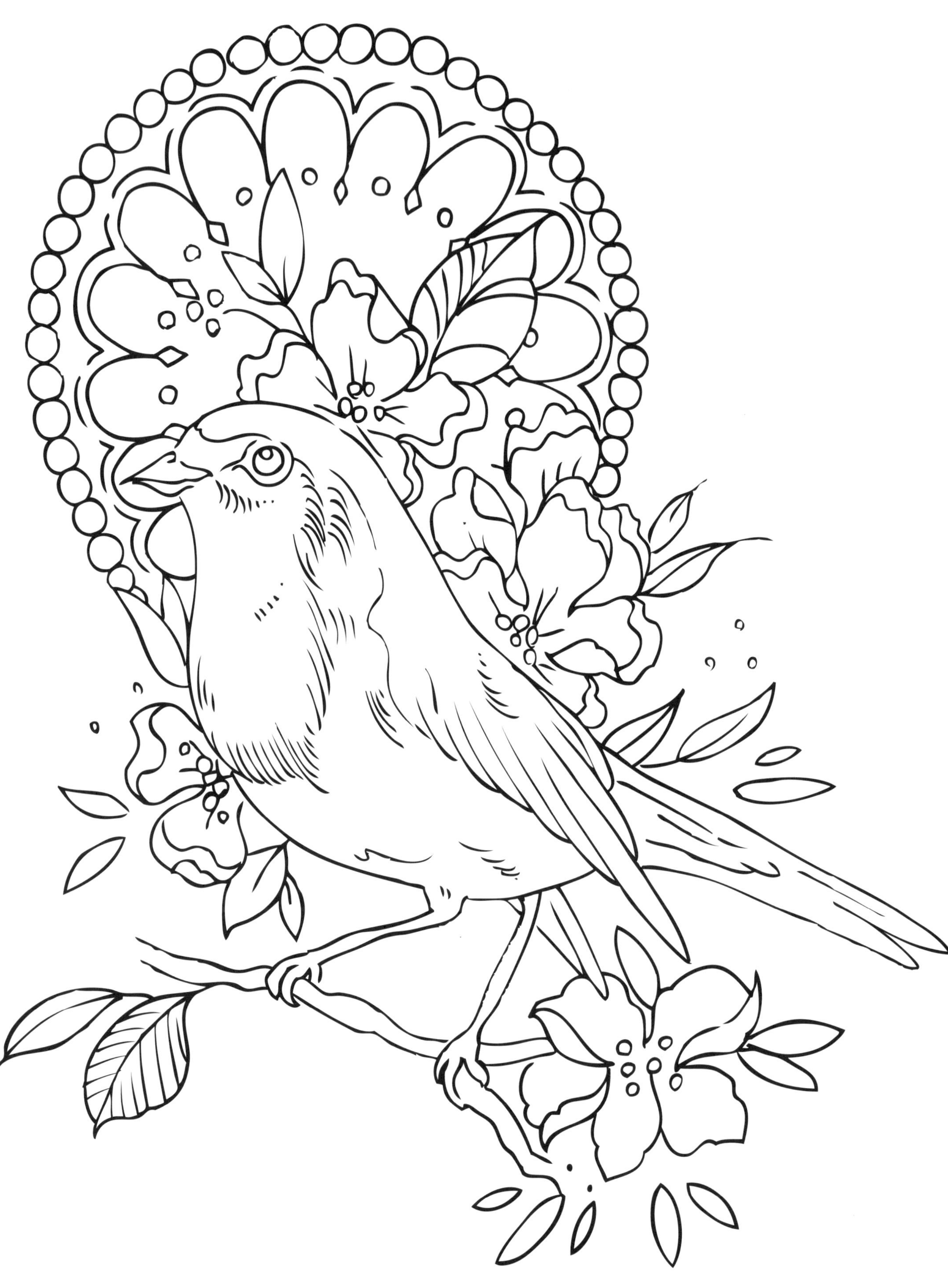

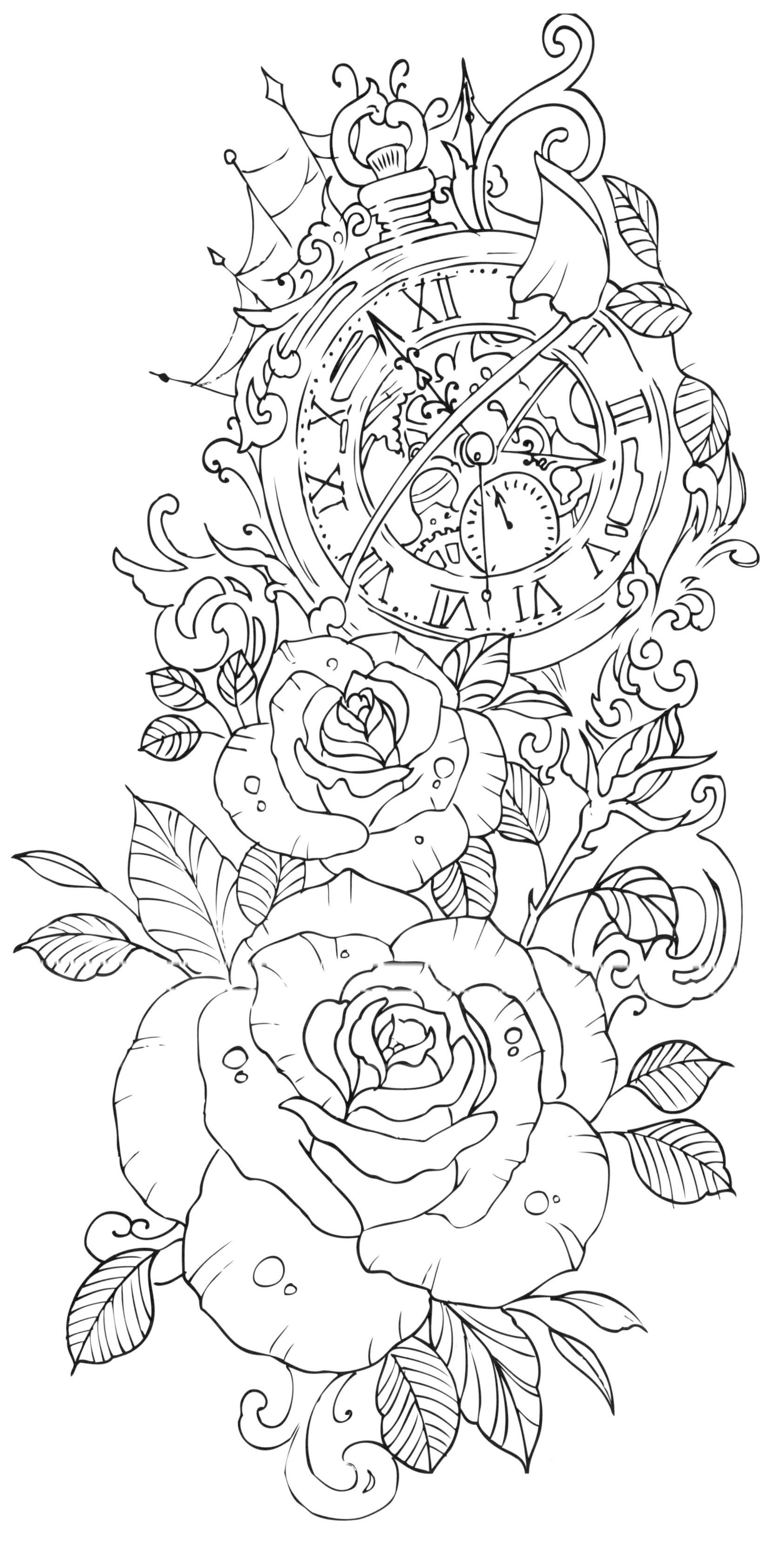

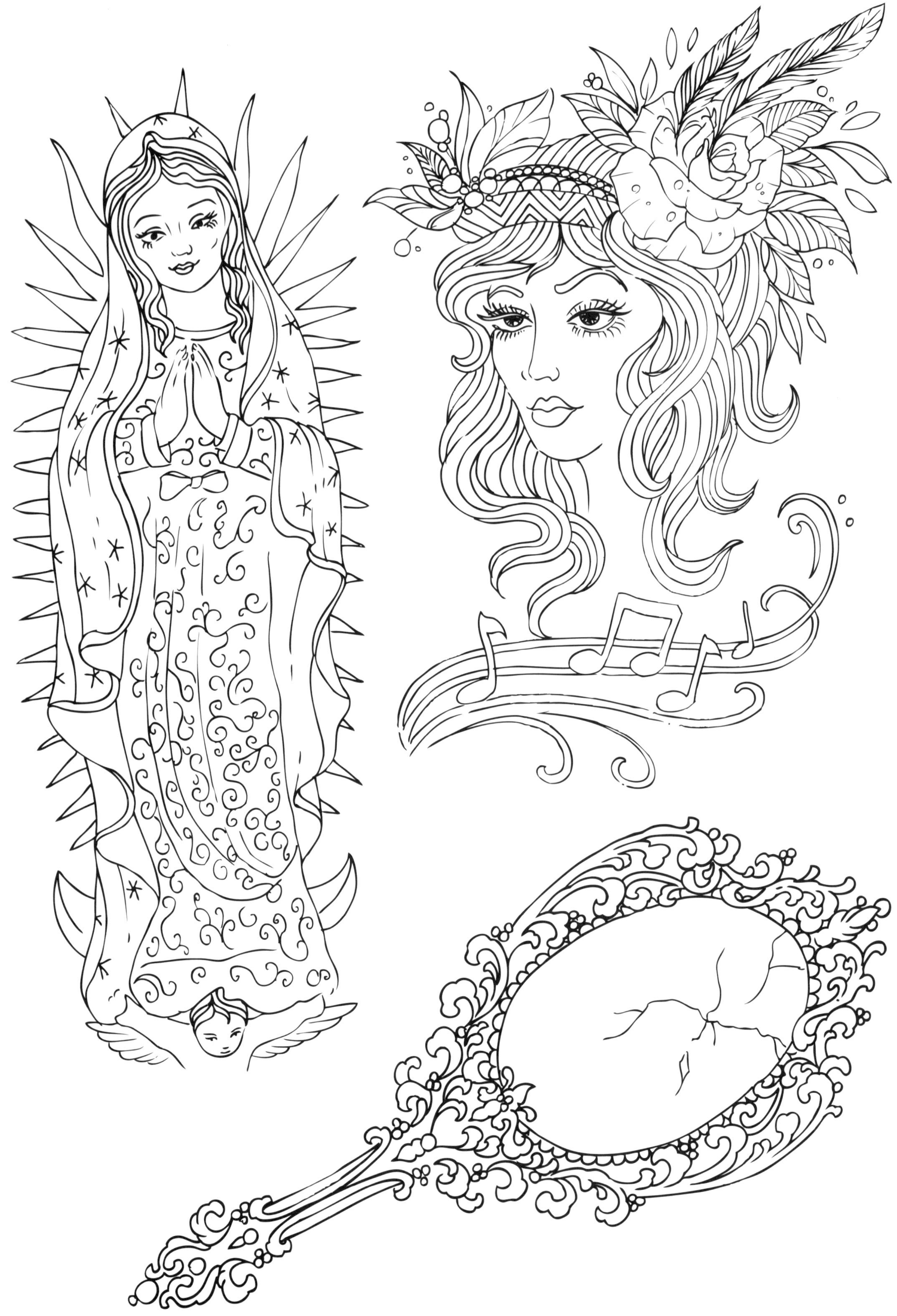

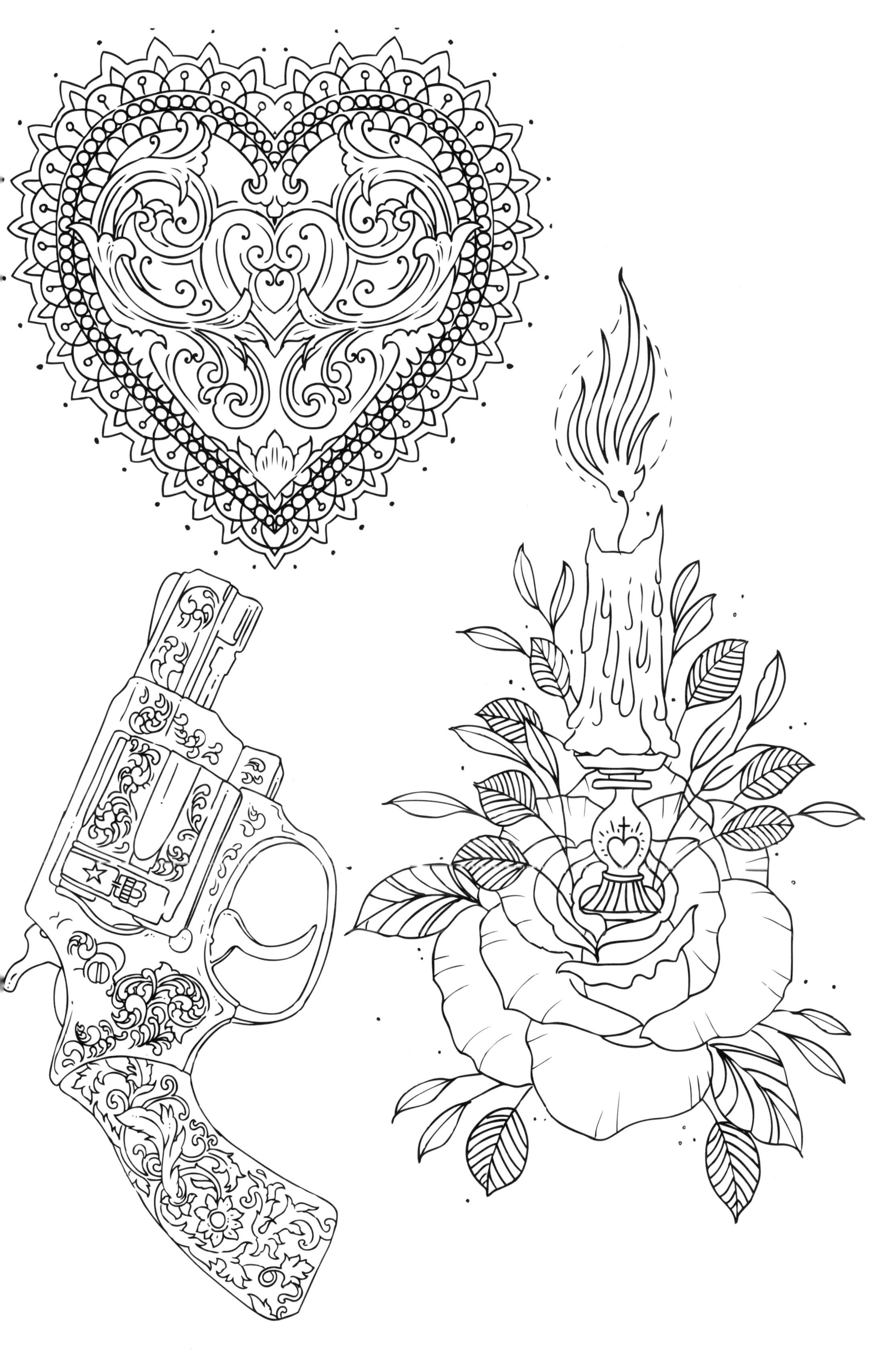

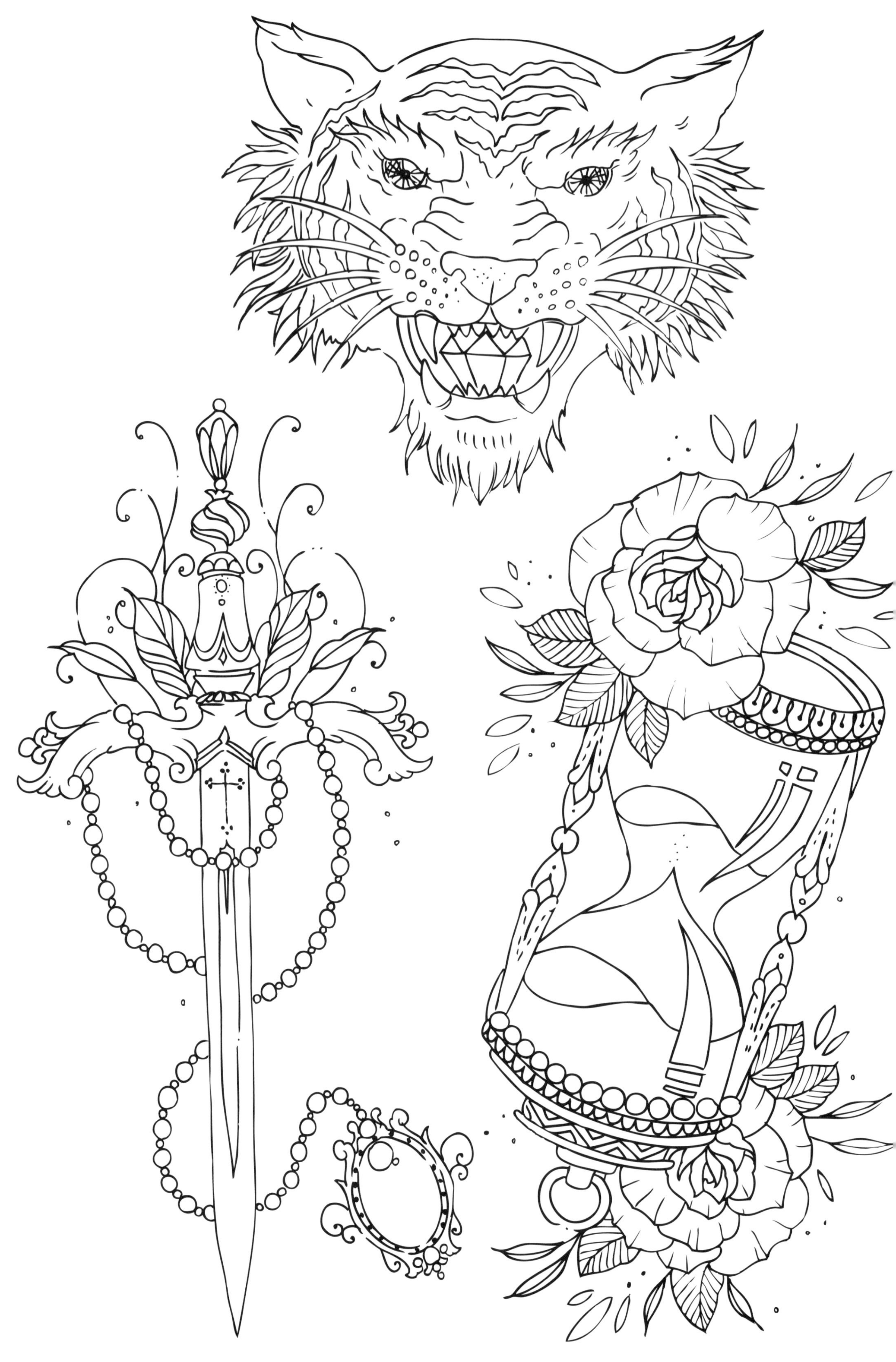

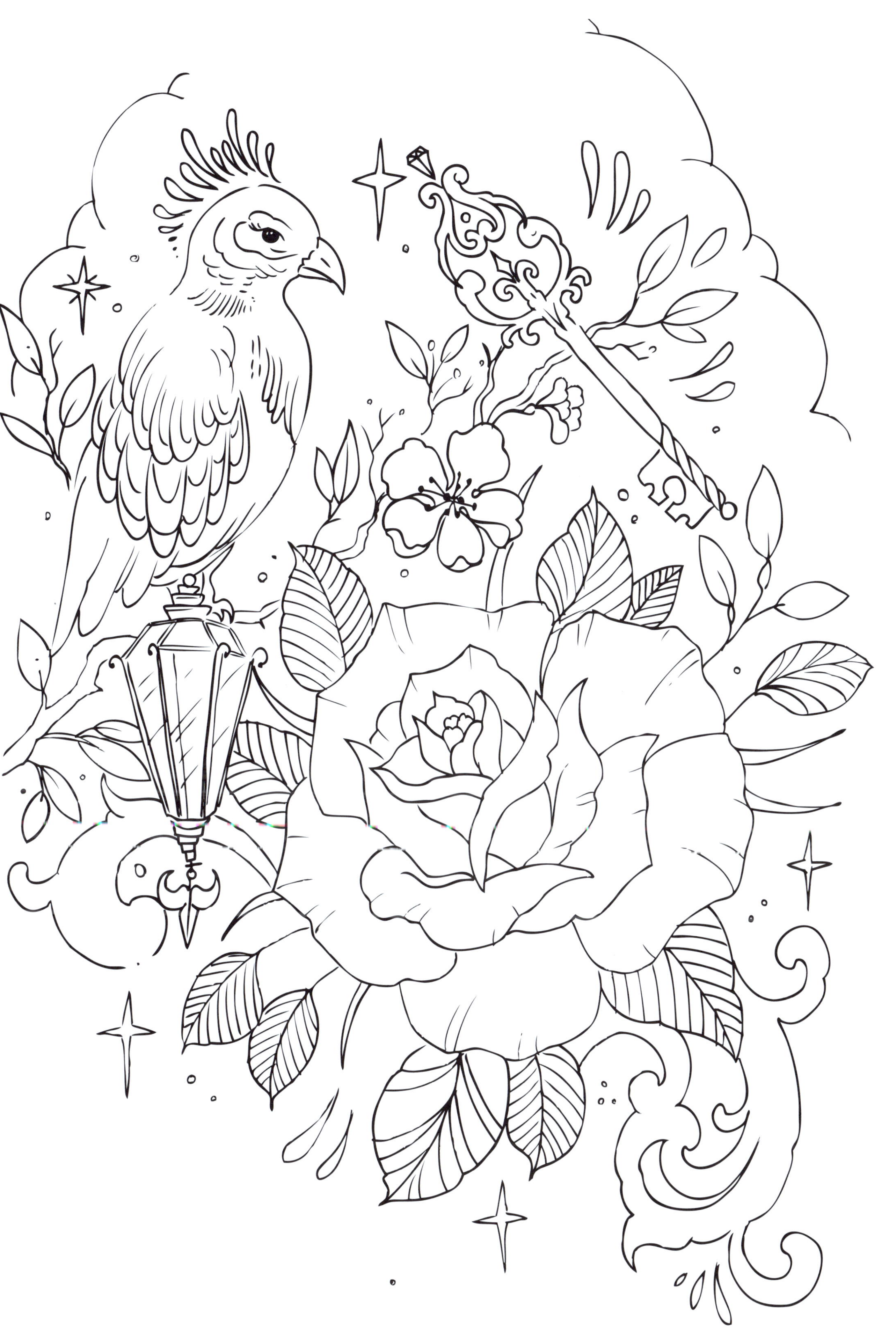

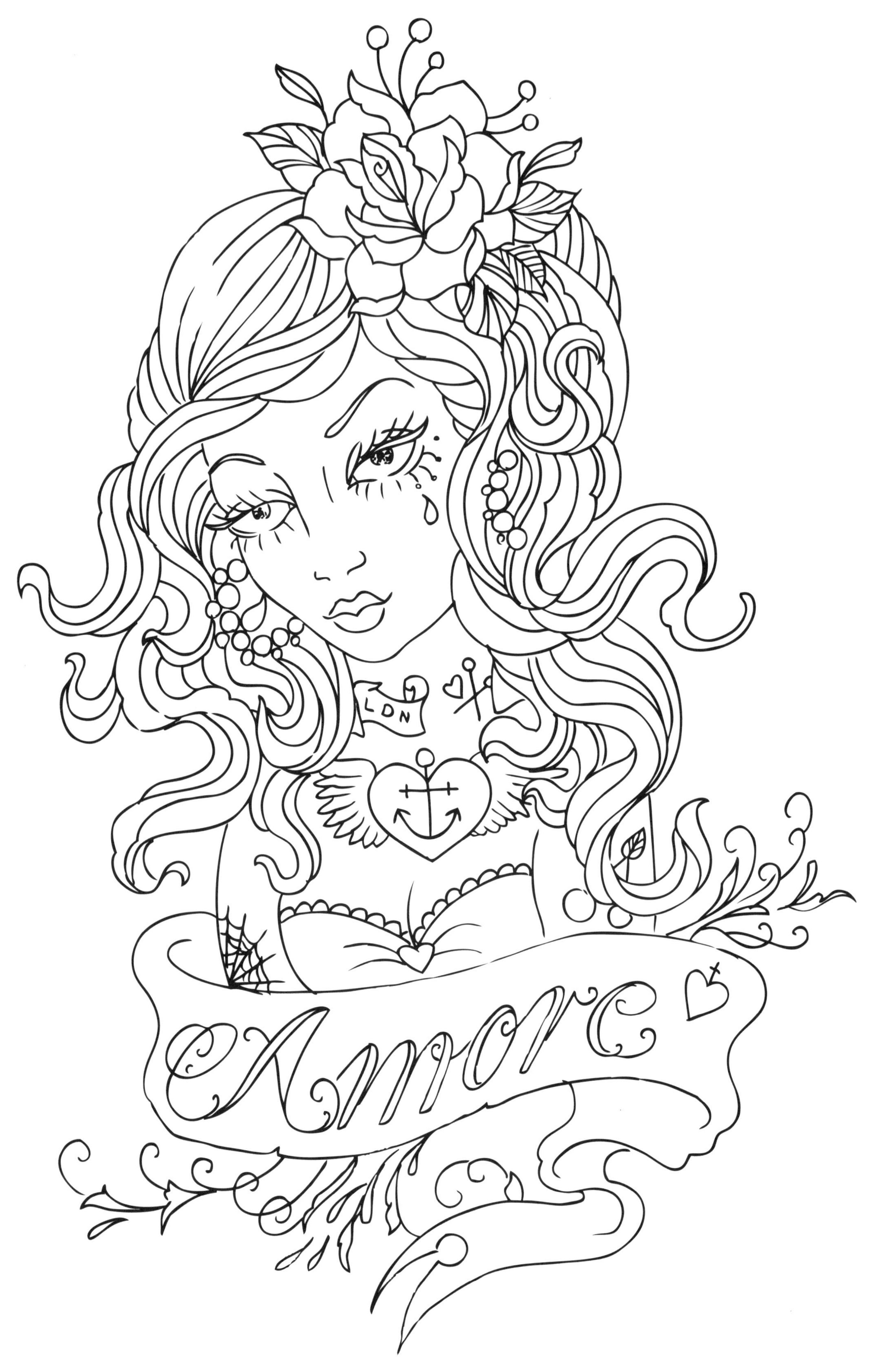
LDN
Amore

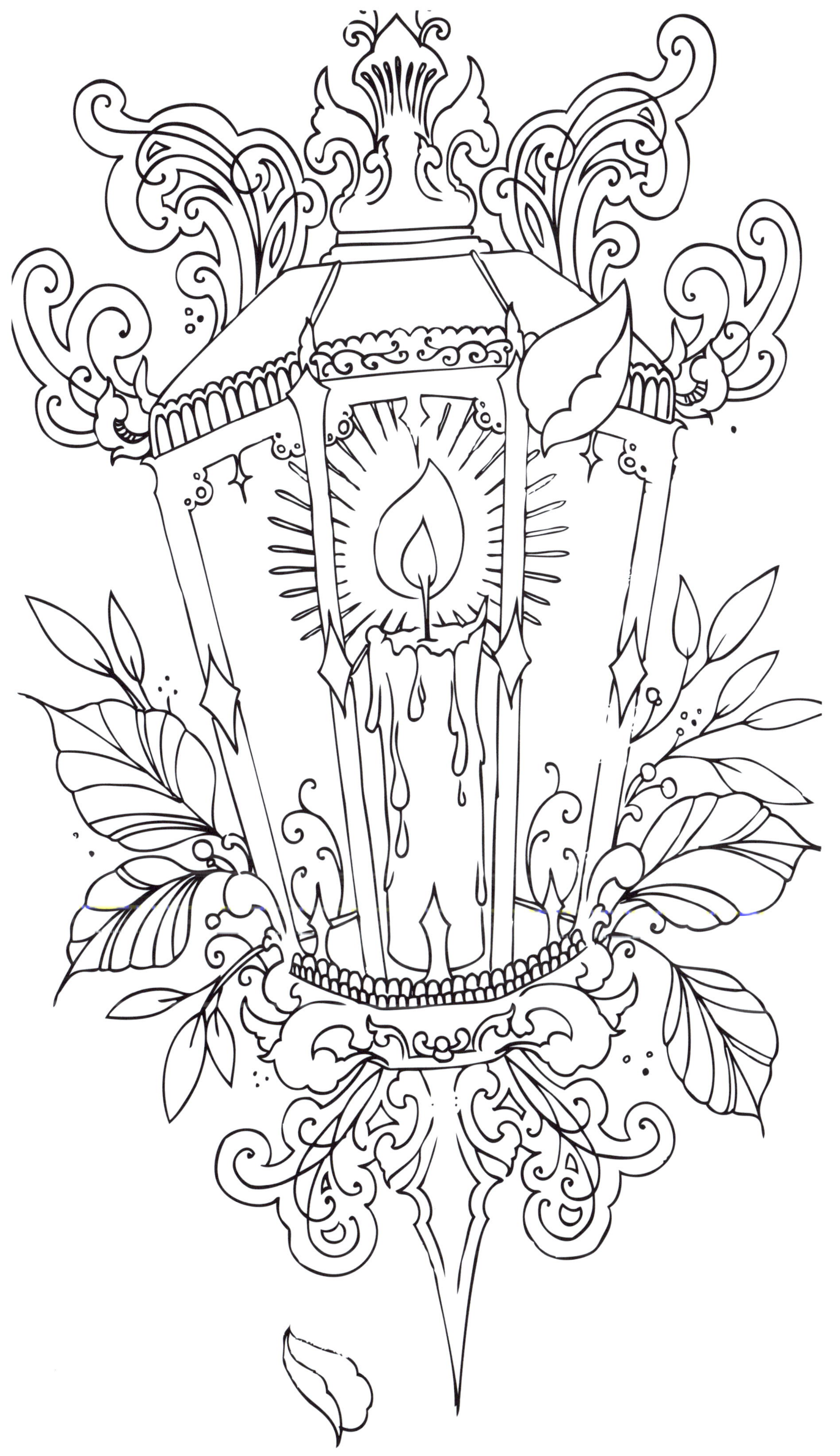

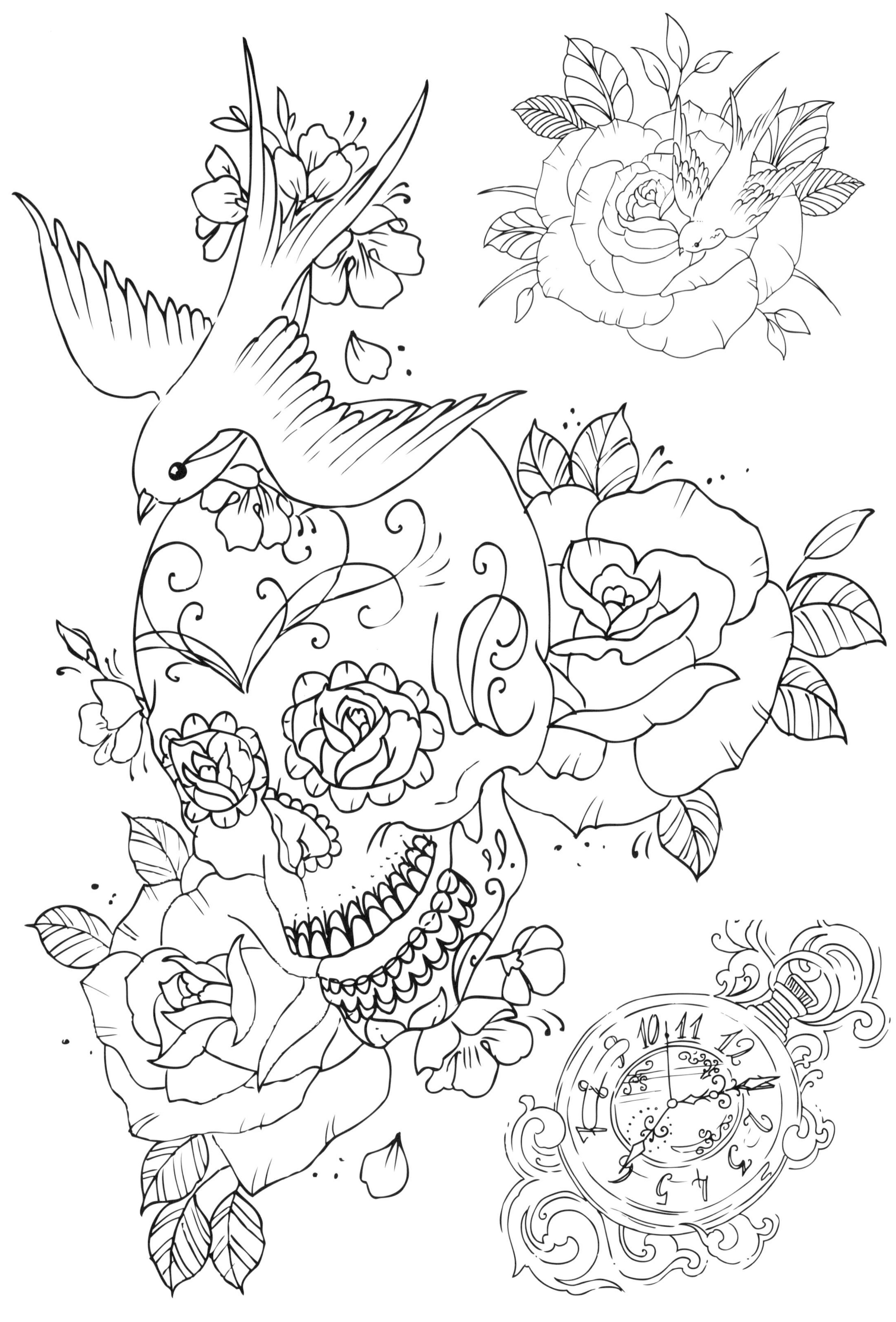
10 11 12

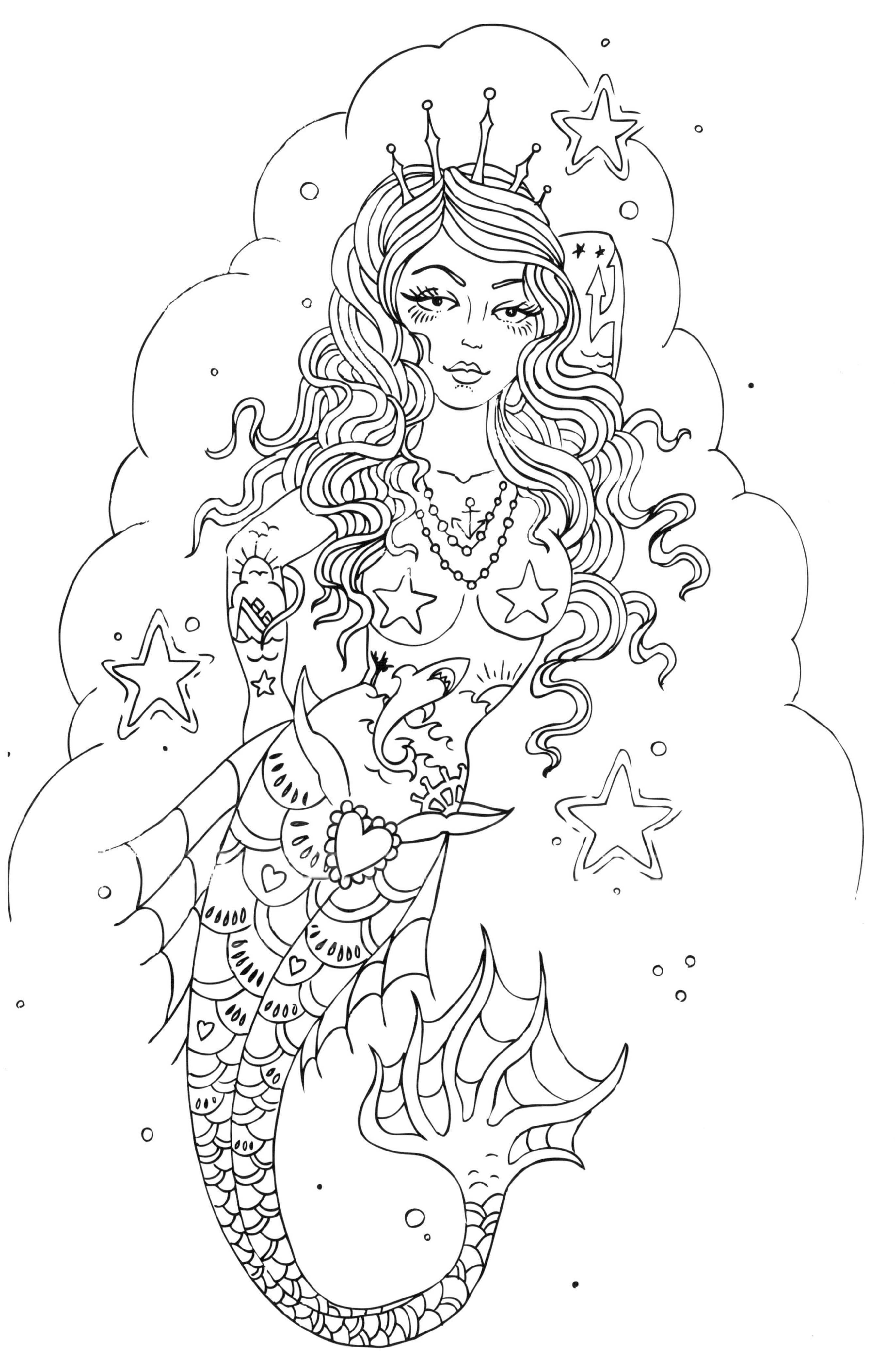

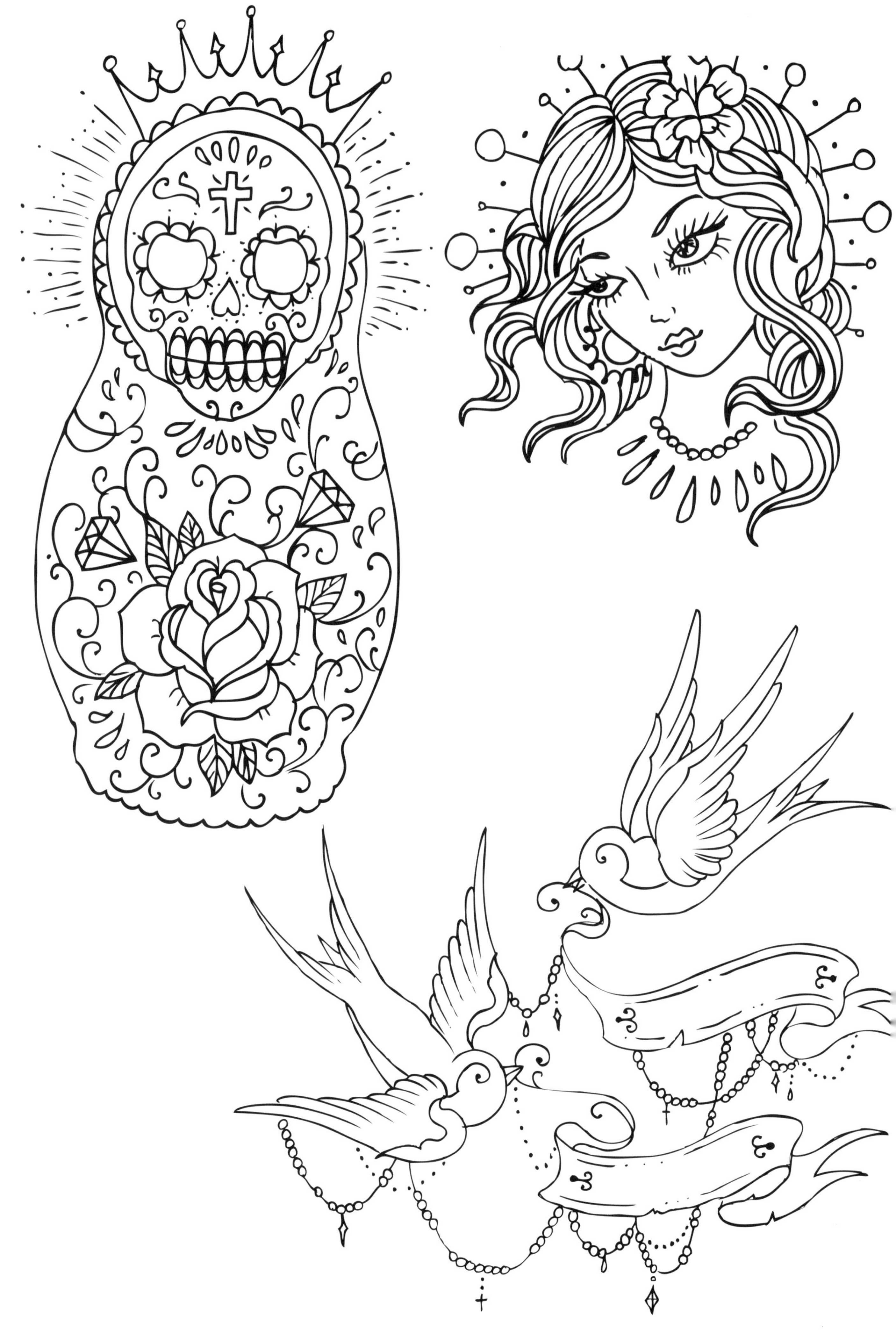

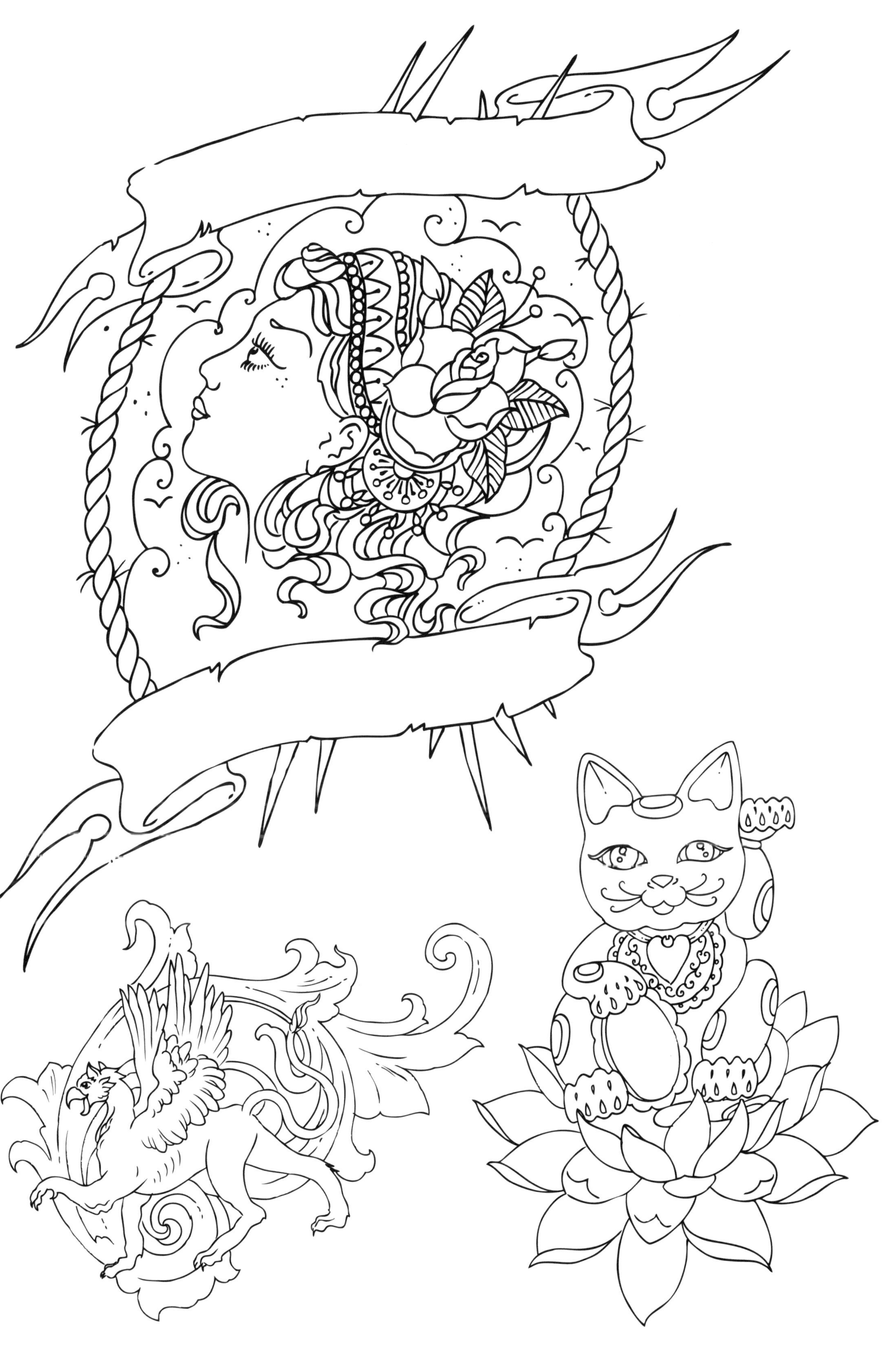

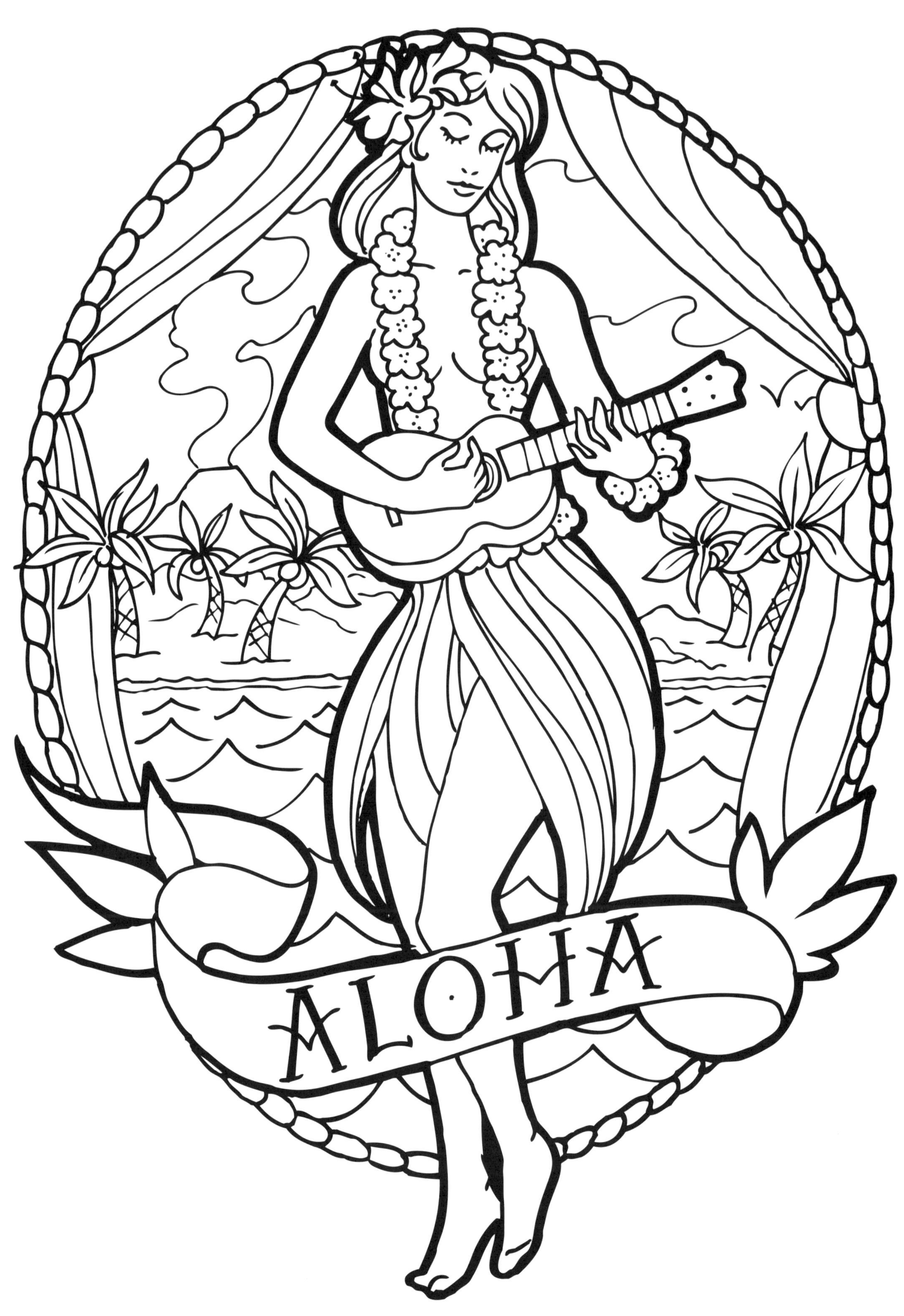
ALOHA

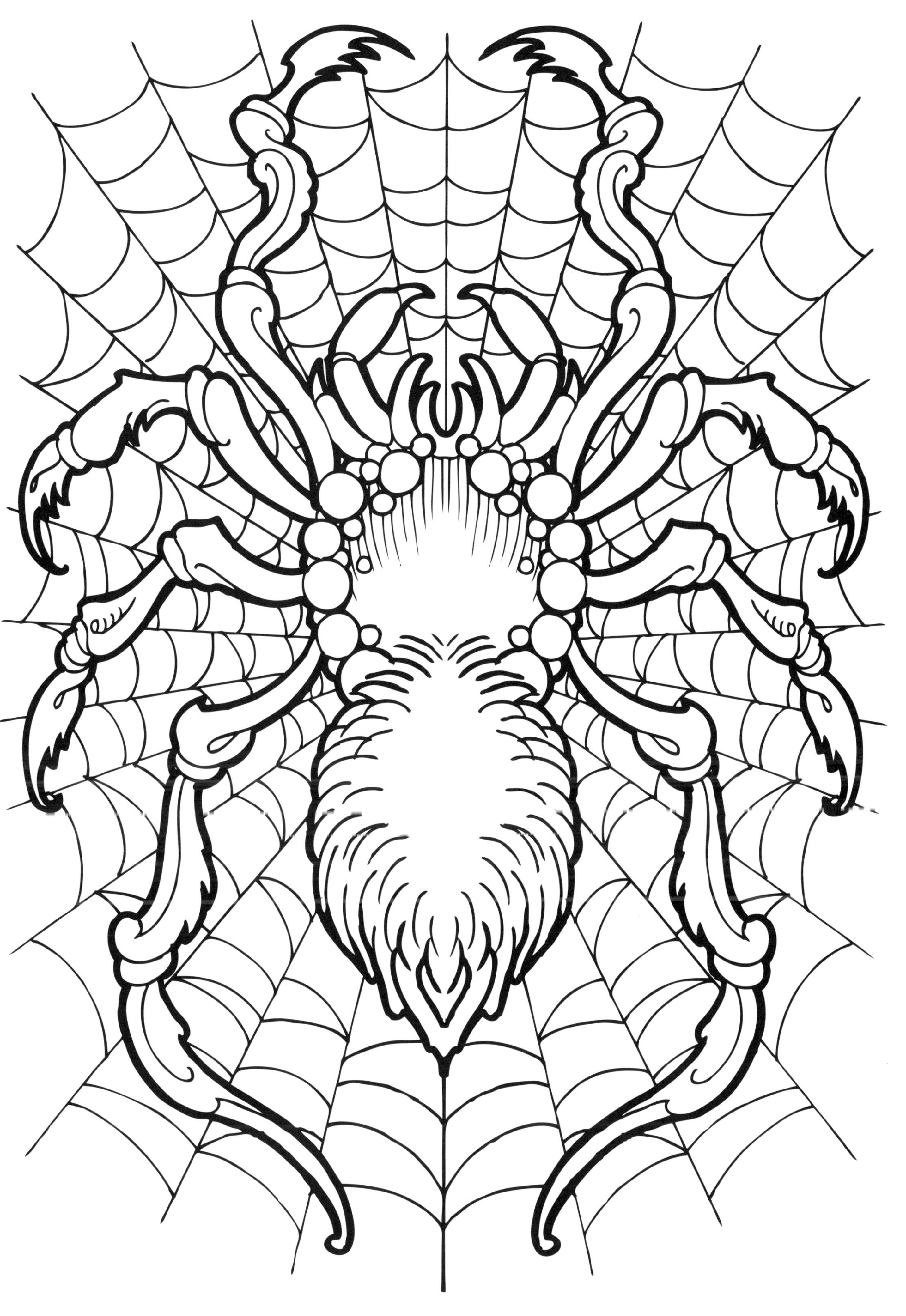

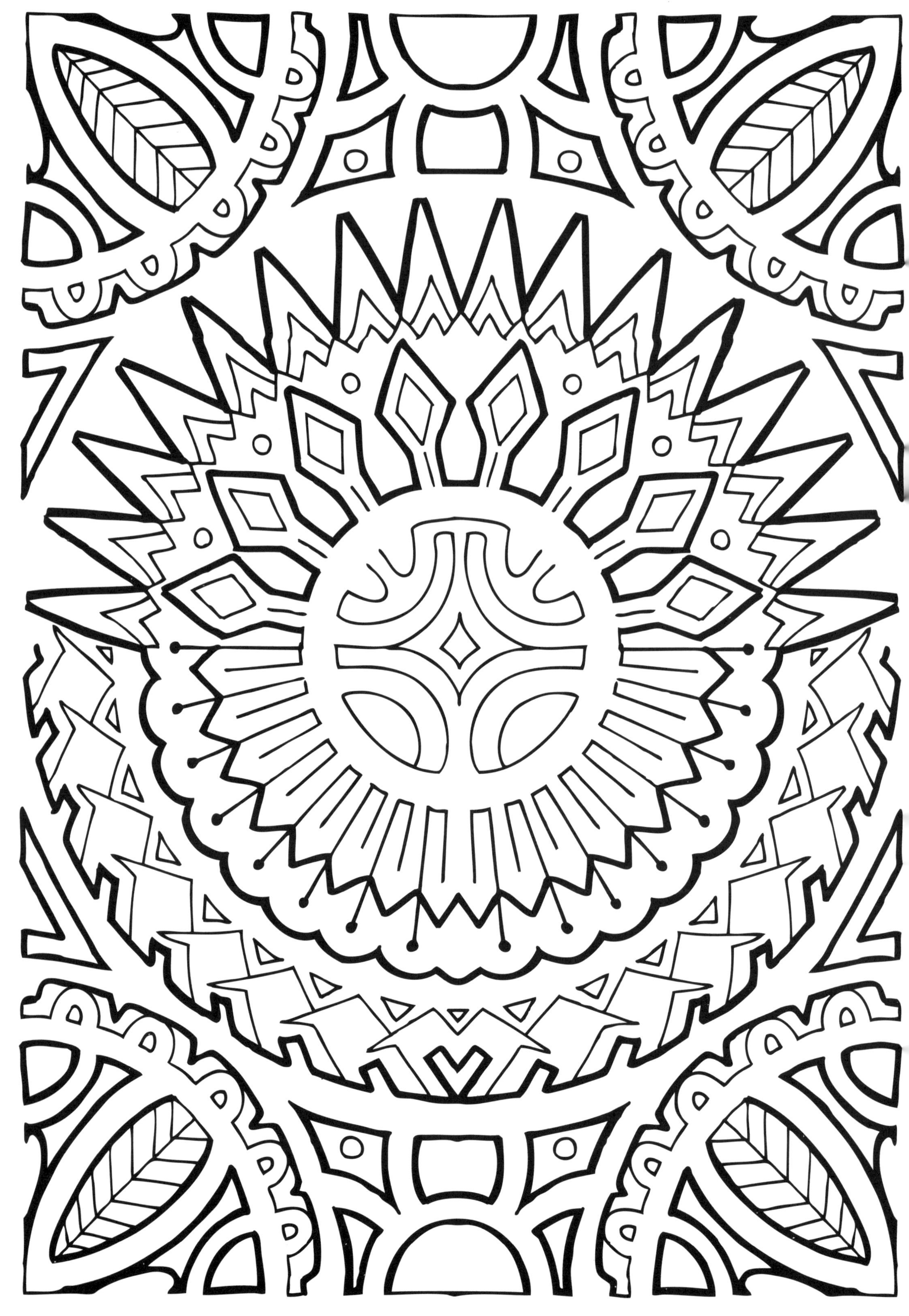

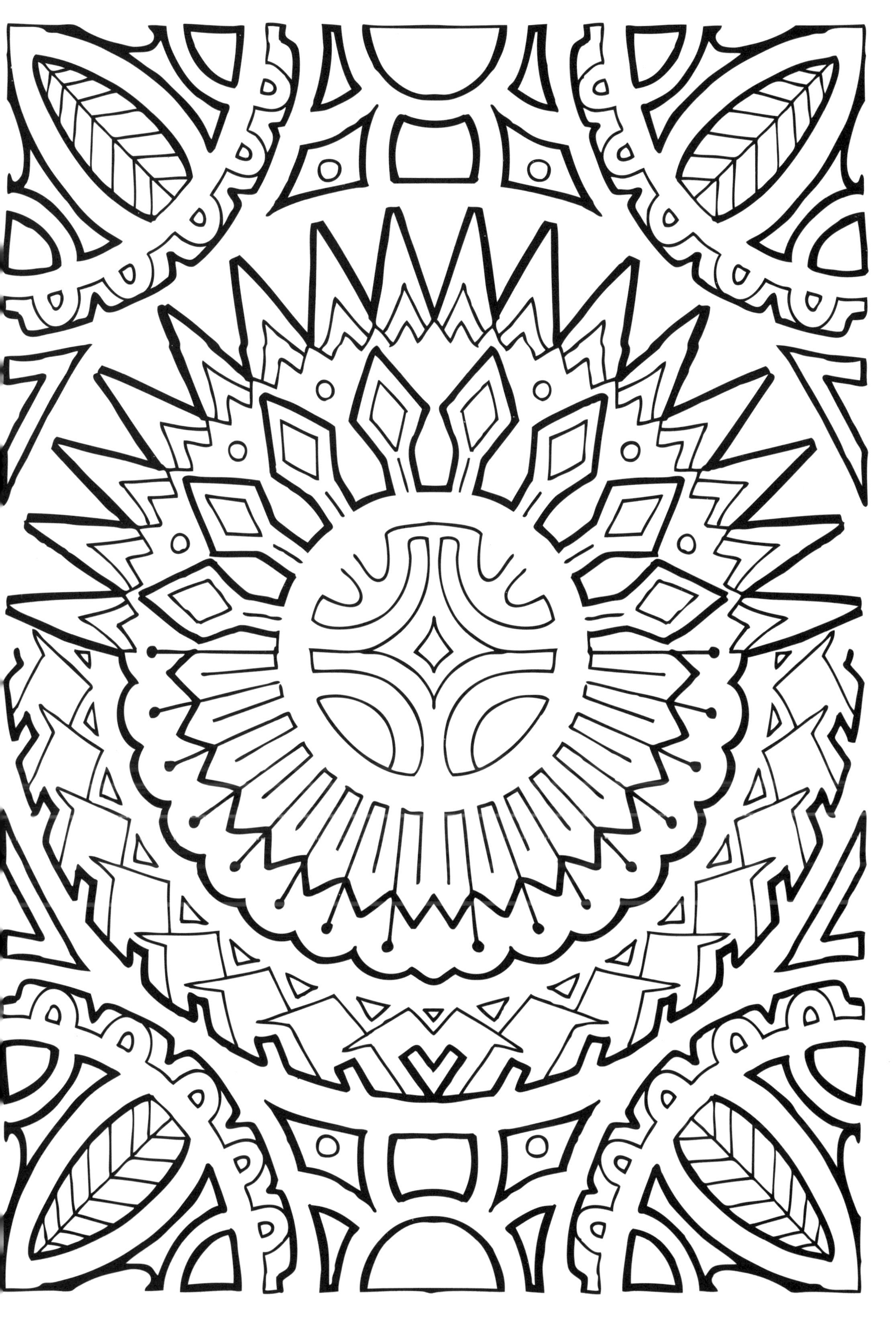

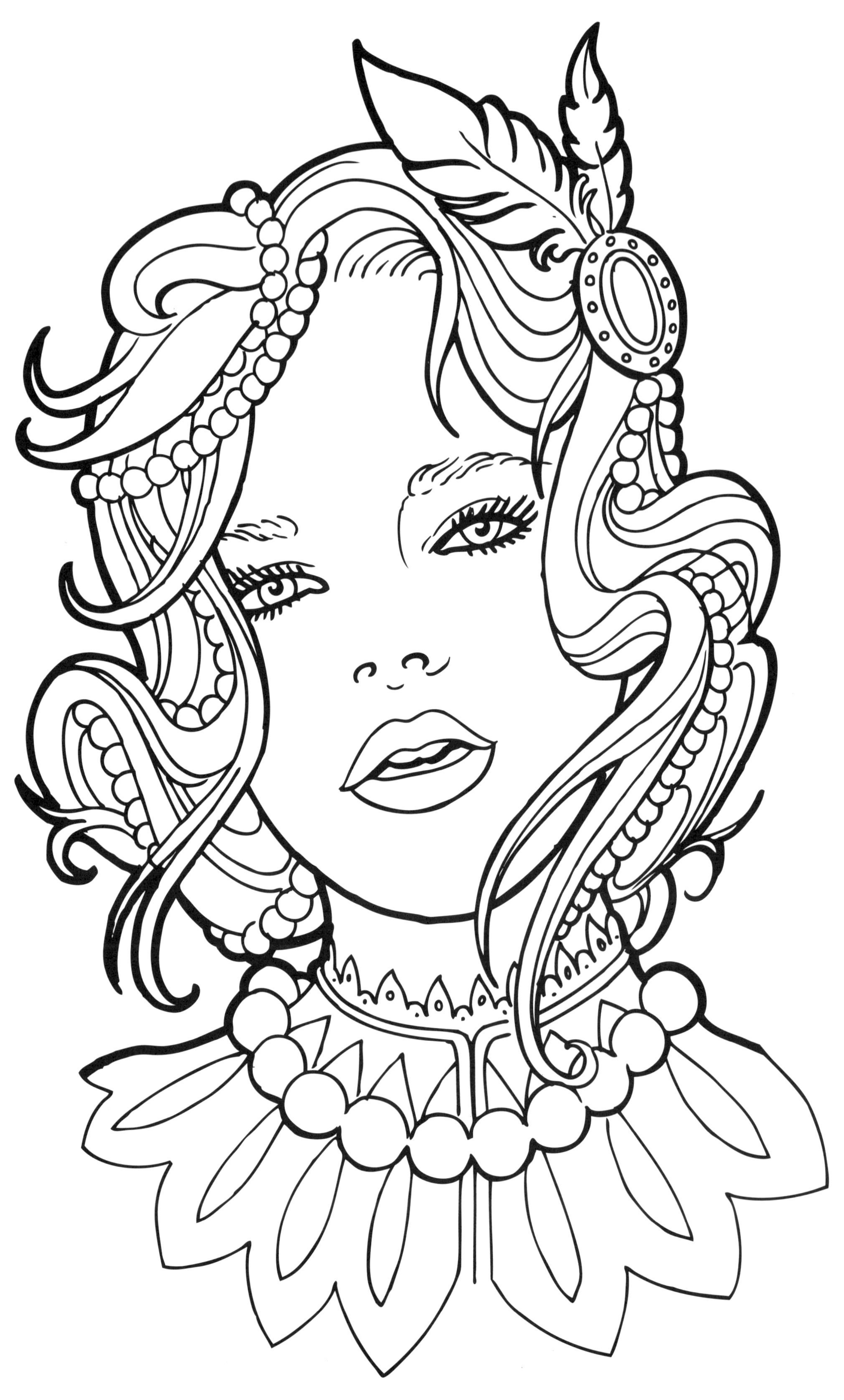

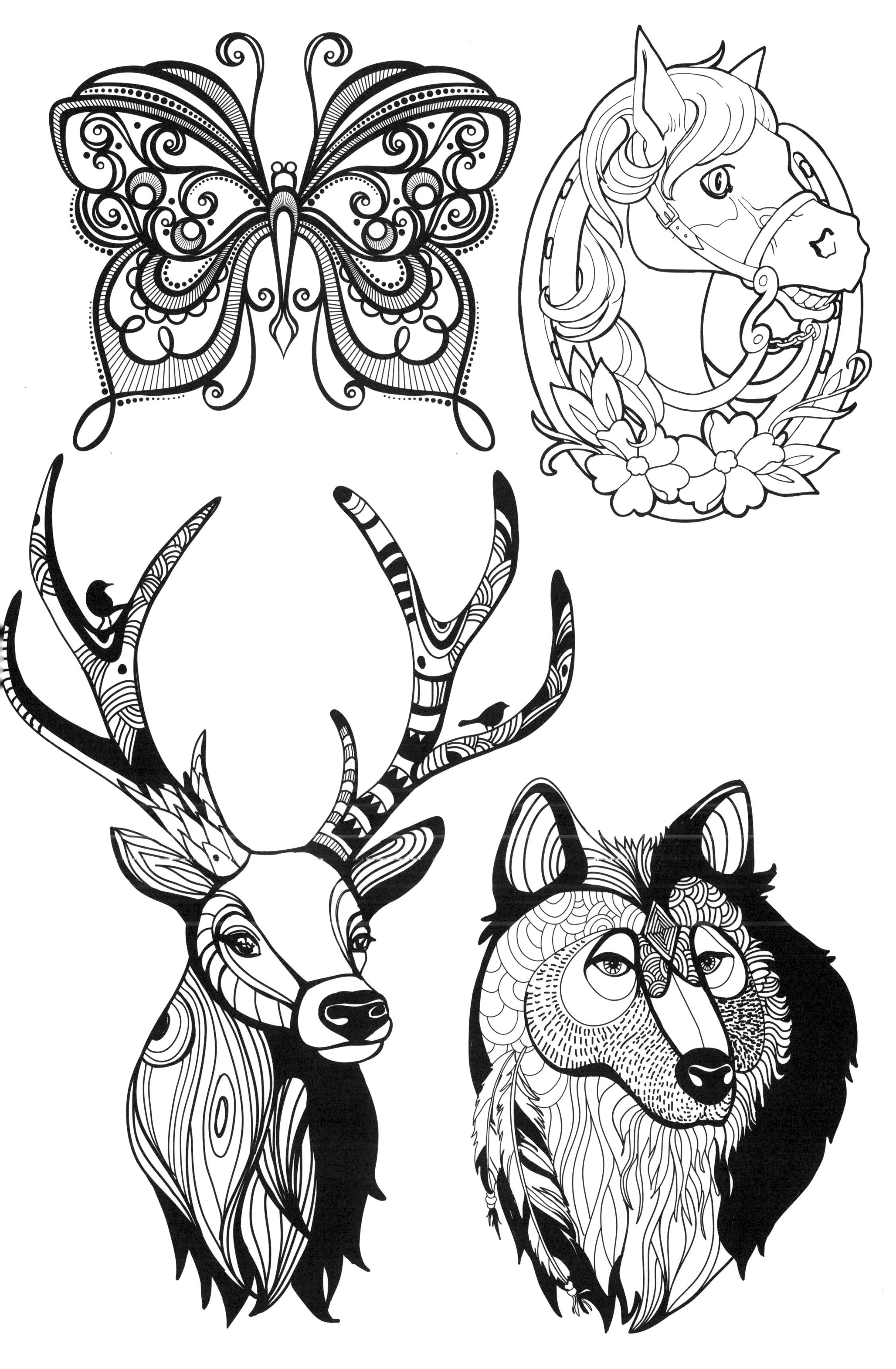

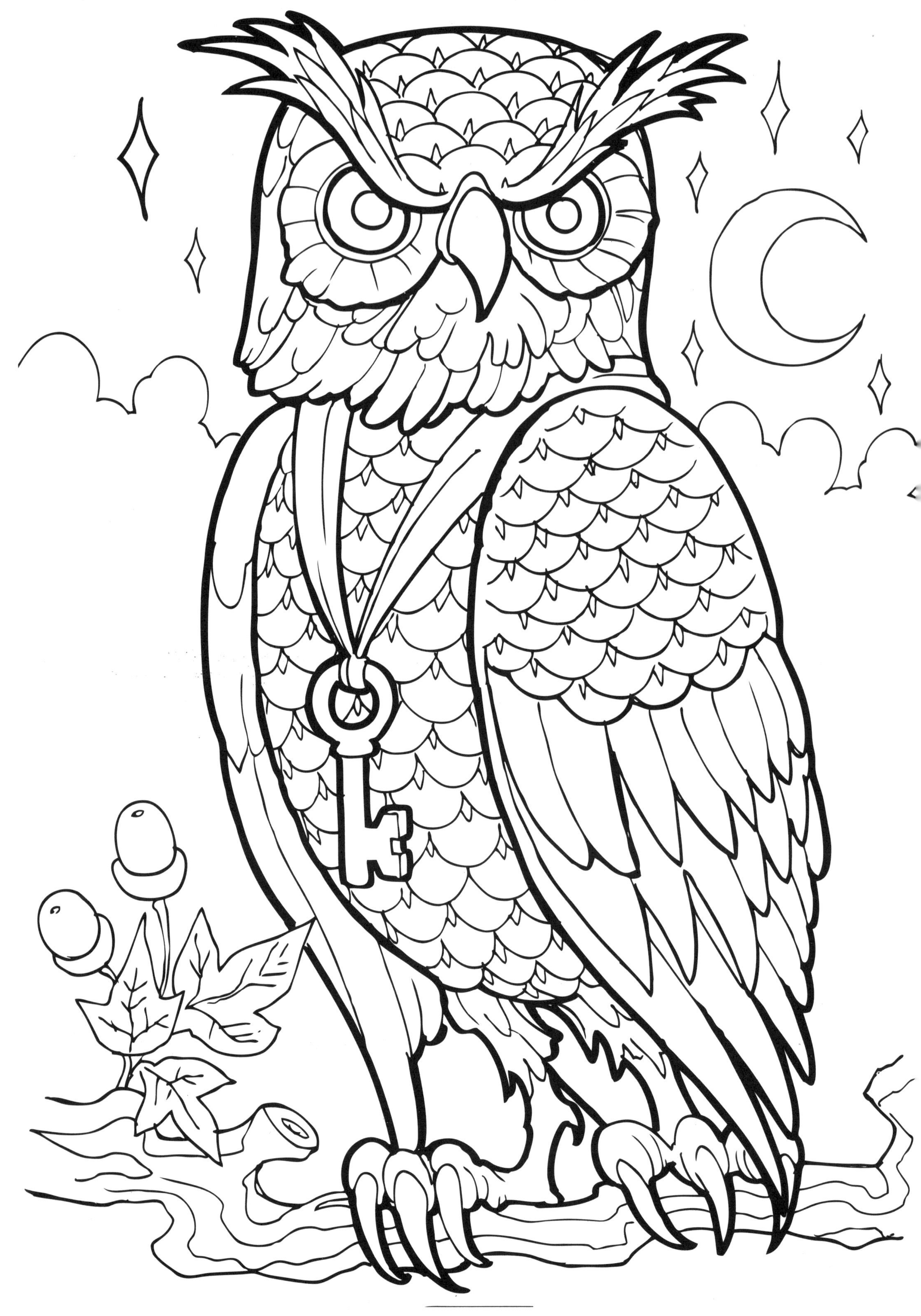